SCREWED

THE PATH OF A HEALER

AMNON GOLDSTEIN, MD

iUniverse, Inc.
Bloomington

Screwed: The Path of a Healer

iUniverse books may be ordered through booksellers or by contacting:

iUniverse
1663 Liberty Drive
Bloomington, IN 47403
www.iuniverse.com
1-800-Authors (1-800-288-4677)

Because of the dynamic nature of the Internet, any web addresses or links contained in this book may have changed since publication and may no longer be valid. The views expressed in this work are solely those of the author and do not necessarily reflect the views of the publisher, and the publisher hereby disclaims any responsibility for them.

Any people depicted in stock imagery provided by Thinkstock are models, and such images are being used for illustrative purposes only.

Certain stock imagery © Thinkstock.

ISBN: 978-1-4502-9435-5 (sc)
ISBN: 978-1-4502-9436-2 (dj)
ISBN: 978-1-4502-9437-9 (ebk)

Library of Congress Control Number: 2011904704

Printed in the United States of America

iUniverse rev. date: 04/01/2011

Dedicated with love and admiration to my fantastic and screwed children: Ravit, Ran and Ori. I love you very much, and I am very proud of you. Only because of your love and support, have I been able to write this book. Thank you so much!

I send my love and thanks to Ettie for the best years of our life, for raising our children to become the great people they are today, and I thank you for the love and support during the worst years of our life.

Ettie, Ravit, Ran and Ori: It was the best of times; it was the worst of time – but together, we did it.

I love you very much.

Finally, I would like to say that if you were to meet me, you would recognize behind the "suave and debonair" façade an Israeli schoolboy with a less-than-perfect English vocabulary. I would also like to express my heartfelt thanks to Elena Watson and a young and talented writer Manasvi who managed to take my "Israeli schoolboy" words and magically weave them into the wonderful story you have before you to read today. It was not an easy task, Elena and Manasvi, but your perseverance and patience made working with you an absolute pleasure. Thank you from the bottom of this screwed man's heart.

TABLE OF CONTENTS

FOREWORD

As a friend and admirer of Dr. Amnon Goldstein, it is a privilege to express my views and comments regarding this masterful life story. You will read about him with abundant pleasure as he takes you on a winding journey, twisting your view of his life's many quirky turns and counterpoints to truly live up to the book's title – "Screwed: The Path of a Healer" – an illuminating, forthright, and soul-searching insight into a man's journey for a better way to help and heal humans.

Dr. Goldstein has devoted his life to medicine, surgery, acupuncture, nutrition, and hypnosis. Ultimately, his profound insights turned to the root cause and source of illnesses and their resolution – the mind of man itself! Dr. Goldstein has traveled the path from trauma and vascular surgery and matters of the heart to what matters most: the actual cause of disease and ailments rooted in the mind and the heart. His life is a testament to the heroic determination of one man to stand alone courageously in the face of institutionalized opinion and threats to demonstrate the power of healing through alternative techniques and methodologies. It is a call to each of us to stand strong in our convictions and never waver from the knowledge we know to be true, no matter the adversity and challenges we confront.

Being of the Christian persuasion, I'm sure Luke, the physician who was one of the twelve Disciples of Christ, must have been beset by many of the same challenges Dr. Goldstein has encountered from his colleagues and his profession. Luke openly embraced a philosophy and a belief that was contrary to his training – a belief that man can be healed by the touch of love and compassion, a touch capable of removing guilt and shame and consequently affecting a cure in the diseases of men; that forgiveness is a remedy for ailments both of soul and body.

From his early life to the autumn of his years, Dr. Goldstein has shown that living life with the courage of one's convictions has its own reward, despite popular view that would have us believe that the general opinion and consensus should always rule. Dr. Goldstein is indeed a humanitarian who has dedicated his life to improving the health and wellbeing of others. His impact upon mankind is yet to be totally understood and appreciated; his battles, both personal and private, have not once caused him to waiver in his dedication and commitment to the cure and amelioration of pain and illness in his fellow man. Norman Cousins, M.D. wrote: "If something comes to life in others because of you, then you have made an approach to immortality." This surely speaks of Amnon's life and purpose – he has resurrected the dead and dying and has devoted his life to the benefit of his fellow man.

With best regards,
Ron Watson
President, American Press Association

INTRODUCTION

The superior doctor prevents illness; the mediocre doctor attends to impending sickness; the inferior doctor treats actual symptoms.

—Chinese proverb

I live in what society calls The Golden Age, but I often wonder where the gold is, or if there has ever been any gold. I wonder about life that seems wasted without any notable achievement or success story to tell. I have felt myself to be special and was blessed with many wonderful gifts in this life: a high IQ and talents in many fields. I have received an excellent education and the most valuable thing in my life, the love and support of my family and friends. In spite of my hard work, in spite of helping thousands of people, I did not achieve anything notable, and I see an insecure financial future. Will I need financial, physical, or mental support from my children or anybody else? Will I be a burden to anybody or to myself? Will I torment my soul?

I am left to wonder about the things that passed me by. As I look back on my life, I realize that only a few people have experienced so much in such a short lifetime. I feel these experiences should be shared with the world. So I have decided to write this book for my children and for myself. In it, I am sharing my life with you.

The book was originally handwritten in Hebrew, as I find it easier to express my views in Hebrew than in English. Writing this book has been a wonderful experience. It has made me relive everything that happened to me. It has been like a second lifetime, only shorter and written in ink. I have felt satisfied, happy and accomplished, depressed, filled with sorrow and sadness. Many of the handwritten pages have been spotted with tears, as were the days they speak about.

Now, in my sixties, I feel young and full of energy; my health is good; and I am ready to start a new exciting and interesting chapter in my life. Today, I know that my mission is "to heal and teach." Finally, I would like to say that, if I had only one wish, I would wish once more to find real love, to truly love and be loved. I will ask for a love that is unconditional, pure, a love that heals everything. God is unconditional in loving, and so should we be. Only if the person has found true love has he found God and discovered himself.

People who have read the manuscript of this book or parts of it have said that they couldn't stop. Many have confessed crying, laughing, and, sometimes, being disgusted by some of the descriptions in this book, but everybody has said that they couldn't wait to read the final version.

To begin with, I'd like to dwell on my book's title: "SCREWED." Screwed? Yes, I am screwed, and so are you. In this world, who isn't? We all are screwed one way or another; it is good. Let me ask you: When was the last time that you looked in the mirror and saw the real you? I am referring to the face behind the masks we wear when we are in the company of other people or even when we occasionally look at ourselves. Are we so screwed that we are unable to see the real us? Is this world nothing but a big stage full of people acting, playing parts, wearing makeup, and hiding their true selves behind the masks? If that's the case, then where are the real "I," the real "you," and the real "us?"

It begins from the day we are born – maybe even earlier – that we are brainwashed, taught, forced, often preached at to lose our real selves; and one day it's lost behind the masks that we are expected to wear in society. No, our real face can't be lost and is never lost. It's just hidden beneath layers of habits and knowledge. It waits and waits for us to find it. It is not an easy task – oftentimes very difficult and quite impossible. Ralph Waldo Emerson, the American essayist, said it best: *"To be yourself in a world that is constantly trying to make you something else is the greatest accomplishment."*

This book is not an autobiography. It is more of a way to show through my life and work as a healer, and through my professional and personal experience, how screwed some of us have become, starting from our self-image and relationships, to friendship and sexuality, health and finances, and so on. In this book, I am not judging or criticizing anyone. I am just presenting my personal point of view.

*

Experience is an author's most valuable asset; experience is the thing that puts the muscle and the breath and the warm blood into the book he writes.

–Mark Twain

*

I use the term *healer* and not *Doctor of Medicine* because I see the first term to be much more appropriate. Not every M.D. is a healer, and vice versa. Healers are usually people who remove pain from the lives of other people.

During my life, I have moved from one country to another. As far as my medical experience is concerned, it includes surgery, holistic medicine, pain management, practicing and researching electro-medicine, nonsurgical facelift, hypnosis, and more. Everyone who has met me once knows that I try to get to the depths of everything I involve myself with. I have never been superficial in any of my endeavors.

I have been blessed with many talents and skills – surprisingly, I haven't been taught most of them. Are they the result of my previous births? Lately, I have begun to believe that to be the case. From a very young age I knew how to knit, sew, do woodwork; I knew about electrical works, plumbing, and everything in the house. My culinary and baking skills are at par to professional. I love interior designing and decorating. I needed a big painting for my living room, so I painted one. I am sharing this painting with you: it is on the cover of my book. I have named it "*The Flow of Energy.*" I love music and my dearest hobby is photography. In the early days, I used to take pictures as well as develop and print them. I have won prizes at international amateur contests. Today, with digital photography, things have become so much easier.

*

If you never cease to stand like a curious child before the great mystery into which you were born…you will never grow old.

-Albert Einstein

*

Looking back, I can say that I have lived a very interesting life. I have accumulated a lot of experience as a healer, treated thousands of patients from the homeless to royalty, as well as everyone in between. By sharing my life with you, I hope we all can see how screwed many of us really are, and I hope that together we can find a way to make a better world and a better life for all of us.

People always take the meaning of the word *screwed* negatively. It is not always negative. It could be positive. An actual screw can go up and down, but as a person, one can get stuck along the way. I often use the word *screwed* in its different meanings: sometimes to express my emotions, my sadness, sometimes to express my disagreement or irony over many evils that prevail in our society.

This is my first book. I hope it won't be the last. In my next book, UNSCREWED, I would like to do some unconventional writing. I would welcome your opinions, reactions, comments and everything that you can think of regarding this publication. I will try to add them as much as I can in an objective way. Please send me your comments, suggestions, solutions, and thoughts to screwed@amnongoldstein.com.

*

You will find, as you look back upon your life, that the moments when you really lived are the moments when you have done things in the spirit of love.

—Henry Drummond

*

I was married to Ettie for thirty-five years. We moved across countries and continents, never staying in one place for a long time. The longest time we've ever lived in one house was four-and-a-half years. One of my friends often asked me, "What are you looking for? Who are you running from? Where are you running to? Remember one thing: when you run, you always take yourself along with you."

The same goes about cars. Like a lot of men, I used to change the cars quite often. My friends used to joke: "When the ashtray in your car gets full, change the car." Now, I have been driving the same car for the past ten years, perhaps due to the fact that there's no ashtray in it. The grass looks always greener on the other side of the fence. Now that I live on a golf course in Florida, the grass is lush and green all year round. It may be the right time to stop looking for the greener grass and devote more energy to things that really matter: love, healing and teaching.

My life has been very interesting and unusual, but it has never been an easy life; sometimes, it was more of a rollercoaster, where every day, every moment had its ups and many downs. Now it is time to get off that rollercoaster and stand on solid ground, time to look forward and believe in good. I was, I am, and I hope to be a rebel to my last day, the one to stand up and fight for something I believe in. I hope that with the help of my children, Ravit, Ran, and Ori; Ettie, their mother; my friends; and you, my readers, I can do it. We can make this world a better place, and, possibly, unscrew it. Do you hear John Lennon singing? *Imagine all the people living life in peace; you may say that I'm a dreamer, but I'm not the only one. I hope someday you'll join us, and the world will be as one.*

Chapter 1

Born at War: Seeking Peace

I t is said that memories start forming when we get a certain identity of ourselves. Our memories are strange but beautiful things that define our lives. One of my earliest memories is a Passover dinner at my grandparents' house. I was only two years old. The dinner was about to begin when there came a knock at the door. It was a few British soldiers who quickly entered the house and were all around us, storming the place, picking up things, opening the closets, searching everywhere, perhaps looking for the weapons. I remember my utter horror at the time as I ran up to my mother and hugged her trying to hide from the soldiers. I do not remember what happened next, but I could never forget that early childhood experience.

The memory goes back to my kindergarten. I remember a feeling of happiness as we sang, danced, drew, played and listened to the stories. The walls were covered with pictures of fruit, plants, animals, letters and our own drawings – all bright and cheerful. One afternoon during story time we all sat quietly in our classroom, when all of a sudden the doors swung open, and police officers started carrying in injured people: there was a bomb blast in the center of Jerusalem. I still remember the feeling of complete terror as we heard the groans and saw blood coming from the wounds. I'd say that to make such young children watch all this was a rather screwed up thing to do. It seemed like scaring little kids was part of Israel's national security.

*

I was born on April 28th, 1943 at the Mount Scorpio Hospital in Jerusalem. I am told the skies were magnificently blue, patched with white clouds. Of course, among those clouds was a dark cloud – the cloud of war, a war that would claim many lives. During the Second World War, Israel was under the British mandate. There was sadness and destruction everywhere; every eye sought hope and peace.

What was in store for this child born in the midst of a war? Like everybody who is born on this planet, my life was going to be screwed: a little twisted, a little funny and a little sad; just like all our lives – but mine was just not screwed yet. I was just born, my pure soul untainted by the world. The doctor picked me and gave me a few gentle spanks on the butt. That's how we welcome a newborn baby: a few good spanks and we are ready to see the world! It is from this moment on that my life began, the moment I let out a cry. That was a beginning of my story.

*

In the 1940s Israel was still under the British rule, and we had to abide by their laws. During those days, the British did not allow the survivors of the holocaust from Europe to come to Israel. Instead, they were sent to new concentration camps in Cyprus and Mauritius in order to keep the country refugee-free. Many families were torn apart, and millions of people lost their lives.

Things got better after the war: the British decided to grant Israel an independent status, and on May 15th, 1948, the state of Israel was born. Immediately after its birth, the Arab neighbors attacked Israel. To maintain and defend its independence, Israel had to fight for its identity and its freedom. There was a mass immigration from East Jerusalem to Israel. Hiding at the bottom of a truck under the feet of the British soldiers, my father, who served in the National Police, was able to escape from the old city of Jerusalem.

We lived in a small apartment overlooking Jerusalem. It was a peaceful place where I spent my early childhood. By the age of five, I made a lot of friends. We used to play outside, on the dirty streets, free from all the hassles of the war, sharing our small secrets, running and skipping, yelling, hiding and climbing. A friend of mine who was the Rabbi's son told me one day: "You know something…" He gave a meaningful pause as if he was about to tell me the location of some hidden treasure. "Soon … we will be going to live in our own state." The news did not matter much to me: I was happy and protected in my own world.

I never saw the ugly face of the war before. I did not know how it affected the lives of many people, until one day I had to experience it myself. It was the day when a bomb landed in our garden. The skies were clear; the day was very bright. My brother and myself were playing outside in the garden when suddenly the bombing started. I was scared; I did not know what to do, and there was destruction everywhere. Our mother came running and picked my baby brother in her arms. I was dragged away by my young aunt. As we were walking up the hill to the center of the city, an old woman came out of a house, and told my mother that she should take care of her children. She asked her not to run around outside when there was a war going on and bombs were falling from the sky. Taking her advice, my mother took us inside the house, and the old lady went out to close the window shutters. As we waited for her to return, we heard an explosion – she was killed, hit by a bomb.

A few months after the incident, we moved to an apartment in the center of Jerusalem. I could still remember that building, my new home. I used to look down from the fifth floor at the old town below us. Sometimes there was darkness outside as the smoke rose from the city, and the war continued.

My father served as a police officer and my mother was working as well. During their absence, I was the one responsible for my younger brother and our safety, taking him with me to the basement whenever the siren went off. Arab forces were surrounding Jerusalem. They prevented the food, water and supplies from coming into the city, and ice was delivered on trucks. To get ice for their iceboxes, people used to line up for hours. I also waited outside in the line. All of a sudden, we heard the buzzing sound of bombs. We barely had any time to run, as a bomb landed, killing many of those who were lining up to get ice. That episode haunted me for many years to come; it was, perhaps, the reason for my future decisions. Being just a kid, I kept wondering: "What was the fault of the people who just died? What wrong have they done? Is standing in the line to get some ice so big of a crime that it must result in death?"

*

The war continued for months. Mothers lost their sons. Wives lost their husbands. We all lived in constant fear. One day this fear, sadness and uncertainty finally came to an end. It was the day when Israel proclaimed its independence and became a free State. The resources of the country had been depleted. There was very little water and food available – the government had to come up with a new rationing system. People were given food coupons. Food was distributed based on the size of the family. Some people sold their coupons, and my parents bought them to feed my brother and myself.

Our life in Jerusalem was simple: to have fresh eggs, my parents kept hens in the veranda, and there was a continuous supply of milk. It was my grandparents' job to supply all the neighborhood residents with milk. I still remember watching them, even into their senior years, carrying enormous vats of milk up the narrow stairways of the buildings so that each family could buy a liter or two. They would be going up and down narrow staircases all day long carrying heavy loads of milk – a terribly hard and strenuous job.

Being a strictly orthodox Jew, my grandfather managed to convince my parents to send my brother and myself to a religious school – not such a good move, taking into an account my deeply embedded propensity for rebellion. They soon realized their error: one Saturday (a Sabbath day), a teacher from the school saw me riding in a car to a football game. Naturally she was less than pleased. She asked my parents to withdraw my brother and myself from the school, since we were not acting in a "sufficiently religious" way.

At the same time, my father was appointed as the Head of the Income Tax Bureau in charge for the entire southern part of Israel. Luckily we moved to Beer Sheba, a desert town in southern Israel that, at that time, was very small; in fact, so small that if you blinked for too long while driving through it, you would have driven right through it without even noticing.

As soon as we heard the news of the potential move to a new city, we started packing. We had lived in Jerusalem for a long time; Beer Sheba was an entirely new place for us. We were excited about the move: new people to meet, and a new house to explore. Along with the good news came the bad one: we were told that terrorists had been attacking cars in that part of the country, so we were advised to carry weapons. Luckily, we didn't encounter any terrorists and, traveling under the hot desert sun, reached the town of Beer Sheba. I was very excited to see our new home and surroundings.

We settled comfortably in the town of Beer Sheba when a short period of peace was interrupted by another war. October 29th, 1956, was the beginning of the Sinai Desert War. As the war devastated the land, things became difficult again. Sirens often pierced the nights. As soon as we would hear the sirens blaze we would run towards the dark and dingy shelters where we crammed together to save ourselves from the raining bombs. During our hideouts in shelters, many rumors spread among the children.

One of the rumors was about the new teacher: "We are going to have a new teacher, and she is very tough and mean!" The rumors ended when the teacher came to our class. Her name was Miriam and for me she was not just a teacher, but also the undisputed savior of my academic life. She proved to be, without any doubt, the nicest teacher I had ever had; also, by far, one of the strongest influences in helping me become more than a dropout. Thanks to her, not only did I manage to get into a medical school, but her guidance and friendship never left me throughout my entire educational tenure. She accompanied me as a teacher, an educator, a friend and a counselor for many years even after my graduation.

*

We were about to begin high school, and an IQ test was required to determine our future abilities. Every student was supposed to write an essay. I wrote that I wanted to be an aeronautic engineer. A few weeks later my parents were called to meet my teacher. I wondered what the teacher would tell my parents. Why had she called them? I thought I had failed the test. Will I be allowed to get to high school or not? To make matters worse, I was asked to stay out of the room during the entire time they were talking about me.

As I kept speculating what was going on inside – having a feeling of being screwed again – the door opened and I saw my parents with a big smile on their faces. I got 168, the highest score, on my IQ test. Miriam praised my talent and told my parents that later on in life I could do whatever I decided to do. Now I knew that I was screwed with a high IQ. What was this IQ anyway? Was this what helped me get good scores in exams even though I hardly studied? Was my ability to do so many things like sewing and knitting, doing woodwork and plumbing, etc. also explained by the high IQ?

Chapter 2

High School

Being a small town, Beer Sheba had all the problems of a small town. To begin with, there was only one high school. I often wondered if there were more children outside the school than inside – it seemed to me that if all the children had come to school at once there would not have been enough room for everyone. The school consisted of two small residential buildings and several former houses that were made into classrooms. Everything was very close and tight and there was no room outside for us to play soccer.

During my freshman year there were about seventy students divided into two classes. Luckily, most of my friends were in my class. As far as the atmosphere was concerned, things were pretty cool, the children were really chirpy like any other high school kids, and the teachers were nice and friendly. In fact, they were so friendly that we were allowed to call our teachers by their first names. I loved my teachers, and they all liked me except for three teachers who used to give me a bad time. That was really annoying!

The lady who had almost burst a vein in me with her annoying remarks was the principal. She looked funny – short and overweight. She lived near the school and had a damn good memory, knowing every student by name. The only bright spot in her personality was that she was usually full of energy and did a good job as a principal. We would call her "the ball of mercury." She used to pick on some of the students, usually the weak, and, ironically, the ones who were overweight. On one occasion she picked on one of the girls in my class and started yelling at her. She told her that she was lazy and fat. It was particularly funny to see her scolding other fat kids. At that moment, I could not help myself, and, being perfectly screwed, jumped forward and snapped, "Look who's talking! The fat cow!"

Everyone was speechless, including "the ball of mercury," who simply left without saying a word. I guess she never expected retaliation from a student. Later on, some kids from another class and a couple teachers came to shake my hand and tell me that I acted very bravely, and that I was a very good friend. After the initial euphoria of being the school "hero" died out, I realized that I was in a screwed situation. I now faced the prospect of being expelled from the school after having yelled at the principal in the way I did. Fortunately, my high grades and good relations with the teachers prevented that from happening. The fact that my father held a very high position in the city was also in my favor. Despite what might have happened, I don't to this day feel any remorse over my emotional outburst.

Then the inevitable happened. My parents were invited to come to school. My father knew that on his way home from work he had to stop by the school. The chances were that his screwed-up son must have done something wrong during the day.

I didn't look for trouble, but if someone messed with my friends, I was not one to keep quiet. That incident changed many things at school. Every time the principal insulted any of the students in my presence, I always stepped in to defend them.

The other teacher in my school that I didn't get along with was the French teacher. I have heard that the French are very polite, but that woman didn't fit the stereotype. She was, perhaps, the only teacher who didn't let us call her by her first name. As far as her looks were concerned, she was a middle-aged woman and was very unfriendly to her students.

Another irritating thing was that in a country like Israel with so many Arabs, we had to learn languages like French. Why not Arabic as a third language? I thought it was ridiculous, and since I did not like the French teacher, I decided not to study.

The third teacher that I did not get along with was the physical education teacher. I could find no apparent reason for roasting kids in the heat of the Israeli desert. You see, I was never athletic and I did not care for the physical education classes. Today, of course, things have changed. Now, due to my knowledge and experience, I know the importance of exercising. But I am still unable to understand the reason for grilling students in the heat.

Chapter 3

"I Want To Be A Surgeon"

Eureka! I've got it.

—Archimedes

I t is time that I tell you the reason I became interested in medicine. My Eureka Moment is different from the one by Archimedes, although I could have been taking a bath as well. My story is not that far from being a sudden realization. One night I woke up because I heard my father screaming in pain. Something was very wrong with him. Immediately the doctor was called and my father was diagnosed with kidney stones, and had to have surgery to have them removed.

Unfortunately, a few months later he was told that the problem hadn't been solved, and he would need another operation. The stones developed again, or maybe the doctors were screwed-up in our city! My father decided to see a private urologist in Jerusalem who was known to be the best in the country. It was better not to take any chances. The operation was going to be expensive and my parents decided to start saving money for it.

It was the day of the surgery when I went to Jerusalem to see how my father was doing. When I walked into his room I saw the IV line attached to one of his arms and the blood infusion line to the other; the oxygen catheter was attached to his nose; another tube went to his stomach. There was a catheter for urine and a drain with blood dripping out. I felt sick and shocked at the same time. I had never seen my father so weak and with so many tubes attached to his body. I passed out. I was happy my father was asleep at the time and couldn't see it.

When I got up, I found myself outside in the arms of my mother; my family was standing by my side. I had a headache and I felt nauseous. I lost consciousness and bruised my head. When I recovered, I said, "I'm going to be a surgeon." My family thought that because I had sustained a head injury, my mind had been screwed. But in my heart I knew what I wanted to do. I didn't want to be a doctor who prescribes drugs. I knew I wanted to be a surgeon. In those days the definition of a lawyer was a Jewish boy who cannot stand the sight of blood. Here I was, a Jewish boy wishing to become a surgeon, but who fainted after seeing his father with tubes attached to his body.

My father recovered quickly. The high position that my father had working in the government meant that he had many friends in society. Some of them were heads of the departments of the new hospital that was just completed. They visited my parents often. When I told them that I wanted to become a surgeon, they tried to convince me to choose another profession, but failed. On the other hand, I convinced the head of the E.N.T. department to let me watch an operation. At first he looked a bit skeptical, but later on agreed. I think he must have thought I would pass out again at the sight of blood and would change my mind.

On the day of my first surgery, I was very excited. Wearing complete surgical attire and a mask, I was ready to step into the operating room. I felt like a doctor myself; I was introduced to the team as a medical student. My heart pounded. It was hard to breathe with the mask on. The operation was about to begin, and the surgeon held the scalpel in his hand ready to make an incision in the patient's neck to perform thyroid surgery. At this moment, I grew dizzy and the room began to spin around me. I almost lost my balance but managed to get to a nearby chair and sit down. Slowly the room stopped spinning and I regained control of my senses. I stood next to the surgeon when he proceeded. It was an amazing experience!

I laugh today: Why I was the only one who felt that the room spins? Perhaps the room had been spinning before the surgery; only the other doctors were used to it.

The surgery went well, and at the end the surgeon and the team shook my hands, telling me they were worried for a minute that I was going to faint because I looked very pale. That experience definitely made me stronger, and the operating room never spun again.

*

Starting from that day the hospital became my second home. Spending time there was a lot more enjoyable than the French classes or physical education exercises. The doctors, nurses and other workers in the hospital grew to know me well and taught me many things: how to give injections, suture wounds, and put plaster casts on fractures. I worked with different surgical units and eventually decided that general surgery was what I liked and what I wanted to do.

As always, when you are enjoying something, time runs fast – the time in the hospital ran very fast – and the first year of high school came to an end. I divided my time between school, friends, hospital and home. All these activities kept me busy and happy. I was enjoying what I did, whether it was at school, at home or at the hospital. Everything was exciting and interesting. We got our report cards – my grades were very good with the exception of physical education and French. Not that I expected them to be. I had always been kind of screwed in those subjects. The principal stated that unless I passed the French exam by the end of the summer, I would not become a sophomore.

During the last two summers I had worked in order to help my parents pay for my school tuition. That summer I had to work, study French, and work at the hospital. There was a lot to be done. There were certain issues I had to deal with, like my French, for example. It was time for some damage control. I knew that my chances to pass the French exam were very slim. It was about time I got some help. I hired a French tutor and asked her to teach me how to talk and read. There was no chance that I'd learn to write in such a short time. She initially objected, but later agreed and warned me that I would not be able to pass the exam without writing. She didn't know that I had a plan that would get me through the exam without the written section.

The day before the exam I put my plan in action. I went to visit my friends in the emergency room and asked them to give me some Plaster of Paris bandages. I made a cast of plaster and fixed it around my right forearm from the hand to the elbow. Now the stage was set. All I needed to do was keep my act together and the plan would succeed. The next morning I was ready to take the exam. I showed my "injury" to the teacher and told her that I had broken my forearm. This meant that I would not be able to take the written section. She agreed to test my speaking and reading ability, and because I had learned enough French to speak well, the oral exam was relatively easy for me. I passed.

*

To earn some money I had to work, so I began giving private lessons to children. I don't know how they had managed to learn anything before having me as their tutor. As a result, their grades began to improve, and I managed to save some money to buy myself a small motorcycle. I was very happy and proud when I rode my bike to school. Again, "the ball of mercury" at our school just would not leave me alone – it is very irritating that some people just can't stand to see others happy.

As I stood at the entrance of the school next to my bike chatting with my friends, the principal came out and told me not to enter the schoolyard. I was surprised and asked her why. She told me that motorbikes were not allowed on the school premises. Annoyed, I pointed out that there was no traffic sign saying so. She replied by saying, "I am the traffic sign."

Since my reputation as a school hero was at stake, I retorted, "If you are the sign, then why don't you get stuck in the ground like the other traffic signs?"

She walked away. I don't know how I should have felt about what had happened – all I knew was that she had never stopped me again. One thing

I must say is that, I was not proud about what I said. I still wonder today what my reaction would have been if one of my children said something like that to their teacher.

After getting the motorcycle my life became easier. It was easier to go to school, work at the hospital and meet my friends. Israel was not at war during those days (for a change), but terrorist activity happened all around us. The Medical Center in Beer Sheba was the main hospital for the southern part of Israel, so most of the wounded were brought to the hospital by helicopter. Whenever I heard the sound of the helicopter, I would run to the hospital to help out.

Once, during a school break, some of my friends invited me to hang out with them at the nearby garden. They had brought cigarettes with them. That day I had my first cigarette; unfortunately, it was not the last. I felt dizzy and nauseous, but that didn't stop me – smoking was a very cool thing to do during those days. After all, I was the one who was screwed up. Another of my so-called "heroic" thoughts was (since I already had a bike) that knowing how to smoke would help me attract girls.

The end of the year approached. We found out that about twenty students out of the seventy who started high school would be promoted to the next year. The ones who passed would be divided into two classes: the first one had mathematics and physics as the main subject and the second class had sociology as its main subject. I chose the second class with sociology because my best friends were in it. No one wants to get bored in a class where there are no friends.

The summer vacations were great. I worked in the emergency room at the hospital. I was happy. Not only did I get a chance to do what I loved the most, but also I was paid for doing it. During the summer I helped out during surgeries. My job was to hold retractors so the surgeon could see the operating field.

On one occasion, a young lady came to the emergency room. She had a dislocated shoulder and was in a lot of pain. The orthopedic surgeon on call decided to do something I had never seen before. He decided to do the reduction under hypnosis instead of general anesthesia. I had not heard of such a technique before. It was an unforgettable experience. There was a lot more to medicine that I wanted to know. The patient had no pain, and within a few minutes the shoulder was back in place. I was excited and wanted to learn hypnosis. I started hunting for books that would clarify to me what hypnosis was about and how to perform it. Such books did not exist. I was frustrated and tried to enroll in some of the courses at the hospital, but was refused because I was only sixteen.

My junior year started. There were just twelve students in the class, and the teachers were friendly. All in all, it was a great year and I spent a lot of time at the hospital. The staff accepted me as one of them, and I enjoyed every moment I spent there. I participated in many surgeries. One of them was the most memorable: it was the day when they let me cut the appendix during an appendectomy. It was an overwhelming experience. After that moment there was no doubt in my mind – I was going to be a surgeon.

Chapter 4

Screwed

By the end of my third year, three of my best friends who had just graduated were called to join the Army. A few weeks later parents' day was held at the Army camp where family and friends were allowed to visit. Because it was quite far from where I lived, I thought: *Why bother with the long journey? I would rather go to Tel Aviv and stay there with my relatives and then go visit my friends at the camp.*

When I reached the camp I was very excited to see my friends. They were all grown up, dressed as soldiers. We had a really good time catching up on the "good old days." It was rather melodramatic to put it that way because we had been away for just a few weeks.

It was very hot and muggy when I reached Tel Aviv, and I decided to go out and get some fresh air. There are many beautiful parks in the center of Tel Aviv. The park I went to was quiet and peaceful. The trees bowed gently under the breeze, the birds chirped. I sat down on a bench under an old oak tree, thinking about the events of the day, relaxing and enjoying the evening.

A young fellow strolled toward me down the alley. He too was trying to find refuge under the shadow of the trees, away from the heat and noise of the main street. He approached me and started a conversation. The stranger seemed to be slightly older then myself, very friendly and polite. I found out that he was discharged from the Israeli Army.

We talked for a while, then he asked me if I wanted to join him for a drink. I agreed. As we walked, he pointed to one of the houses across the street and told me that it was where he lived. He invited me to his apartment for another drink and some classical music. As I sat there enjoying the music, he took off his shirt. It was very hot inside the house. Then I felt his hand touching my body. Something was very wrong here, I thought, something was very screwed.

He pushed me and I fell on his bed. I tried to resist him but I could not. He was much stronger than me. He took off his clothes and started to take off my clothes. I tried fighting back. I tried resisting. Everything went blank. I was raped. I don't remember what happened afterwards, or how I got out of that man's house, or how I got to my relatives' house. I do not remember anything.

All I remember is that after I had reached my relatives' home, I took a very long shower. I couldn't sleep. This time my nightmare was real. I felt ashamed. I felt like I was pulled into a dark whirlpool. It was suffocating. I felt that I could never escape this feeling. I felt that I was drowning.

*

I could not go home like this. I took a bus to Jerusalem where my grandparents lived. I told my grandparents that I was not feeling well. They welcomed me and let me stay. I was full of guilt and uncertainty. When my grandparents left the room, I reached for the drawer where my grandfather kept his medications and took as many pills as I could. I had no idea what those pills were. I put them in my pocket and returned to my parents' home.

The next day I called the hospital and said that I was ill. I spent the rest of the day in bed, feeling violated, deteriorated, molested, abducted, humiliated, lost and unclean. I felt that my life was over and there was no hope for the future. I decided to end my misery. That night, I swallowed all the pills I had taken from my grandparents and I went to bed, awaiting my death.

The next morning I woke up nauseous, but still alive. I could not face anyone. None of my family or my friends could understand anything like this. I spent most of the day in my room smoking and crying, trying to make sense of what had happened, submerged by my guilt and humiliation. When I returned to the hospital, nothing was the same. It was not the same world. I was not the same man.

*

The senior year of high school started and my grades deteriorated. I felt very depressed, emotionally and psychologically wounded. I lost all hope for the future and considered leaving school and getting a job. After time my teacher told me that if I continued to procrastinate, I would certainly fail. During that period my parents were very concerned about me. They called my dear teacher Miriam to see if she could help. My parents felt that she was the only person who could talk some sense into me. They told her that they didn't know what was going on with me, but I was seriously considering quitting the school.

Miriam was alarmed and invited me for to dinner at her house. Her husband was an M.D. – I don't know if she told him about my problem or not – but he was very nice to me, sharing his experiences as a doctor, and telling me how much he enjoyed his work. To hear words of encouragement from an experienced doctor was very soothing at the time. Miriam placed her trust in me and told me that she believed in me and I would certainly make a great surgeon in the future. She told me I should get on with my life and study as hard as I possibly could if I wanted to make my dreams come true. I followed her advice, and slowly my grades began to improve. Things began looking up.

However, on a personal level, no matter how hard I tried; things were not the same as before. I did not attend social functions. I saw my friends, who were happy and active; on the other hand, there was me, a seventeen-year-old, raped and pretty much screwed-up. This was my first sexual experience, and it was awful. I was confused about sexuality, about trusting people, and about life in general. Every time someone touched me I jumped with fear of being hurt. This demon followed me everywhere; it haunted me every moment I lived, and it made my life miserable. The only thing that mattered to me and the only thing I knew was that I still wanted to be a surgeon. It was the only desire left in me, the only thing that kept me moving, except for one problem – there was only one medical school in Israel. It accepted fifty students out of over a thousand applicants. Why couldn't they have opened more medical schools if they had so many people wishing to become doctors?

I filled out my application, and my father arranged for me to meet with the Vice Dean. He was a rather haughty fellow. When we met, the only question I was asked was: "What do you think your chances are of getting into medical school? You are not a student from one of the developing African countries or an Arab." What a question to ask an aspirant! It sounded as if he were discouraging me from joining the school instead of encouraging me. He told me that my chances of getting into the medical school were very slim. As if I didn't have enough problems, there was another one: during that period the Israeli government supported the African developing countries by providing scholarship to their students to attend Israeli universities. Obviously, large numbers of students from those countries were admitted this way. Something was very screwed in this system. Israel had only one medical school, and students from other countries had a better chance than Israelis of being admitted.

I knew there was a long road ahead of me. I had to take two entrance exams: Science and Bible Studies (the second one was my choice, because I was very good at it). I thought that even if I had not studied biology in school at the level required for the examination, I would study with Miriam, my teacher, during summer vacations and pass the exam. Then, if I succeeded, I would be invited for an interview.

During the last year at school, as we readied for Matriculation examinations, the teachers went on strike – the school year was interrupted. With only twelve students per class, some of the teachers invited us to their homes and offered help preparing for the exams. I needed help with English and Hebrew grammar, so I studied with the grammar teacher and improved considerably.

Finally high school ended and summer vacation started. That meant work. I had to study and prepare for the Biology and the Bible Studies exams. When the day of the Biology exam arrived, I felt anxious and nervous. The questions were too simple. I thought that, perhaps, I didn't understand them properly. Miriam was waiting for me outside. She had already seen the exam paper and knew that I gave the right answers. A few weeks later I found out that I had scored very high on both of the exams. Now it was time for an interview.

On the day of my interview I was nervous, but, hey, who wouldn't be? It was a chance of getting into the medical school. Regardless, I was ready to give it my very best. In the room were three professors from the Medical School. They fired many questions at me. In Israel at that time, there were many cases of violence against doctors in hospitals and clinics. One of the professors asked me: "As a doctor, you know that these days there are so many incidents of violence, how would you protect yourself?" I replied, "When I chose medicine as my profession, I accepted the risk. I don't want to be a banker sitting behind bars like they do in the banks. I am sure that if I show compassion and interest in my patients, they will have no reason to attack me." I had passed the interview even though I did not know it at the time.

A few days later the results of the Matriculation exam came in, and I found out that I had failed English. Other than that, I scored high marks in all the subjects. It was clear to me that unless I took a second English exam and passed it, I would not be admitted to a medical school. I studied hard and retook it. Unfortunately, I found out that even if I did pass English, my chances of being accepted were very small.

I told my parents that I would like to go to the United States to study medicine. The announcement came as a shock to my parents, but they knew that if I had made up my mind, there was very little they could do to change it. I worked very hard for next few months and managed to save some money for a trip to New York on the lower deck of a very small ship. I was told that there would be twelve people sharing one cabin. The thought of traveling by myself was scary, and sharing my room with a bunch of other people brought back the memory of being raped.

Chapter 5

The New World

The day of the voyage arrived. It was April 1962. The ship was at the docks ready to leave the port. My parents, my brother and my grandmother were there to say good-bye to me. Everyone was crying. Still sobbing, I boarded the ship as my family watched me from shore. As I stood on the deck, lonely and scared, my heart was filled with many different emotions: I felt like jumping off the ship. I wanted to be home with my family.

The vastness of the blue sea spread out ahead of me and the New World was inviting. The sea was calm and the sky was clear. I looked around and was pleased to find other young passengers. Together we had fun visiting various Mediterranean ports. I visited Naples, Italy, the French Riviera, and Gibraltar. The fine luck at sea did not last long, however, and when we were crossing the Atlantic the sea because violent. The ship rocked and was slammed by the huge waves. Many passengers suffered from motion sickness and were puking overboard.

On my nineteenth birthday I was invited to join the captain and the crew for dinner. As we ate our dinner, one of the crewmembers told me that there was a telegram for me. I thought that something had happened to my family. To my relief, it was a happy birthday wish from my parents and my brother. My journey became easier knowing that my family was okay, and their wishes came as a cheerful reminder of their love for me.

In a few days we reached the port of New York. As we disembarked from the ship, I bid goodbye to the crew and many young friends that I had made during the journey. I got off the ship with three hundred dollars in my pocket that were supposed to help me start a new life in a new country with new people, a new language, and new culture. I felt like I was screwed again, but I knew everything was going to be okay.

My aunt met me at the port and told me she did not want me to come to stay with her. It was only after my grandfather wrote her a letter that she agreed. I felt as if someone had dropped a bomb on my head. What kind of an aunt did I have? I had come all the way from Israel just to find out I couldn't stay with her. I was surprised and disappointed. It certainly did not expect such a welcome.

After I settled in, I wandered the streets of New York and found a totally new world that I had never seen before. Everything was wonderful and surprising. Even using the subway every day to go from Brooklyn to Manhattan had its own charm. I had been warned about the city's high crime rate, especially in the subways, but that did not stop me from exploring. I was only nineteen years old. I felt like an explorer, bold and fearless.

I was comfortable in this new city. There was so much to do and see. I applied for pre-med study at three different universities: NYU, Columbia, and Cornell. I was required to pass the entrance exams. More exams! Since I had prepared hard for the examinations in Israel, I passed easily and was accepted into all three universities. Now I had to make a decision. The major problem that I faced was the tuition fee of $4,000 for each of the universities.

Another major problem was that, because I was a foreign student, I was not legally allowed to work – very different from Israel where the foreign students are paid to study. I had no idea where I was going to get this money. I was still pondering the problem, when one day during the summer vacation I saw an advertisement for Hebrew-speaking counselors for a summer camp near Philadelphia. I applied for the job and got it. I was delighted! I thought it was a nice opportunity to spend the summer away from my so-called loving relatives who almost made me flee the day I had arrived, as well as save some money.

The summer camp was different from Israeli camps, and I had a great time. There, I met Becky, one of the students' counselors. We used to meet every day, go for walks and talk for hours. It was only a matter of time when we fell in love. I was still facing my demons, and since I had been raped, everything about sexuality and relationships frightened me. Things were different with Becky. She was about my age, born and raised in the USA. She was always so full of life; we were happy together. Anyone who knew us or even saw us would have said that we were very much in love. Before the end of the summer we decided to get married. We were young, in love, just like any teenager who falls in love, everything seemed right to us.

Since my arrival the United States, I wrote to my parents once a day, but I had not written about our decision to get married. I also sent a letter to the medical school to consider my application for the coming year because I had passed my English test. In the beginning, they were reluctant to do it, but later they said that I would have to come for another personal interview. Eventually, after a lot of persistence, they agreed.

It was Parents' Day at the camp, and Becky's parents came to visit. When she announced our decision to get married, they almost fainted, but asked to meet me first. When Becky called, I was afraid that her father would not approve of me. Luckily, her parents were wonderful, and we spent a delightful weekend together. Becky's father called me for a serious talk – a usual kind of a talk that a girl's father would give to his daughter's potential partner – and told me that he was impressed by me and would not mind us getting married. Then he put his hands on my shoulders and said that his wife and he would give us their blessing, but we would have to wait a few months.

Becky's father was a big industrialist, and because Becky was the only child, he wanted me to come and work with him so that I could learn the tricks of his trade and would eventually get ready to take his place one day. He explained to me that after the marriage the factory would be Becky's and mine. I tried to reason with him, insisting on my desire to become a surgeon. I had always wanted to be a surgeon and I had no intentions of running a factory.

Becky's father tried to talk me out of it, but I was adamant and refused to accept his offer. That made him furious and I was asked to leave. Obviously, after that incident, Becky's parents refused to let Becky see me anymore. I was upset, but I could not stop life from moving on. The summer ended, and at the end of my vacation I returned to New York. I did not see Becky again. A few weeks later, I found out that she was killed in a car accident.

*

I chose Columbia University. I was still not sure where to get my funding. Time passed, and I still didn't know. Yom Kippur arrived. My aunt and her family were very religious – I was the only one who was not. Remember the time when I was expelled from the religious school? I didn't have many religious inclinations. It was a very hot day in Brooklyn. The only place you could find a breeze was the staircase where I spent most of the day lying on the steps. In the morning a telegram arrived for me. Again, something to worry about. To add my anxiety, my aunt received it herself. Because it was a holy day, she said I would not be able to open it until the end of the day. Time stopped moving forward. I thought the day would never come to an end. Eventually, at the sunset, my aunt handed me the telegram that read: "YOU WERE ADMITTED TO MEDICAL SCHOOL. COME HOME".

The very next morning I found out that there was a special offer for students traveling from New York City to Israel. I took advantage of it and immediately bought a ticket for $300. My vacation in the U.S. was coming to an end, and I was anxious to go back to my country and be with my family. I packed all my stuff and in a few days boarded a Boeing 707. That was my first flight ever. Below us, I could see the never-ending blue vastness of the Atlantic, and then, many hours later, finally, we landed in Israel where I found myself in the arms of my family.

Chapter 6

Medical School

The next morning I was on my way to Jerusalem to make sure that I was actually admitted to the medical school. There was no mistake: I was a freshman at Hebrew University Medical School in Jerusalem.

It was 1962. The summer was over and the winter was yet to begin. It was the month of October, and the school was about to start. When I saw my name written on the white paper pinned to the green board, my heart was filled with joy. I made it! I was going to become a doctor!

We were divided into two groups: the Israelis, and those from the developing countries, mostly from Africa, for whom the classes were to be conducted in English. During my freshman year I took the basic courses: Science, Physics, Math, Biology, and English, which after spending six months in the U.S. was an easy subject. I could read and understand a lot of material published in English.

Most of the students in my group were older than myself, with twenty-two being an average age. We devoted mornings and afternoons to studying, while at night most of us had to work. I remember hanging out by a public telephone booth waiting for my parents to call me so I could share my new life with them. "Only six more years minus one week are still left," I blurted to them at the end of the first week.

Unlike the Israeli students, the African students were getting their stipend from the Israeli government and had a lot more time to dedicate to studying and having fun at night. Now, how screwed and unfair could things get? That's what I'd like to know! Being an Israeli citizen, you don't get any support or help except for student loans, while foreign students were actually paid to study in Israel! As a result of this policy, they performed better than Israeli students, and the teachers were constantly teasing us regarding our poor grades compared to those of foreign students.

*

Since the time I watched an orthopedic surgeon perform a shoulder reduction with a patient under hypnosis, I have been interested in hypnosis and studied it as much as I could to understand how it worked. Now, as a medical student, I was sure I would be able to study more about hypnosis and the techniques to reduce pain though it. One day, I gathered all my courage and asked several of my teachers where and how I could study hypnosis. Instead of guiding me and quenching my curiosity, they seemed annoyed by my question and answered rather sternly that, "In a medical school we teach real medicine – not magic tricks." That was a pretty screwed up answer, I thought. I had seen a doctor use that technique on a patient and it worked! The whole medical procedure was performed without anesthesia, resulting in no pain on behalf of that patient. They simply couldn't answer my question and regarded me as a "quack" for asking it. I realized that I would have to discover it on my own.

As the year passed, I became engrossed in studies and work. By the end of my first year, I was hired at the hospital. Now, for the first time I was a real medical student and not a young child who wanted to learn about medicine. I had grown up.

After a brief summer break, I started my second year. While the first semester was still dedicated to basic sciences, the second semester marked the beginning of the nightmare of Anatomy. There was not enough money to buy all the necessary books, so used books were given to the Israeli students, while the foreign exchange students received brand new ones!

On the cover of one of the Anatomy books that I received from the school was inscribed: "In case of fire, throw this book in it."

I assure you, those three anatomy books were very scary. All three of them were ridiculously thick, and written in a language I could not understand. To me, those books seemed more like three big monsters trying to swallow me up, rather than regular textbooks. I was sure they came alive when I was going to sleep every night. I had a feeling that the study of anatomy would not be easy – more like trying to learn a telephone book by heart. There was always so much to remember, so many terms, some in Latin and some in English.

The sophomore year was primarily dedicated to the Anatomy of the brain and extremities, implying a detailed analysis of every contour of the brain without any explanation of its multiple functions. I mean, isn't it easier to remember a hundred or a thousand phone numbers while associating them to real people? Then there were all those nerves, roots, and so many other things that had to be learned by heart.

The funny thing is that during my work at the hospital, I found out that most of the doctors didn't remember their Anatomy. The stuff they did remember was the practical Anatomy, the things that we deal with daily. I figured that the information to be retained would, probably, constitute fifty percent of what I had learned in the medical school. At the end of my sophomore year we had to take an anatomy exam. Many students failed and, yes, I was one of them. (Finally, the monsters got me!) We were told that we had to retake the exam by the end of the summer, and only those who passed would continue with their junior year studies.

To make things worse, during the summer I heard many rumors. There was talk about immigrants moving to Israel from Romania. Some of them were medical students. Someone then told me that because there were not enough seats in the medical school, they were going to fail some of the Israeli students. That was the reason why they had made the anatomy examination harder than usual. I could not take any chances and spent hours preparing to retake the exam.

The phantom of anatomy haunted me throughout the summer. Finally, came the day of the exam. It was an oral exam. The examining professor would point to something on the cadaver and we would have to identify it in Latin. One of my best friends failed the exam again. He had to repeat the second year. I was shocked and scared by the possible outcome. Seeing your friend fail does give you a feeling that you might follow in his path.

For better or for worse, I was supposed to be the last student to take the exam. By the time my turn came, the sun had gone down. I was sweating under the burden of the impending torture. At nine-thirty at night, I entered the examination room. The tension, fear and anticipation of what was about to come almost paralyzed me. As I entered, I saw that the examiner was one the toughest professors in the department. He was very strict and never smiled – at least we had never seen a smile on his face. His face seemed to have been made out of cement: emotionless and cold.

When all was said and done, I passed the Anatomy exam with flying colors. For once, everything seemed right. It was 11:00 p.m. when I came out of the building. I rushed to the nearby telephone booth. I wanted to call my parents. The telephone receiver was wet with my tears. I was ecstatically happy, and so were my mom and dad.

The third year started. The first semester brought more Anatomy to learn. There was also a Nursing course where we were trained to become nurses – fairly funny to us young Israeli guys. Nevertheless, all the knowledge that I acquired working in the hospital as a nurse gave me the opportunity to work more efficiently during the evenings and night shifts at the hospital. By the second semester of my third year we began learning specific medical subjects that taught us how to record a patient's history, conduct a physical, take blood pressure, pulse, etc.

*

There was an issue of imaginary ailments. The more we read about a certain disease, the more symptoms characterizing it we discovered in ourselves. Along came Pathology, and every day one of us would discover that he miraculously, almost overnight, became a recipient of some rare, bizarre illness. Isn't life much simpler for those with just a limited medical knowledge? There was a course in Pharmacology, where we studied all about the medications for those weird ailments we diagnosed ourselves with during Pathology classes. A good thing was that we were not allowed to prescribe yet – otherwise there would have been quite a number of drug addicts among us.

As the fourth year began, things changed for good. We moved to the new Medical Center built in Jerusalem with a new building of the Medical School attached to it. This was the first year that I really enjoyed. Finally we were doing stuff that only doctors were supposed to do, rather than fighting the monsters in our medical books, or cramming up on all those parts of the human body. On top of it, we got to wear white coats. It felt so good putting it on and looking like a doctor. We had to take care of patients and their needs, including taking a case history, examination and auscultation – examining a patient with a stethoscope. Not only did the stethoscope help us listen to the patients, but it helped us feel somewhat more important. It added to the personality of a doctor: The white coat and the stethoscope were my fantasies since I was a child, and they had come true.

Chapter 7

My New Cars

I was given a choice of either staying in Jerusalem or moving to one of two other hospitals. I chose the hospital that was the farthest. It was located on a beautiful beach – could not be any better.

My father quit his job as the Head of the Income Tax Bureau in the southern part of Israel and opened his own office. Since I was on my own, and the rest of the world didn't trouble me at all, I felt free to do many things that I could never do before, like buy a car. Even though I worked very hard and saved some money, it was not an easy thing to do. I didn't need any unnecessary attention on my behalf. I didn't want my car to become a subject of rumors and gossip (the son of the Head of the Income Tax Bureau driving a car!) in a small town where everyone knows everyone and where it was almost impossible to remain incognito.

After struggling with these thoughts for a while, I finally decided to get myself a car.

A few months later, my mother opened a gift shop in one of the main hotels in town, and our financial situation started to improve. By the end of the summer vacation I managed to save 500 Israeli pounds. I was delighted by the prospect of getting a car and was daydreaming about cruising in it on the roads of Israel. Accompanied by a good friend of mine, I went to Tel Aviv where I found an old 1948 Ford. Though it was a bit rusty and looked more like a World War I relic, it still was in a reasonable condition. The upholstery and the seats were torn but it was still moving.

To be frank, I didn't expect anything better for 500 pounds. It really didn't matter. What mattered was that it was my new car. I bought it and the same evening drove back home. I will never forget the expression on my parents' faces when they saw me. I was driving a rusty old car with torn seats. It looked as if I had just had an accident. But they were my parents, and they were happy for me.

The next day, I went to the Arab market where I managed to find some upholstery material and I fixed the damaged seats in the car myself. I thought that was a smart thing to do since my American relatives were coming to visit us and I had to pick them up at the airport. It was their first trip to Israel, and the sight of my car was rather shocking to them. They came to the conclusion that the Israeli economy had either collapsed or was in big trouble. A month later the ashtray was full and my parents and friends convinced me to sell the car, saying that it was in "great" condition, but it looked like part of some old-time legend. Also, there was a chance that I'd be holding just the steering wheel of my car by the time I reached Haifa. Haifa was the place where my new hospital was located. It was the place where I was supposed to work and study that year.

After a small discussion about the car, I surrendered, for the first time in my life I accepted money from relatives. For 1,500 Israeli pounds, I bought my second new car, which looked more like a toy than a war machine. This time it was made out of fiberglass (I was warned not to park close to camels because they might chew on the fiberglass). The car was of old model, but it ran very nicely. I also noticed that it had an empty ashtray and my friends suggested that rather than emptying it when it gets full, I should consider getting a new car. They must have been jealous, I thought. After all, I was the only one to drive around in a car.

*

Before relocating to the hospital campus I loaded the car with all my stuff and the next morning, as the sun rose and its light scattered all over Beer

Sheba, off I went to start my fifth year of school. A good friend of mine and I moved into a fully furnished two-bedroom apartment located in the hospital yard. Despite the junky, deteriorating decor of our new home and the pungent odor of decomposition coming from the drawers, we were really happy.

There were just six students that worked at the hospital at that time. Whenever any one of us was missing in action, everyone immediately noticed it. So much for sneaking around and cutting classes – we had to act like international spies to escape even for an hour or so.

One morning I woke up and looked outside. It was a beautiful morning. I called Bertie, my roommate, and we decided to spend the morning on the beach together before school started. The refreshing sea breeze, the crying of the seagulls, the softness of the sand under our feet, the rhythmical lullaby of the waves – we were in a world far away from our hospital duties and the professor of surgery who was giving a lecture at noon, submerged and hypnotized by the vastness of the turquoise Mediterranean ahead of us. As the tide hit on the shore, the spray of water splashed on my skin. I turned my head and saw the secretary in charge of the students running towards us. She begged us to return or else the professor would get really mad. Not wanting to get her in any trouble, we did as we were told.

The beautiful morning on the beach was over.

*

It was a wonderful year. We learned and practiced a lot. Since there was just a few of us, we did not have to share the same patients with each other, which offered each one that extra time needed to become good specialists, the ones who know their patients and care about them on a daily basis. As the result of this constant contact with our patients, we became much more aware about the multiple symptoms of certain kinds of ailments.

Bertie and I worked in the kidney transplantation unit. There, we worked for most of the evenings and nights watching and treating patients with kidney transplants. It was a brand new procedure at the time, and our job was to carefully monitor the patients. We spent most of our time in an immaculately clean room that was a restricted area: all communication with other people was done through a microphone installed above the window where we got the medications and supplies for the patients.

After the late nights at the hospitals, there were many mornings when we were very sleepy at the time of our classes. But my job had its own advantages: it gave me an opportunity to make some money which helped me cover some of my expenses – including the car that I would change later on when the ashtray became full. (After all, I had to maintain my image.)

Chapter 8

❧

The Six-Day War

During those days, Israel was not engaged in an official war. But since the end of the Sinai War there had been terrorist activity, especially in the southern part of Israel. Retaliation from the Israeli army was almost part of the daily news. Every day it grew worse. I was born during the war, and was still hoping for a peaceful solution in Israel. As tension and violence penetrated the world, the struggle for power broke out between the East and the West. This led to the Cold War between communist Russia and the United States. It sparked the uprising in Hungary against the communist dictatorship that was brutally crushed by the Soviets, and to the Vietnam War. There was struggle and war all around me. In my own country, the tension between Israel and the surrounding Arab countries escalated. It was very clear that another war was imminent. Soon, after, the hospital went into high alert and we were discharged from our studies.

The first thing I wanted to do was to reach Beer Sheba Hospital. I drove as fast as possible to reach my destination. At Beer Sheba, I went straight to the hospital before even seeing my parents. Everyone was happy to see me, and I quickly joined them in their duties. The Head of the Department of Surgery, who always had treated me like his own son, took me on his team. I was almost a doctor now.

*

It was Friday evening and I was in the emergency room on duty with another doctor. Suddenly, the doors burst open and an ambulance crew pushed a gurney through the door. On it was the Head of the Department of Surgery, Dr. Gliksman, my very dear teacher and close friend. Half of his body was paralyzed. He was unable to speak. He'd had a stroke. Using his good hand, he gently squeezed mine while trying to mumble something I could not understand. We turned his office into an ICU. As he lay there receiving treatment, he looked at me, and I knew from the look in his eyes that he wanted me to go back to work. He wanted to tell me that life has to go on. The situation outside the hospital was getting worse. When I was leaving the room, I saw something that closely resembled a smile on his lips.

Indeed, the situation outside the hospital was quickly deteriorating. Long convoys of army vehicles moved to the south. There were many accidents as well. But I noticed something different, something that I had not seen before: I saw people becoming nicer, friendlier. The drivers on the road were more polite, and, generally, people were willing to help each other. Perhaps it was the tension of the war, which had brought out the better part of all of us. I still find it unfortunate that very often we act kind to each other only in the times of trouble, but it was still nice to see such a change in human behavior.

A few days later, our surgical team was called for a meeting, and we were introduced to the new Head of the Department of Surgery, Dr. Eger. Dr. Eger was in his late thirties, and spoke with a very heavy Hungarian accent. He barely spoke any Hebrew. After the nationwide revolt of 1956 and the brutal Soviet invasion that followed, he was one of the Hungarian refugees that was fortunate to escape. Dr. Eger had been working for a while in a hospital in central Israel. Everyone who had worked with him previously told us that he was a great surgeon.

The lights in his room glowed brightly, and, to my surprise it was full of smoke. I didn't know that he was a smoker. Since many of us were, he offered each one of us a cigarette. It was my turn to be introduced, and Dr. Eger stepped forward to shake my hand. When I told him that I was a medical student who worked as a doctor, he gave me a big smile, and, somehow, from the look in the surgeon's eyes, I knew that I had found the one I was looking for.

Dr. Eger was indeed a wonderful man. As a doctor, he was miraculous. His surgical experience was outstanding. To watch him perform surgery was like listening to music played by a master pianist. The art and the rhythm of his work were simply magical. His hands worked very fast, as he precisely made incisions. The operating field was so clean that one could hardly see any blood. He employed delicate instruments to separate tissues rather than using his hands as many other surgeons did, calling it "untraumatic surgery." The results of this kind of surgery were far superior. Patients had fewer complications, less bleeding and infections, and most importantly, recovery was much faster.

As we spent time together working, I began to idolize Dr. Eger who took me under his wing and became my teacher, mentor, friend and second father. I got to know his family better, as we got closer. I became their good family friend, and his son became more like a brother to me. His wife was a very nice lady. She was a proficient cook, and prepared delicious Hungarian food. From that day onwards, I was consulting him and his wife about everything. Even though they did not know Hebrew, we communicated a lot, mainly in English. Language is never a barrier if people really care for each other.

*

It was the 4th of June 1967. I was on duty in the emergency room with a doctor from the Department of Neurosurgery. We were very busy. Recently there had been many accidents. Mainly the accidents involved victims of military vehicles. Early in the morning we received wounded soldiers that were being rolled in one after another. They were inside the first tanks that had crossed the Israeli border into the Gaza Strip. This Six Day War claimed many lives and left many wounded, creating a deep political resonance for many years to come.

As soon as I found free time from work, I rushed to my parents' place. They were still sleeping, unaware of the recent developments. I woke them up and told them that the war had begun. My parents had seen so many wars, and this was just another one to claim more innocent lives. Quickly, I took some clothes, cigarettes, and some other things I would need for a long stay at the hospital, and left. There were many other lives to be saved. When I arrived at the hospital, I saw wounded soldiers everywhere. Many were from the Gaza Strip and Sinai. The war was being fought on three fronts of the country: Egypt, in the south; Syria, in the north; and Jordan, in the east.

Dr. Bormann, from Jerusalem, was in charge of our team. He specialized in heart and chest surgery and was also a great general surgeon. My eyes were dry from lack of sleep. I worked nonstop for four days and nights, going to the emergency room when called and the surgical wards to take care of I.V. lines. Finally, the sleep deprivation was taking its toll. I began to lose focus. On the fifth day, during surgery, instead of cutting the silk thread after the surgeon had sutured, I cut his glove. Too bad for the glove, but at least I did not do any more serious damage!

Dr. Bormann was very understanding and asked his first assistant to take over. Then he took me to the ward and insisted that I catch some sleep for a few hours. I fell asleep the very same moment my head touched the pillow. An hour later, a nurse woke me up saying that they needed some help with a soldier after his surgery. It was time to return to work.

At the end of the war, Israel had seized the Gaza Strip and the Sinai all the way to the Suez Canal from Egypt, the Golan heights from Syria, East Jerusalem and the West bank from Jordan. There were injuries, deaths and losses. Caring for the wounded was difficult, both physically and emotionally. They suffered from severe burns, amputations of arms and legs, and many other injuries.

I spent the whole summer working at the hospital trying to reduce the pain and sufferings as much as I could. Soon the summer ended. I returned to Haifa for a short while to say goodbye to my teachers, instructors and friends before starting my last year of medical school. The unique experience and the words of praise from many doctors reinforced once more the desire to become a surgeon.

School started, so it was time to change the car. It was going to be my fourth car. This time I bought from a dealer in east Jerusalem that a few weeks earlier had been under Jordanian rule. It was a big, nice American car, not edible by the camels, and didn't look like a world war artifact.

The territories seized by Israel offered a new way of getting from Jerusalem to Beer Sheba via Hebron. As a result, the travel time was shortened. Now it took only forty-five minutes. As my car sped on the black road surrounded by the desert on both sides, the radio played the Six Day War songs. One of them, which was pretty famous, kept playing again and again, which was ironic considering its lyrics: "I promise you, my little girl, this will be the last war." It rhymes very nicely in Hebrew. That little girl who was being referred to in the song is probably in her forties today, and she did not have even a day of peace. Many songs are too good to be true. This was not the last war.

Chapter 9

Shalom: שָׁלוֹם

The war ended, and life in Israel returned to normal. People started their routine activities: rudeness returned to the roads, neighbors were unfriendly again, politeness vanished from businesses, and even doctors spent less time with their patients. As soon as the dark times were over, as soon as the war ended, the kindness and compassion gave way to rudeness and indifference.

All the above is rather strange. The word "hello" in Hebrew is "shalom," which literally means "peace." It is used as a greeting, or when you are bidding goodbye. However, it also signifies welfare of every kind: sound health, prosperity, security, contentment, wholeness, perfection, and even harmony and rest. But, of course, the most important meaning of "shalom" is "peace." As I dwelt on all those things while driving around in my car, I wondered if, perhaps, for some unknown reason people had forgotten it.

The war was over, but peace was still far away. It was hard to believe, but another war was about to start along the Suez Canal, and it was going to be an exhausting long one. Since Israel had occupied many Arab territories after The Six Day War, the Arabs who lived there were not friendly any more towards the conquerors. Driving through these new lands became increasingly dangerous. The hospitals were still occupied by the wounded, and many of them were still coming to Beer Sheba, rather than checking into the new military facility in Sinai.

We worked in different departments, and usually in pairs. One day Bertie and I arrived at the psychiatric hospital and had to take medical histories and examine the patients. On one occasion, a woman that I was treating complained of being pregnant for the past few years. She had been living in an illusion that there was a baby growing inside of her. After having conducted a thorough examination, I discovered that she had developed a large-size tumor in the lower part of her abdomen. (The human mind is, indeed, a marvelous device allowing us to believe or find an excuse to believe in anything we want). So, I reported the diagnosis to her attending physician, who explained the news to the patient and told her that she had a growing tumor that had to be surgically removed. Needless to say, the woman's fallacy about pregnancy vanished soon after the surgery, and she was back to her normal state of mind.

*

During my graduate year I studied Ophthalmology, Dermatology, Otolaryngology, Psychiatry, Pediatrics, Obstetrics and Gynecology. I'd say that Pediatrics, when it came down to actually holding and treating very young and very ill children, was the hardest thing I had ever done. I love kids. Children are the purest of souls on earth and to see them suffer the way they did was very, very painful. There were cases of terminally ill children and those with life-threatening conditions. Even today, with forty years of experience as a doctor, and after having treated many children, it is still very difficult for me to stick a needle in an infant's scalp to give him fluids.

The year came to an end, and we shifted to a higher gear – our finals. Each examinee was to be tested by three Professors of Medicine who specialized in the given subject matter. It was a real thing: each medical student was assigned a patient whom he had to examine. That included obtaining the medical history, evaluating the symptoms, and coming up with the differential diagnosis, assessing reasonable prognosis and suggesting various treatments.

Out of all the exams, I particularly remember one. It was the exam in Gynecology and Obstetrics. I spoke to the patient and examined her. I completed my report and entered the examination room full of confidence over the assessment I had done. There were three professors of Gynecology. I presented my patient's medical history to them, stated my findings of the examination, and, as I began suggesting the right treatment, the professors of gynecology asked me a question, "What will you do as a doctor who has just met this patient?" I began giving him the answers, but every time I said something, he'd shake his head. "No, what will you do before that?" I tried to come up with possible answers, but everything I told him, resulted in "no."

I became really nervous. All confidence left me. I started sweating. I feared I was going to fail. My throat was dry and it felt as though my tongue was glued to the roof of my mouth. I could hardly say anything, but after a long pause, I gathered all my strength and mumbled, "I don't know." The doctor smiled. "Always try to make a connection with your patient. Let them know that you care. Put your hand on her arm. Give them a feeling that they are in good hands."

It was something that I would never forget in all of my years of practicing medicine. I do not necessarily put my hand on the patients. These days in the U.S., I most likely would be sued and accused of sexual harassment. But I always listen. I show them that I really care and really want to help. If I really listened to the patient, I probably would not be able to see as many patients as is required. That's one problem with modern medicine.

*

My last exam was in Surgery. It was scheduled for December 5th, 1968. Everything in my life so far suggested that I should pass that exam with flying colors: the day I saw my father after his kidney stones were removed; the spinning operating room when I was sixteen and my first appendectomy; the memories of my dear Hungarian teacher and mentor; the long night shifts treating the wounded in Beer Sheba during the Six

Day War. My confidence was high, and there was no way I was going to screw up, I thought.

Well, well, well … I examined the patient and did the best I could presenting the detailed analysis of his case to the Examination Board. During that time, there was a brief interruption and one of the professors had to leave. He was called to the emergency room. I had to finish my presentation to the remaining two professors. Questions followed. I waited for the results. The news came: I got the highest score! For once, I had my head screwed on right! I was overjoyed and could not help smiling. I was a Doctor of Medicine.

As I was about to leave, the door opened and the third Professor of Surgery, the one who had left earlier, walked in. He saw a big smile on my face and probably thought it would be a clever thing to do to ask me a question or two. This time, for sure, I was screwed, blued and tattooed as the smile slowly left my face. Instead, I got dizzy and had no idea what the correct answers were. After this debacle he brought down my grade from "excellent" to "very good." After the exam, I asked my friends who were surgeons if they could answer his questions, but none of them could. It did not really matter, because now I was a real doctor, and not a bad one.

I hurried to my car. I wanted to get to my family; I wanted to share my happiness with them and the rest of the world. Before driving home, I stopped at the Health Department and got the sticker that said "Doctor of Medicine" for my car windshield. I couldn't wait to see my parents. As soon as they heard the news, they hugged me and told me that they were very proud of me. My mother went inside and brought me an envelope: it was my graduation present. I opened it. There was a check inside with the name *Doctor Amnon Goldstein* written on it.

Chapter 10

The Cutting Edge

The next morning I woke up to the first sunrays. I woke up in anticipation of the new life that was awaiting me. It was my first day as a medical doctor at the Department of Surgery in Soroka Hospital, Beer Sheba. This place became my second home during the years I was studying to become a physician. As soon as I opened the front door, I heard, "Shalom, Dr. Goldstein." I smiled – that was my friend, Dr. Widdny. "Doctor?" Was he actually greeting me? It was funny to hear it from him. We had known each other for ages. I was and still am very happy and proud of the title that I had earned, but prefer when people call me simply Amnon, by my first name, whether they are friends, colleagues, or patients.

That same day, Alberto, a doctor from the ENT department, gave me a good piece of advice. He told me that when I present myself to officials or while ordering Kosher food, I should present myself as an M.D., which will ensure that I receive a faster and more professional service – or a better piece of steak – while, on the other hand, when dealing with service providers like car mechanics, plumbers, etc., I should just tell them my first name. "If they know you are a doctor making a lot of money, they will charge you more," he reasoned. One might think it to be a pretty screwed-up advice, but unfortunately it was, and still is, true.

I was visiting friends who lived in Savion, a very prestigious neighborhood outside Tel Aviv. I parked my car outside their house with my "Doctor of Medicine" sign on it. It was about midnight when the doorbell rang, and we saw a man who looked panicked – his son was choking. I immediately rendered help. Upon the boy's recovery, his father, feeling relieved, asked me in front of everyone who'd been watching the scene, "How much do I pay you for your help?" Before I managed to answer, "I don't need to get paid," my friend Jim jumped in and said, "Pay him as much as you would have paid a plumber to open blockage in your sewage at this time of night, or pay him half of what you were ready to pay before he saved your son."

This sudden answer from Jim was not what the man was expecting. He was taken aback and started stuttering. I realized that the sudden remark from Jim might have embarrassed him, so I put him at ease and told him I expected no payment.

*

The pace of work at Soroka Hospital was very fast. We had to deal with a lot of wounded soldiers and civilians. Like most young doctors, I thought I knew everything, but very soon I found out that I had to learn so much more in addition to the knowledge acquired at med school. That was just a foundation. It was there, at Soroka, that I started taking my first steps to becoming a healer.

After the ashtray of my last car filled up, I bought a new car, and for the first time it was really brand new. The new car and the title of a doctor had made me an eligible bachelor, and yes, every now and then someone would give me this envious look. I hated when people stared at me. The reason was that deep inside I was still hurt and trying to heal from that sweltering hot day in Tel Aviv when I was physically assaulted. I felt very uncomfortable whenever there was a slight discussion about sex or sexuality to the point that I had to get up and leave at one time. The nearest escape was my work and my patients to whom I wholeheartedly dedicated my time and love. As the admitting physician working in a surgical unit, I had to know every little detail about the patients: the case history, the full physical examination, the result of the tests, as well as conduct differential diagnosis to be presented to the surgical team. Every day I had to undergo yet another struggle of fighting death of those admitted and prayed to God to help me cope with it.

Working in the hospital was not just an escape. I loved my work. Everything was so different from being a student – now human lives were in my hands. I had to attend to patients before and after surgery, change the dressing, and renew the IV line. I spent most of the day in the operating room three times a week, assisting during surgery and performing operations while being supervised by a senior surgeon.

The fact that everybody in the Department knew me from my college years started to pay off. The years of intern practice at Soroka had put me at the same level of expertise as other resident physicians. I spent more time in the operating room than other young physicians and had more responsibility. Two to three times a week I was on-call working in the ER, taking care of everything from simple sutures to treating very severe injuries and other surgical conditions.

One Saturday night, the ambulance delivered a female patient accompanied by her husband. The patient was sedated and covered with a blanket so that we could not see the extent of the injury. She was hysterical, screaming and crying. When the cover was removed, we all saw that she had extensive injuries to the lower abdomen, her pelvis and legs. On top of that, there were severe second- and third-degree burns to about 40 percent of her body.

As it turned out to be, the family was spending a weekend in the Gaza Strip. Before reaching it, the husband got out of the car to get some drinks when an Arab terrorist threw a hand grenade into their car. The two young children, a boy and a girl, were killed instantly. Pretty, their mother, had no desire to live, but survived after having gone through a sixteen-hour surgery conducted by a team of general, orthopedic and plastic surgeons. After the operation, her condition was critical but stable.

Having seen her two young children's instant death, Pretty was determined to give birth to another boy and a girl. She had her own private room, and her husband Bob was next to her day and night doing all he could to comfort her psychologically, and to help prepare her vegetarian meals. Changing the dressings on the burned areas was extremely painful, even with all the pain medication she was on, but Pretty knew she had to go through agony and pain to give life again.

Pretty stayed in the hospital for about half a year and, overall, had about thirty operations. There was no doubt that even with the extensive trauma to her pelvis, nothing was going to stop her from becoming a mother again. When Pretty and Bob, her husband, went home, we all had to cry. For years we stayed in touch with the couple. A year went by, and one beautiful spring morning we saw them standing in the doorway holding in their arms a little baby boy. Two years later this little boy had a sister. They named the children after the two little angels they had lost in the horrific terror attack.

*

They teach you in medical school not to get too attached emotionally to your patients. I guess I am a bad student. Even today, after more than forty years of being a physician, I am still emotionally attached to many of my patients. The joy of seeing them healed and the sorrow of losing some of them is still a big part of me.

Soroka hospital was and still is the hospital that serves all the southern parts of Israel. Besides serving the civilian population, it also accommodates the troops that are stationed in the south, as well as the Sinai desert and the Gaza Strip. Military helicopters delivered most of the wounded soldiers there. We were busy all the time: days, nights, weekends and holidays. The hospital staff constantly remained in a state of high alert. Any minute there could be the sound of a chopper or the piercing siren of an ambulance rushing in yet another victim.

Dr. Eger, the Head of the department of Surgery, my teacher, mentor and a second father, whom I admired and respected in so many ways, once told me privately that one of his goals was to train me to take over his work one day. I told him that I felt privileged, and would do my utmost to become as good a specialist as he was, or even, with God's help, better.

Besides being a general surgeon, Dr. Eger loved vascular surgery and spent a great deal of time teaching and training us in this field. We had an experimental lab for vascular surgery conducted research. Working there provided a special treat. It was more like a hobby compared to the exhausting long shifts and drills. Dr. Eger's wife, Suzan, was a wonderful lady who used to bring us strong coffee and delicious Hungarian food when we worked long into the nights.

One afternoon, a woman was screaming as if she'd been stabbed was rushed to the ER. Her face was covered with a towel. She was in a trance repeating over and over again: "He took my eyes out! He took my eyes out!" I entered the cubical where she sat on a bed and tried to calm her down, with no success. When I asked her quietly if she could remove the towel from her face, she refused and continued screaming. With the help of Edith, the nurse, we removed the towel and almost passed out. It was the most horrifying thing I had ever seen. Both of her eyes were hanging from their sockets, all the way down her face on a thread of tissue. What a horror! What madman could have done it to her? Immediately, an ophthalmologist was called. He told us that very little could be done. She would be blind for the rest of her life. The neighbor who brought her in reported that her husband found out she was having an affair. In a rage, he tried to strangle her and when her eyes were bulging out in agony, he took both of them out using his fingers.

*

Every day I listened, learned, worked and gained a wealth of experience. There was not a single day when I would not learn something new, as there are no two people, and consequently no two patients that are alike. I loved my work and was very happy. There is no routine in surgery. Every day was different.

But it was time to take a break and change scenery. I had saved enough money during my internship for a travel adventure, and now decided to have one. I was going to visit Europe this time. At the travel agency I met two students about my age, Miri and Gila, very nice and friendly ladies.

We started chatting and discovered that we had a lot in common. We decided to go on this trip together.

We visited Holland in the early summer when all the Dutch tulips were in full bloom; then London; and afterwards, we drove all the way to Scotland. We journeyed along the French Côte d'Azure to Spain and then took the Orient Express from Madrid to Italy. After visiting the ancient ruins and fountains of Rome and singing on board the gondola along the canals of Venice, we returned to Milan from where Miri and Gila went back to Israel, while I took a boat to Greece and the Greek Isles. I needed to be alone for a while, away from the rest of the world, away from Israel, away from the emergency room. I spent a relaxing week on the Island of Hydra. It felt as if I was on a different planet where all the buildings, houses, Orthodox churches with their gilded domes, steps and arches, were pure white cascading down to the tranquil azure waters of the Aegean Sea. Quietly, I was carried away into the world of the Greek Gods and legends.

Chapter 11

Love Is in the Air

Time at work passed quickly. Talk about my new car started to die out. During one late night shift I went from the emergency room to the surgical unit. As I passed the nurses' station I saw a new girl who must have joined the staff just recently. She was dressed in white. I looked at her face – she was pretty – and instantly I was attracted to her. That night I could not get her image out of my head. I had to know more about her. I had to know who she was, and what her name was. The desire to know her, to make her part of my life became stronger every moment.

I called my friend David, an anesthesiologist who was on duty that night, pointed out the nurse out to him, and said, "She is going to be my wife." He looked at me with surprise and asked, "Do you even know her name?" He laughed at my childlike declaration of my future marriage. He looked at me again and said, "You are a screwed and tired man. Go get some sleep."

But sleep was miles away from me. I decided to talk to the girl. I introduced myself. Apparently she already knew who I was. I thought it to be the right moment to ask her name. She smiled at me and said that her name was Esther. As I inquired more, I learned she was a student at the university. She studied mathematics and had her classes during the day. She worked part-time as a nurse at night to cover her expenses.

Passover was approaching, and I realized that I would have five days off during the holidays. Nothing would have been better than to spend this time with the woman I was going to marry. With no hesitation, I asked her to join me on a trip to Galilee, the mountainous region in Israel's north with high peaks, many streams and brooks, evergreen forests, valleys and lakes. It's a very beautiful area, especially in spring. She was surprised by my sudden request. Her immediate reaction was, "No, I don't know you." It is really strange when people want to do a certain thing, but say no the very first time they are asked to do it. I chuckled and said, "I just introduced myself to you. How can you say you don't know me?"

We must have talked for half an hour or so, interrupted many times by patients. Finally, she agreed, but on one condition. That I meet her parents first. They came from Austria and requested that their only daughter, Ettie, introduce any new male friends to them. I agreed. I had to meet my future wife's parents, after all.

Ettie and her parents lived in one of the suburbs of Tel Aviv. Their house was small but comfortable. As I entered, I sensed an atmosphere of strictness and discipline surrounding Ettie's life. Her parents were very nice, and we got along really well. I found out that they had escaped from Austria when the Nazis came into power. Ettie's father later joined the British Army while her mother studied and practiced nursing in Scotland. After a lot of painful turbulence, they reunited and settled in Israel. I liked them and found them to be friendly, but aloof.

The next day, we traveled to Haifa for the annual flower show. Ettie and I then headed to Acre, one of the oldest sites in Israel, dating back to 16th century B.C. where, according to the Greek myth, Heracles found curative herbs to heal his wounds. We visited the old defense wall fortified during the mid-18th century by Daher el-Omar, that a century later would survive Napoleon's siege. From there we watched a most beautiful sunset as the colors of the sun changed from bright yellow to deep orange, finally setting in the Mediterranean, painting the sky with subdued lilacs and azures. The sound of the waves as they crashed against the yellow stones of the wall on the shore filled the evening. It was just the two of us at that moment, a definitive moment, a moment of love. A beautiful flower that lay on the golden sand caught my attention. I picked it up and asked Ettie, "Will you marry me?" She looked in my eyes and said, "Yes".

Now was the time to announce the news and receive the blessings of our parents. There were no objections on their part: Ettie's parents suspected that something like that was about to happen, while mine got very emotional and told me that was the best surprise they had ever had. At a Friday night dinner at my parents' house, my mother announced that it was my birthday the next day and everyone was invited to our engagement party. And she meant everyone. There were more than seventy people there.

The next day our house was decorated with all sorts of flowers, decorations and lights. Everyone was cheerful. Ettie arrived. She was dressed in a beautiful white dress. It was a bit too short, according to my father who could not help himself. "Does she not have enough money to buy a bit longer dress?" We all laughed at his remark.

The party was filled with joy and laughter. My mother was an outstanding cook who loved to entertain guests. She had prepared everything possible, even though it was the Sabbath and all the shops were closed. Somehow she managed to stock ahead of time everything needed for the big feast. It really was love at first sight, and everyone saw it. I really fell in love with Ettie. I think, even today, Ettie does not quite believe me, but maybe when she reads this chapter dedicated to her and her alone, she will see how much I loved her and how I had fallen truly, madly and deeply in love with her the moment I saw her.

Rumors spread fast in the hospital and the city. So did the gossip. Some assumed that Ettie was pregnant, and that was why we were getting married in such a rush. It was annoying and not possible – we just met a week ago. The preparations for our marriage started and were followed by all the required fuss of a wedding. The dresses, the decorations, the guest lists – it all kept both of us busy. Between all that planning and work, I had to find time to make it to several fittings with the tailor. In those days, everything had to be made from scratch. Finally the wedding day was announced. It was July 13th, 1970. I was nervous that day, but when I saw Ettie dressed up in her long white wedding dress, all my fears were gone, and my heart was filled with the love I had for her. She was so beautiful. I remembered the time we had spent together, those three months that had passed us by, and now we were to be a married couple.

After the wedding my parents called Ettie and myself with a surprise. They gave us the deposit to buy our own apartment. We took a mortgage, too. We were excited and started to feel like a married couple. However, we barely got to see each other. Occasionally we would run into each other during our shifts as a doctor and a nurse, but we always saw each other in the dining room or in one of the corridors of the hospital. With so much time spent apart, we were still in love and very happy.

Chapter 12

Welcome, Ravit

The year went by and Ettie was pregnant with our first child. I could not wait to see my child and become a father. I counted days until her arrival, and on October 28th, 1971, our daughter Ravit was born. It was the day I could never forget. It was the day I became a father.

But before all that, we had to go through natural labor and pain. The magic of the epidural was yet to be discovered by the civilized world, and it was quite common to have complications. Our family friend, the Head of the Obstetric Unit, whom we had known for years, was going to help deliver our daughter. Being a doctor, I was allowed to be present, an unusual situation in those days. A screaming woman in the maternity ward was a pretty typical thing to hear. There were no complications during delivery. It was after midnight when I first saw our baby daughter Ravit. I was filled with love, a new kind of love, and this, too, was love at first sight. The midwife congratulated me with my blonde baby daughter. I was looking down at the baby as she got smacked (the usual welcome to the screwed world!) and yelled out her first cry. Welcome to the world, my daughter Ravit.

I looked down at her small head and noticed that her hair was dark. "The color of the baby's hair will change. Look at her eyebrows," replied the nurse, "They are light, and so your daughter will be blond." That was a rather smart deduction, I thought.

In the morning I walked into Ettie's room. It was full of flowers. I had never seen so many flowers in one room, and there were flowers outside the room as well. Surrounded by all the flowers, Ettie was lying in bed, crying. I was scared. Terrible thoughts came into my head. I thought something had happened to the baby.

Ravit was in an incubator and her birth weight was low. The pediatrician wanted to do a spinal tap, because, according to him, she appeared to be rather lethargic. It was a false alarm. The baby was fine. My parents visited us soon, and when my father saw his granddaughter for the first time he asked me, "Are you going to tell me that someday this little creature will turn out to be a human being?" Indeed, it was hard to imagine that the tiny little underweight baby girl would become overweight in a few years.

The birth of the first child changes everything. It seemed that it even changes your DNA, your values, emotion and, certainly, priorities. The things that were so important to us up until now suddenly faded in their significance, giving way to the most cherished and loved creation, our newborn baby. Even a person's driving is affected when there is a baby on board. I used to be a fast driver, but not anymore. I couldn't risk my life. I had to be around to love and take care of the new member of my family. You have to be a parent to understand it. Life will never be the same, not even after your children grow up.

Like all new parents, Ettie and I spent many sleepless nights caring for our new baby. Time flies when you are having fun, and pretty soon Ravit turned one year old and was admitted to a nursery while Ettie returned back to work. The nursery was a great place for working mothers. The babies were well taken care of and fed several times during the day. After Ettie picked up Ravit, she would feed her again around 4:00 p.m. Ravit's grandmothers and her mother were constantly worried that the little girl was starving, and in no time we were the happy parents of a plump baby girl. I asked the grandmothers to stop overfeeding the child, and they thought I was the bad guy for even thinking that way. I mean they really screwed me over, treating me like some evil villain who was preventing his daughter from being fed enough. Now, am I totally screwed-up or is it western society where 50 percent of the population has weight-related problems? I assure you, it all starts in childhood when our mothers are overfeeding us. And Ravit? Well, she'd pay a dear price for it one day.

Ettie went back to work. She began teaching at a nursing school, and I got busy with my duties at the hospital. A few months later Ettie was pregnant again. We were both happy and expecting our second child to come soon. Suddenly tragedy struck us. It was when Ettie got sick with measles, and so did Ravit. Luckily, they both recovered very quickly. However, Ettie's mother, who was also a nurse, told us that children to mothers who had measles during pregnancy suffered from severe birth defects. She had seen it on her job. She told us that we are going to have a child with birth defects, and to not expect any help from them.

I decided to look into the matter, and after consulting many experts we came to the conclusion that the pregnancy had to be terminated. This was a very accepted medical practice under these conditions. The gynecologist tried to convince us not to do it, but eventually he agreed to stop Ettie's pregnancy.

I will never forget the moment when he came out of the surgery room holding a small bottle. He put the bottle in front of me and said, "This could have been your baby." I broke down. Were we screwed or was he? How could anyone say such a thing to a friend, a doctor, and a father? That was a very difficult and tragic time for us. He told Ettie that after the abortion she might become infertile. As any woman who had to have an abortion, Ettie was going through feelings of guilt and remorse, and the only thing that could help her cope with this tragic loss was to have another child. After a short period of time we were very happy expecting our second child.

Our family was expanding, but our apartment was very small. We decided to buy a lot in a small developing community called Omer, near Beer Sheba, and build our new house.

Finding the right house is never an easy task, and after having seen several lots, we eventually settled for one. It was 100,000 square feet and located by the side of the road. There was no heavy traffic. We paid $5,000 and became the new owners of piece of desert in Omer, a small community surrounded by Arabian Bedouins and camels – everyone we knew thought that I had a loose screw. My plan was simple. I decided to build two houses instead of just one; sell one, and then we could use the profit to build the house we had always wanted.

Chapter 13

Dr. Eger

There are days that just go by, and then there are days that bring with them the startling news that no one can ignore or forget. This time the news came, and it was about my dear friend and teacher, Dr. Eger. He had been diagnosed with advanced lung cancer. He was only forty-one years old. The news came a day before my brother's wedding.

I was the one who took him to the hospital in the center of Israel. The next day his wife and his young son came to my brother's wedding. When I saw them, I could not control myself, and the tears began pouring down my cheeks. The sorrow was so great that I was unable to cope with my emotions throughout the wedding. I could not break this news at my brother's wedding. I tried again and again to tell myself to stop crying and not screw up my brother's wedding because he had no idea what was going on with me.

A few days after the wedding, my boss had surgery followed by radiation. As soon as he was fit to walk again he came back to work. We all knew it was only for a short period; we all knew his life's light would soon cease, and the man who was a teacher and an example to many of us would soon have to battle death. Even though he was terminally ill, he kept treating and guiding us as young doctors. Until his last day he was dedicated to his profession, devoted to his colleagues and patients, and determined to defy death by sharing all his wisdom and talent with a team of surgeons who at any minute were ready to take over his responsibilities and duties.

Alas, he was indispensible. In fact, he was the most important part of our hospital's foundation, and it was hard to imagine things without him. Besides being such a great general surgeon, his real passion remained vascular surgery. At the hospital we worked hard in this field and many new developments in vascular surgery came out of our department. We were the first hospital in the world to replant an upper limb of a soldier that was cut off by shrapnel. There were other instances of replantation of an upper limb, but those injuries were not sustained in war. We were also the first hospital in the world to reconstruct the blood flow to a lower limb in a patient whose arteries and veins were stripped by mistake during an operation to remove varicose veins. We were able to save her leg, and all this had happened under Dr. Eger's supervision.

Those acts of surgery had their own bittersweet moments. I remember how a red-haired soldier for whom we re-implanted the arm gained full movement and control of his arm. A few months later when I was on duty in the ER, I saw him walking in with a towel around his arm. I got worried and feared that something terrible must have happened to his arm that we had joined a few month ago. Later I found out that he got in a fight and broke his arm. I was relieved that he had his arm still attached to his body, and not in the icebox. The arm was broken, and after receiving proper treatment he was discharged, and promised to stay out of trouble.

Meanwhile, Dr. Eger's condition was deteriorating. He was very sick and refused to be treated in the hospital. I started treating him at home with the help of his wife and other doctors. I stayed next to him for most of the days and nights. We did not want his son to see his father suffer, so his twelve-year-old boy was sent to stay with friends. The last four days of his life, he was mostly unconscious. I had to administer high doses of morphine to control his severe pain. He woke up once and demanded angrily, "Stop screwing yourself over this. Let me die." He died the next morning. He was forty-two years old.

Hundreds of people came to his funeral. It was quiet and dignified. The rabbi said, "God judges you in justice and makes you die in justice." His words cut me like a sharp knife, and I screamed, "Where is justice? A great person who helped thousands of people, a good father, teacher, husband, and friend died so young. How can you call it justice? If this is justice, then I don't want any part of it."

I knew it was inevitably that my friend would soon depart. It's all part of the Divine Plan, and each one of us has his path to follow.

Chapter 14

My Father-in-Law

When I returned from the funeral, the telephone was ringing. It was Ettie's mother – she was panicking. Her husband was bleeding severely from his stomach. Since the day I had met Ettie's father, he suffered from an ulcer. As a young doctor, I had contacted his attending physician and asked him about the possibility of surgery to solve the problem once and for all. What he said was pretty irritating to me. "There are certain people who need and want to be sick in order to get the attention from others."

I exclaimed, "Why would anybody do that?" But the physician advised me that I should listen to him and do nothing about it, because if I cured his ulcer, he would then develop some other disease, and God only knew what it might be.

I was amazed to hear such a thing from an experience doctor. It was really unacceptable for me to see that there are doctors that would give such a screwed-up response. Who would want to get sick and suffer to get more attention? I did not believe him. Today, with some forty years of experience, I do not doubt his words. He was right and still is. Let me tell you something: even the best doctors in the world cannot heal a person who does not want to be healed. Most people would seek a cure for their diseases, they would say that they want to heal and be healed, but deep inside their subconscious mind, under hypnosis, we could find the need to be sick. A doctor or a healer can only help and guide a person who's ready to be healed. All healing is self-healing. It is the person who heals himself. No one can cure a person who wants to make himself sick.

I told Ettie's mother to call an ambulance and get her husband to a hospital because he needed urgent surgery. She said, "Herbert refuses to go to the hospital and says that unless you come to see him, he was going to die at home." It was about a two-hour drive. I was on my way to see my father-in-law. He was very sick, pale and vomiting blood. I tried to explain to Herbert that he needed urgent blood transfusion and surgery to stop the bleeding. To my relief, he agreed, but demanding that I should be the only one to operate on him, otherwise he would refuse any treatment. I tried to reason with him, explaining that he was in no condition to be in the car for two hours to get to the hospital where I worked. I suggested that he'd better be going to the nearby hospital. I let him know as well that I do not operate on relatives. After all of this, I still was unable to convince him. That was another turn of the screw. I ended up taking him to Soroka, the hospital where I worked.

There was no time to lose. We started immediately by giving my father-in-law blood and fluid to stabilize his condition and prepare him for the surgery. I asked Dr.Lewis, a senior surgeon, to perform the operation, but Ettie's father refused and agreed to have it done only if I was to operate on him. He acted like a stubborn child. So Dr. Lewis and I together proceeded with the surgery. We had to remove about two thirds of his stomach in order to stop the bleeding.

The next day a physical therapist came to give Herbert treatment and make him cough. There was a reason behind it: being such a large man and a smoker, it was critical to make the patient expectorate the phlegm from the lungs to prevent a chance of developing pneumonia. Again, all our attempts were in vain, as he refused to cough up and hawk his phlegm out, complaining that it was too painful. Exactly two days later, he developed severe pneumonia and was in critical condition.

I was very concerned about him and asked the best hospital pneumologist to take care of him. He was connected to a respirator but still managed to talk and say things that really angered me. I felt like there was no use trying to help some people. He spent four days in the ICU, and luckily, despite his bad attitude, managed to recover and was discharged from the hospital.

Chapter 15

Yom Kippur War

After the death of my dearest friend and mentor, followed by the illness of Ettie's father, I was emotionally exhausted; but there was more to come. It was September 1973, right before the Jewish New Year, when we moved to our new home. It was a beautiful and large house where Ravit had her own bedroom, and there was another bedroom waiting for the newborn.

It was October, the holy day of Yom Kippur. The sky was clear blue with a few puffy white clouds at a distance. I decided to spend some time in the garden – it was a quiet day perfect for gardening. We had planted several fruit trees, shrubs and perennials, and it was time to water everything. While I was pulling some desert weeds, I noticed that the traffic on our narrow road became unusually busy. Yom Kippur in Israel is a holy day, and people usually stay in their homes. Something unusual was going on.

I was still trying to figure it out when the phone rang and I was urgently called to the hospital. Another war had begun. I took Ettie and Ravit to my parents' home and headed for the hospital. By the time I reached the hospital, the war had been given a name, the Yom Kippur War. This time, it was rather unexpected.

I had worked at the hospital during the two previous wars. Too many wars to speak of, but this one was different – there was no warning – and Israel was attacked on all fronts by the Arab neighboring countries on the holiest day in the Jewish calendar. We were continuously watching the news. I remembered Ben-Gurion, the first Israeli prime minister, saying, "The last war in Israel will be the war when the Arabs win." I wondered if his words were a prophecy. Was it going to be the last war Ben-Gurion was talking about? Was this war going to be the end?

The wounded soldiers that we treated told us many tales about the war. They told us how bad it was on all the fronts: hundreds of soldiers were wounded, hundreds of soldiers dead. It looked as if we were going to lose. This war had led to strained relations between the U.S. and the Soviet Union. The whole world was wondering about the outcome of the war. The Israeli army was not one to give in easily, and within a short period regained control. All the enemies were pushed back. The war took a different course. Responding to cowardly attacks by Arabs on the holiest day, Israel struck back with a vengeance. The enemies were forced to withdraw.

All wars have their heroes. In this war, one of them was Ariel Sharon. He changed the course of the war in the southern part of Israel all the way to the Suez Canal. One morning, I admitted Arik Sharon with a bullet wound in his head. He was in good spirits: full of energy, swearing to return to the front. The neurosurgeon, who was called immediately, confirmed it, saying that it was a superficial wound and Sharon was going to be fine.

The war had left many wounded. In fact, the emergency rooms were filled to their full capacity with soldiers arriving hourly. In view of these circumstances, new arrangements had to be made. The hospital lobby was turned into an emergency room. The place was filled with wounded soldiers. Many of them had burns, limbs that were amputated; severe injuries – but strangely, the place was very quiet. One could hardly hear any screaming. Suddenly, the doors burst open and a screaming soldier ran in. The doctors and nurses rushed to help him only to find that as he had opened a bottle and the cork hit him in the eye.

The war was over. We celebrated our victory. You won't believe what song they played on the radio. Remember, that song that goes: "I promise you, my little girl, this will be the last war." Yep, it was all over the radio on all the stations again.

*

I find that it is very important for me to connect with my patients, to get to know them on a more personal level. During the course of treatment, we had developed close connections with some of the wounded soldiers. There was a young soldier named Avi that arrived in critical condition. He had a shattered leg that needed to be amputated below the knee. He underwent a long period of recovery followed by extensive rehabilitation.

Before he left, I invited him to have dinner at my house. On the night of the dinner, Avi wore his uniform and came to our house on crutches. My young daughter, Ravit, was only two-years-old at the time. She was rather surprised to see a person without a leg. She kept looking and looking, trying to figure out where was he hiding his other leg, then gathered all her courage and asked, "Why don't you have a leg?" The soldier, who had never talked to a two-year-old before, replied, "Because your father chopped it off."

Probably I should have prepared my toddler for such a visitor in advance, but I didn't and there was a price to pay. Ravit was shocked thinking that her papa was some kind of a "butchering monster" who cut legs off people and then had them over for dinner. She was really scared. I'm sure it sounds very funny now, but it was serious business when my little girl refused to talk to me for several weeks after the episode. It worked out for the better, though. One thing became really very clear to me – I didn't want to raise my children in the same war conditions that I had been raised. I had made up my mind. I decided that we should leave Israel and find a peaceful place somewhere else in the world.

The words of the song "I promise you, my little girl, this will be the last war" were playing in my head. This time it was my promise to my young daughter and the baby to be born. I would do everything possible to prevent them from going through what we had gone through, even if it meant emigrating from our native land. You might say that my decision was very unpatriotic, but if you had been wearing my shoes, you would have seen that it was very fatherly and humane. We needed peace – as simple as that.

I decided that after my residency was over, I would leave my home in Israel to find a peaceful future for my family. I worked tirelessly day and night at the hospital. The need for a new Head Surgeon was greatly felt after the death of Dr. Eger. Therefore, as a temporary Head of the Department of Surgery, a specialist from South Africa was appointed. He was a very nice and warm person. As far as his work was concerned, he was a great surgeon. I was very happy to work with him, but after a short period of time he decided to leave Soroka Hospital and took with him some of the senior surgeons.

Out surgical unit seemed empty, and another person was temporary assigned as a new Head of the Department. Previously, he used to be in charge of the surgical emergency room. When I started my work at the hospital, Dr. Eger shared his thoughts with me privately about this guy: "In case of emergency, I would let this surgeon operate – he is a very good technician – but I will never ask his advice as far as a post-operative treatment is concerned. Neither will I take from him any other medical advice." At the time, I couldn't really understand what was he referring to, but later on it became quite clear.

The new Head of the Department, Dr. Jillions, was initially friendly. Once he said jokingly, "In order to get a lot of experience, my friend, I have contributed a lot to the cemetery population in my home country." I didn't like his so-called sadistic way of joking. The loss of life is never a matter of laughter. As time passed, many of us came to the conclusion that Dr. Jillions was not qualified enough to head such a reputable Surgical Department, neither did he provide any support to us, nor to the young surgeons during their last year of residency. There was no professional growth with him.

Another doctor and I decided to approach the medical director and share our concerns with him. There was a general meeting where I honestly shared my opinion with the team, but to my surprise, found no support from anyone else. To make matters worse, the friend with whom we started the whole thing just added, "I think he is okay." What a coward! Saying one thing to me the day before, agreeing to support me, and then not having any courage to back me up during the meeting!

Obviously, from that day my problems started. And I was the one to blame, naively thinking that I could help make the change for the better. I felt like an idiot. Dr. Jillions turned my life into a living hell. He used all his might trying to get rid of me. Things got pretty much screwed up for me in the Department of Surgery. Although it was clear to me that general and vascular surgery were what I really wanted to do in life, for now, things had to change, and I decided to make a move switching to orthopedic surgery, neurosurgery, and plastic surgery.

Chapter 16

Welcome, Ran

As I passed my days working and searching for better prospects, a momentous event occurred. On April 20th, 1974, our son Ran was born.

I still remember that moment very clearly. That day Ettie was in labor, and I was in the delivery room. Again, I was reliving the time of Ravit's birth. It was the same stuff – women screaming all over the place. I wonder why we did not use some kind of medicines to ease their pain. The doctor who was going to deliver my baby was the doctor on duty. I did not want to bother the Head of OBGYN on a late Friday night, although my wife, in between the contractions, asked me a few times to call him because he had treated her during her pregnancy. I should have trusted her intuition, but I didn't. Women know best when it comes to having babies!

Ettie's labor was progressing, and then, into this world, came out a blue baby. The umbilical cord was twisted twice around his neck. It was quickly removed, but the baby was still blue, still unable to breathe properly. He got the customary "welcoming" smacks on the behind, but no crying ensued. I was shaking with fear that we might have lost another baby.

I was desperate to get some help, when suddenly, my friend David, an anesthesiologist who specialized in pulmonology, walked into the delivery room. He was my only hope at the moment. I pulled him by his coat and yelled, "This is my son! You'd better make him cry right now." The treatment worked. The baby's color turned pink, and he was breathing normally, screaming and crying. It was our good luck, and all I could think of screaming was: MAZAL TOV! GOOD LUCK!

A week later we brought our son home. He was very yellow. There were blood incompatibility issues between mother and child. Luckily, it was not serious and within a month the jaundice was gone. The only problem we had was this healthy baby who was eating, screaming and sleeping, while we, the screwed ones, were awake for nights.

After our son was born I took Ravit to the hospital to introduce her to her new brother. She was thrilled to see her new baby brother, but somehow it seemed like she knew of the impending sleepless nights that befell us, she said, "Can we leave him in the hospital until he grows up?" Well, this is a fact: little children are very beautiful and cute, but ask the ones who care for them. It is the hard work of many sleepless nights just to keep them happy and laughing. Since Ravit had warned us about the "dangers" of taking the baby home, now every time he cried she would say, "I told you to leave him at the hospital till he grows up." Now, who would have the courage to stand against the argument of the little girl? We all laughed at her one-liners.

As usual, his mother and grandmothers cared for the baby. They were around him most of the time. Well, with three "mothers" caring for the baby, I tried to be with Ravit during most of my free time. The arrival of the new baby was hard for her. All of a sudden she had to share the attention with this new little brother of hers, and, trust me, little children don't like sharing the love of their parents.

The arrival of a baby in the household makes everyone extra cautious. Actually, I'd use the word paranoid. One particular evening I was watching TV. Ettie and her mother, who was a pediatric nurse for many years, came to me. From the look on their faces, I feared that they might tell me about the outbreak of another war, but what they had to say was even scarier. Ettie almost lost her breath as she said, "The baby is not breathing properly – he is blue." I jumped up from my seat and rushed to my son. I found that there was nothing wrong with him. He was sleeping quietly, peacefully, breathing properly, his sweet plump cheeks pink, not blue. Standing next to me were two very scared nurses who scared the hell out of me only a minute ago.

I took a look at my son again, listening to his heart and lungs. Everything was perfectly normal. So there was only one diagnosis – the sickness was in the heads of these women. I tried to calm them down and went back to watch TV. Ettie came back, blasting me with all sorts of things, telling me that I was a bad father and all sorts of arguments about how I did not care about the baby. All I cared about was Ravit.

One would ask – since I was not even given a moment with the baby – how could I shower him with my love and attention when all the limelight was taken by Ettie and her mother. Ettie would not give up and asked me to see the baby again. I went to check on him again, and again everything looked normal. However, Ettie kept insisting that I just missed the moment when Ran was turning blue. That was it!

I told them to get ready because I was taking Ran to the hospital. The doctor on call in the pediatric emergency whom I knew very well came immediately. What followed was nothing less than an epic. After examining the baby, the doctor came back with a brown paper bag. He handed it to Ettie and asked her to breath into the bag – a very well known treatment for hysteria known to decrease the oxygen level in the blood.

As I said, it was the paranoia of the loving mothers, not the sickness of the baby.

While I was being accused for spending all my time with Ravit, she was getting a lot of attention from her mother and grandmothers in the form of sweets. All that sugar was making her chubby. The grandmothers were very happy because she looked like a healthy child, and me – well, I was the bad guy again objecting to the fact that my little daughter was getting too much food and sweets.

The "sweetening" of the children was not limited to Ravit alone. Usually, when a baby cries between meals, he is given some water. The grandmother, who was the nurse, said that we had to add some sugar to the water. Again I objected and didn't like the idea, this love and care would make my children obese. I told her not to put sugar in the water, but who cared what the screwed one said? One day when Ran was crying, I offered him a bottle of water. He refused to take it. The next thing – his grandmother came in with another sugar-water bottle, and, lo and behold, the baby started drinking it.

How come Jewish mothers and grandmothers always know better than their screwed-up husbands and sons? I guess I have just given an answer to my own question, haven't I? I was worried about Ravit, who was two at the time, gaining so much weight, so I asked a pediatrician to examine her. I was afraid that on top of it, the little girl could have had some other medical issues. There were no other alarming news about her, and the only reason she was overweight was due to being overfed. I remember one of my professors once said, "There is no overweight without overeating." This is true, except for a few exceptions that are medical.

The only other thing that her doctor thought was important to do was to schedule Ravit's for X-rays to make sure that her bones' age corresponded to her chronological age. The day of her appointment (the X-ray lab was in the same hospital building where I was working) Ettie took Ravit to the lab and left her there in the nurse's care. I started walking down the hallway towards the Surgery Unit when I heard piercing, loud screams. They were coming from the lab. I made a sharp u-turn and in no time got back to the X-ray room where my daughter was screaming and fighting a technician who was trying to take her hand X-rays. The image of a soldier whose leg was amputated never left her, and she thought that was what doctors did with "bad body parts."

Chapter 17

The Black Continent

Small events change the course of a person's life. Sometimes they lead to something great. Other times they can mess him up. What happened to me was a combination of both. I still recall the day when it happened. It was my night shift. I entered the operating room and saw a young surgeon performing surgery. I had never met him before. I decided to stay and watch him work. I don't think I have ever seen anything like it. It was more like watching a renowned pianist perform one of Beethoven's concertos. Every move, like every note, was crystal clear, polished to perfection, with precision and total control. He had a great technique – he was an artist! Whoever his teachers were! I wanted to learn from him. I wanted to learn more about him!

He spoke English with a different accent, not anything I had ever heard before. "Certainly not from Israel," I thought. After the surgery, I went up to him and introduced myself. His name was Jeff. Shaking his hand, I told Jeff that it was a beautiful experience to watch him operate. I was impatient. I was asking him a lot of questions, and, finally, he revealed his secret. "There is only one place in the world where in a short time you can learn a lot and gain so much experience. There are many patients and the training is excellent – it is Baragwaneth Hospital, near Johannesburg, South Africa."

Jeff explained to me that it was the largest hospital in the world, and it served the township of Soweto. (The term "township" refers to a residential area reserved for black citizens within the boundaries of a city or town.) "There are about two million residents living in Soweto, and this hospital serves them all. The medical staff is also part of the university, an excellent research facility."

Baragwaneth Hospital seemed like the ideal place to get surgical or any other medical knowledge and experience. There was only one problem. I was not the only one interested in joining the wonderful staff of this South African hospital. Doctors from all over the world would have loved to work there, with an average waiting period of three years. "Screw it," I thought to myself. "That is a good excuse to leave this place once and for all."

I took the chance, that life so unexpectedly surprised me with, and a month later, in April of 1975, I was on my way to the airport to fly to Johannesburg. My parents, Ettie and my kids saw me off. While we waited for our flight, my parents met the owner of the vegetable and fruit store where they used to shop twenty-five years ago. They had a good memory, I tell you. The funny thing was that the owner was taking the same flight as I was to Johannesburg (they had moved there many years ago) and invited me to stay at his house during my visit. That was a sign of a very good beginning. It was way better than the one in New York where my aunt first refused to let me stay with her.

During the flight I had nothing else to do but to imagine what it would be like in Johannesburg. I knew it was the largest city in South Africa, but it was still under Apartheid. Was it going to be a jungle, if not physical forest, but the one with mental wilderness instead? To my relief there were no big trees – at least, not as far as I could see – when we landed in Johannesburg. Rather, it was a big, beautiful, modern city. The mental anarchy of a jungle was still in place though. Already at the airport, I noticed that except the porters and cleaners, all the staff was white. They spoke English and Afrikaans, a dialect that is mainly Dutch, and those were the two official languages of South Africa. The language itself was not the only difference. Everything around me was different, including driving on the left side of the road.

Segregation was everywhere: on the buses, in the post office, the shops, restaurants, movie houses. Even the public toilets were separated, having two entrances, whites and blacks. Furthermore, when it grew dark most of the blacks had to leave the city – they needed special permission to stay in "the white area" after dusk. Johannesburg was a beautiful city. It had lush green public parks with gorgeous landscaping and fertile green vegetation, but only the whites were allowed to come in.

Being a gardener, I took a day off to explore this South African paradise. There were so many different species of trees I had never seen before. (They did have big trees there, after all! I found out that there were six million trees in Johannesburg, i.e., 1.2 million within the parks and on the pavements, and 4.8 million in private gardens throughout the suburbs). I saw a brown paper bag sitting on a bench. Being an Israeli citizen on guard all the time looking out for terrorists, I reported to the guard that there was a suspicious parcel on the bench out there. He looked very concerned indeed and wasted no time offering his apology for the fact that the park had been poorly cleaned that afternoon.

The very next thing I did after taking an outing to the Public Gardens was to make a call to the brother of an Israeli friend of mine. He was a very well known doctor in Johannesburg who arranged my meeting with the professor of surgery at Baragwaneth Hospital.

The hospital was huge! By the look of it, one could see how much activity was going on inside. It had 5,000 beds and many outpatient clinics. The general surgical departments had 1,000 beds divided into five 200-bed units. The units had two very large halls, one for women and the other for men. To supervise all this, the Head of each unit had to be a highly experienced surgeon. Those surgeons were, indeed, first class specialists. I was overwhelmed by what I had seen. After I saw the hospital I was sure that it was the ideal place for me to work.

I met the professor of surgery and we had a pleasant conversation. I presented my C.V. to him and was offered a job. He said that I could start as soon as I got my work permit and license to practice medicine in South Africa. I was entirely happy. My dream was coming true, and it was very real.

My brief visit to South Africa came to an end and it was time to return to Israel.

As soon as we landed in Tel Aviv I was stopped by a customs agent and was asked to follow him to a room where I was asked to take off my clothes as the officers searched me, my clothes and my luggage very thoroughly. I did not know what was going on. My first fear was they might have suspected me of being a terrorist. As soon as they were done with me, one of the officers told me quietly, "You ought to thank your neighbor for all this hullaballoo – he informed the custom authorities that you were about to smuggle diamonds from South Africa." All I had brought back from South Africa were a few presents for my family and children. Without any apology or an explanation, I was released. A neighbor sent false accusations to cause problems for me, his neighbor. Whatever happened to the concept of helping your neighbor?

As soon as I got home, I started the procedures for getting the work permit and license to practice medicine in South Africa. It didn't take much time, and in ten months we had all the necessary documents. In March 1976 we left for South Africa. How long were we going to stay there? Were we supposed to ever return to Israel? Was Johannesburg going to be the place we'd find peace after all? Were we going to regret leaving Israel? Ettie's parents and my own folks saw us off at the airport. It was hard for them to watch their grandchildren and children leave – they were so close to them. I told them that we were leaving for two years to get some practice and experience in surgery, but it was clear to me it was going to be longer. At that time my mother was being treated for severe depression. The depression took a toll on her. She got better from time to time, but in general her condition was not that good. She was crying and it was not an easy thing to say good-bye to her.

Chapter 18

Looking for Peace: The Last Paradise

From the moment we touched down at Johannesburg International Airport, located about 5,500 feet above sea level, there was only one question I could not get rid of: "Will I find the peace I am looking for?"

Of course, we needed a place to live. Initially we found a temporary apartment in the doctors' residence on the hospital premises, a small, but clean two-bedroom flat. We had doctors and their families as our neighbors, and as far as I remember, they were all very nice people. A few days later one of the them scared Ettie by telling her that every afternoon there was a march of black people crossing the hospital premises to get to Soweto – an urban area of Johannesburg bordering the city's mining belt in the south – and that she had to watch her children carefully. That added to Ettie's anxiety.

As soon as we settled down, I started my work at Baragwaneth Hospital (Bara for short) located to the southwest of Johannesburg, on the southern border of Soweto. It was Friday, April 1st, 1976. That day our unit was on duty. It was a pretty long spell of time, some thirty hours. Being new, I was warned that "being on duty" implied also working during the weekends. Being a workaholic in love with my profession, I couldn't wait to start.

Our team consisted of three doctors, four interns and six medical students. Since this hospital was affiliated with the University of the Witwatersrand (Wits, for short), our job also implied providing training for medical students. Starting in the afternoons, patients would pour in and the emergency room was full. Even though it was a time of peace, the emergency room reminded me of my many shifts during the war in Israel – it was like living in a war zone all the time. There were many sick and wounded. At first glance, there were more wounded than sick. Those were the wounds of crime assaults and violence, such as knife stabs, gunshots, and blunt force injuries. The first wounded person I saw had a knife stabbed in his chest. I asked if I should call the thoracic surgeon to drain his chest, a general procedure, but everyone found it funny. They explained that here, at Baragwaneth, all the prep work was done by a medical student under a surgeon's supervision.

I saw some serious stabs wounds, many of them resulting in paralysis as a result of penetrating spinal injuries where the victims were assaulted with axes, screwdrivers, garden forks, sickles, sharpened broomsticks, kitchen knives, etc. Most often the weapon was withdrawn by the assailant. Sometimes there were cases when I had to remove the weapon retained in the spine, either partly broken or intact. Needless to say, management of these patients was quite challenging because removal of these objects very often led to neurovascular deficits.

I was told that a lot of victims were robbed while taking a train back home on a Friday night, their payday, after being stabbed in the back and paralyzed, often with sharp objects like bicycle spokes like that poor fellow who was lying on the operating table in front of me. I could hardly see the place where he'd been stabbed.

The results of these massive assaults were quite evident the next Saturday morning while we went to do the rounds of the department. What I saw was something I had not expected: overnight, the official number of patients in the unit went up from two hundred to four hundred. The cases ranged from minor, like stabs in the chest requiring simple drainage, to more severe ones, with some of the examples given in the previous paragraph. Some of the newly arrived victims were positioned on chairs, mattresses, occupying the spaces between the beds and even under the beds, while those with life threatening stabs were sent to the intensive care.

We usually needed a nurse to translate for us when we talked to our patients. Most of them came from all over the country, as well as surrounding African States, and spoke various African languages and dialects. After finishing rounds, we went to the intensive care unit to check on some of our patients. This hospital kept surprising me. Again, as I entered the ICU, I could not believe my eyes. It was beautiful, perhaps the largest and one of the best-equipped intensive care units I had ever seen in my life.

I snooped around and saw that there were about fifty beds, and each one could be closed with a curtain giving the patients privacy. Apart from that, next to each bed there was a nurse who exclusively took care of one patient using the newest and most advanced medical equipment. They had permanent doctors in the unit and, each department sent a doctor every month to study and work in the intensive care unit for the period of one month. Not only did it help to increase the number of doctors, but it also gave the new doctor special experience working with patients.

Bara hospital was not just a gigantic clinic. It was a place for learning as well, and a part of our duty was to teach the medical students and the resident doctors to advance their training. As I worked with the students, I was amazed by the high standard of their knowledge in medicine. Most of them were in the fifth and sixth year of medical school. Their knowledge and experience were certainly higher than what I had seen in Israel; even the standard of interns was comparable to that of a resident in second year in other countries. Well, it was not much of a surprise – we were getting the best training.

In Baragwaneth there was a department for every field of medicine: heart surgery, neurosurgery, plastic surgery, and every other possible field of medicine. Other than that, the hospital had many outpatient clinics. There were about twenty operating rooms, and they, too, were equipped with cutting-edge technology. The medical care that was given to the black patients under the apartheid regime was extremely good; perhaps, due to the conditions they were made to live in, it had become a necessity. The best thing was that every patient paid only 1 South African Rand – equaling at the time $1.35 U.S. dollars – for all treatments, all medications, all required tests, and their stay at Bara Hospital. Healthcare was affordable, and everyone was well taken care of; medication remained within his or her reach, and this, certainly, was commendable.

I wrote a letter to Erik, a doctor friend of mine in Israel, saying, "I wish the standard of treatment in Israel was as good and advanced as in this hospital for black South Africans." The doctors and the staff were very friendly. They did their best to help each other in challenging situations and were outstanding in their desire to reach out and help care for the sick and injured. Every Saturday there was a special training workshop where the surgeons from all over Johannesburg met to discuss special cases – a great place to learn and understand the medical field on a deeper level.

While working under the apartheid system (apartheid means segregation in Afrikaans) there was one thing that I noticed – the majority of the doctors working at Bara were white. There were a few Indians, but there were no black doctors, although the clinic itself was designed strictly for the colored population. The reason was the medical school in Johannesburg did not accept black students (however, the nurses were black). Again, something was screwed! Why no black doctors, but black nurses? I could not possibly understand or get used to the idea of segregation that penetrated even educational establishments in South Africa.

Baragwaneth was a mammoth hospital. It was still growing while I was there. Even after having spent several years working there, I still hadn't seen the entire premises. The work atmosphere was wonderful – many of the doctors were from foreign countries that contributed to Bara's international atmosphere and made the working environment even more inviting.

As the days progressed I took on more responsibilities and learned more and more. One day, while I was on duty, a young female with knife stab wounds in her chest was brought in. One of the stabs went straight into her heart. She had to undergo immediate surgery. I was going to call the heart surgeon, but instead was told that when I was on duty, I was the heart surgeon. If there was anything to fix, I had to fix it myself.

What was rather shocking at first turned out to be a blessing later on. That day I performed my first heart surgery, and after that incident, had more than 250 similar operations resulting from stabs to the heart. The hospital's mission stated: "You see one; you do one; you teach one," and it certainly was working out just fine for me. I saw my share of sick and injured in Israel and South Africa, and with each new case I continued learning and growing.

A few days later the Head of the Department called me. In his office a surprise awaited me. "I am very impressed with your performance, but here you start at the bottom and go as high as your ability and knowledge takes you. I think you will find it fair and challenging." I began working even harder. It didn't take long before I was called again. When I reached the Head's room, he told me that I was promoted to senior surgeon. From now on I would continue to perform mainly major surgeries, but my main task was to teach other doctors, students, and interns.

Imagine. I, the screwed one, the little boy who once called his principal "a fat cow," was now a teacher himself – and in a world-renowned medical school!

Being a teacher had added responsibilities, but I loved the fact that I was not involved in any of the paperwork. My work was pure medicine. To be frank, I found the paperwork a bit boring. At the end of each operation I dictated the report while I scrubbed for the next surgery. I had to report only to the Head of the unit, Dr. Andre, a great man and great surgeon.

Other than my work, I had a family to care for. While I was working at the hospital, Ettie was taking care of the children in her excellent manner. There were some problems to be solved: the apartment we had rented was just a stop-gap arrangement. We needed a bigger home, with our children growing, and, as always, I feared an uprising by my little children for more space. The first thing I did was to go hunting for a house spacious enough to live in. Pretty soon, with the help of some friends, Ettie and I found a house in a good neighborhood for rent. The price was fair, and in no time we were moving to our new home. It was our first house in Johannesburg, located in a Jewish neighborhood with a lovely lake for sailing, fishing, and spending the day outdoors.

As we moved in, we were pleasantly surprised when our new neighbors welcomed us with flowers, cakes, food, and wished us all the best in our new location. Now this is what I call a beautiful welcome, certainly different from my Israeli neighbor sent a letter to customs, falsely accusing me of smuggling.

The area we lived in was obviously inhabited by whites. Most of them lived in nice houses with beautiful and well-maintained gardens. Attached to the house were the servants' quarters. Each family had at least one black maid working fulltime, except Thursday afternoon and Sundays. There was usually another one to take care of the garden, the yard, clean the cars, and do other jobs in the house. The maid took care of the children, cooked, cleaned, and set food on the table.

In many houses there was a small bell on the table, and all you needed to do was to ring the bell when you needed service. She would come to clean the table or do whatever needed to be done. After dinner you could move to a nearby room where drinks were served, and, of course, the maid attended to all the dishes. As far as the laundry was concerned, all you had to do was just throw the dirty clothes on the floor and magically they would be cleaned, ironed and hung in your closet the same day – and yes, the maid was also a babysitter. We were free to get out in the evenings without worrying about our children.

People were dependent on maids who very often were mistreated by their so-called employers. The servants were routinely carrying out various chores around the house and in the garden, and in return "their masters" would once a week go out and buy food for them, which they cooked and ate in their own quarters. For all their hard work they would get board and lodging, and a very small salary. Under the apartheid law you could only employ the black people who had a special permit to stay in the white area.

Sometimes in the evenings or at night, the police would search for the illegal blacks that would be routinely arrested and sent back to where they came from. The odd thing was, however, that there was no police interference with what was going on in those areas where those illegal immigrants lived – a breeding ground for a wide array of South African train assaults, violence, robbery, rape, gunfire, etc.

A few days after we had moved to our new house I went to the servants' quarters and was absolutely shocked. All that was there was a broken spring bed, a shaky table that they used for cooking and eating, a few broken shelves on the wall to keep their food, clothes and other belongings. The bed rested on red bricks. I was told that this was to keep the little devil named Tokolosh away, so he would not conjure up the spirits of the dead to haunt anyone sleeping in that bed. Whether Tokolosh or Apartheid were to be blamed for the way those poor people had been treated, I could never tolerate anything of that nature, and together with Ettie we painted and renovated the servant's quarters and bought them decent furniture. The screwed "white" mentality of other people living in our neighborhood came to light when we wanted to pay a higher salary to our staff. What came next was a protest from our neighbors. They told us not to do it because if we did, all the neighbors would have to be forced to pay more, which according to them was not acceptable.

Our maid Anna, who was so lovingly taking care of all our needs and more, became an integral part of our family. Our children loved her and she loved the children. We trusted her completely, and she was always as good as her word. Perhaps, the utmost sign of devotion and love on behalf of Anna was when she started carrying two-year-old Ran, whom she tied up with a blanket to her back while doing her daily chores. He would fall asleep immediately, being rocked in his sleep by his African nana's footsteps. I will never forget the image of Anna, our black South African friend, with the white two-year-old toddler on her back. Anna was very gracious and humble, still unable to accept the fact that she was no different from us. Whenever she was invited to join us for dinner, Anna would say "no" politely and eat on the floor in her room just like all her ancestors did, despite the fact that we had bought her new chairs.

A friend of mine said, "This is the last paradise on earth." But I asked myself: "How can it be paradise when the black majority lives in hell? Is our world so screwed that being in hell or heaven is determined by the color of the skin and not by personal acts?"

There were a number of rare ailments that were quite common among the black population, namely esophagus cancer, which, sadly, had a liking for the black population of the country. This cancer was so rare anywhere else in the world – but abundant in South Africa – that in all the years of practicing medicine in Israel I had seen only two cases of it, while in Johannesburg I saw about twenty a day. This was again the result of a poor diet, or rather absence of one. There was something very morbid about this cancer. In all the years of working in Johannesburg, I didn't see a single patient that survived more than a year from the day he or she had been diagnosed. Most of the victims checked into Bara with very advanced stages of esophagus cancer, and that made things really difficult for doctors to treat. While the white population consumed large amounts of meat for every meal – breakfast, lunch and dinner, contributing to South African statistics at the time of being a number one leader in the world in the areas of heart disease, high blood pressure and atherosclerosis – the blacks were starving or surviving on whatever junk they could find that was edible. It was "the food" and/or absence of it that was slowly getting a grip on so many impoverished black South Africans.

Chapter 19

Student Uprising in Soweto

In the middle of June 1976, two-and-a-half months after I started working at Baragwaneth, another war of a completely different form, broke out. It was Wednesday, June the 16th, 1976, and our unit was on duty. As the afternoon approached, the door to the emergency room opened and we were deluged by dozens of stretchers being rolled in one after another. Young teenagers, high school kids, most of them bleeding from severe injuries and gunshot wounds.

For a moment it seemed as if I were back in Israel again. Panic inundated the hospital. I wondered what might have happened. We did not understand what was going on, but soon we found out that there was an uprising in Soweto, the black township near Johannesburg. That day, the Soweto high school students started protesting against The Bantu Education Act, which compiled a curriculum that suited the "nature and requirements of the black people" by boycotting the instructions in Afrikaans, one of the official languages of the apartheid. Police responded with teargas and live bullets.

According to the author of the legislation, Dr. Hedrick Verwoerd (then Minister of Native Affairs) "Natives [blacks] must be taught from an early age that equality with Europeans [whites] is not for them." Black South African population was not to receive an education that would lead them to aspire to positions they wouldn't be allowed to hold in society (hence: absence of black doctors at Baragwaneth), but were to acquire skills that would help serve their township community better or skills required for working in laboring jobs under whites.

The uprising started by Orlando West Junior Primary School, followed by seven other Soweto schools and was the culmination of years of suffering and injustice that had broken free that day. "Our parents are prepared to suffer under the white man's rule. They have been living for years under these laws and they have become immune to them. But we strongly refuse to swallow an education that is designed to make us slaves in the country of our birth," wrote one of the students to *The World* newspaper.

The hospital went into high alert. Everyone working at Bara was instructed to report to work. I had to perform surgery in three operating rooms simultaneously. Our rescue work turned into a swift mechanism that was evolved by us. I would let one doctor start, then it was my turn to move in and do the main part, and, finally, let the first surgeon finish, as I moved to the next surgery. In the midst of this swift-flowing rescue mission of trying to save as many lives as we could of young teenaged kids, there came an announcement: "Please don't panic – they are trying to set the hospital on fire." As soon as the words echoed through the hospital, some of the black nurses disappeared from the operating room, while we doctors continued to do our job. We were there fighting, struggling and trying to save as many of these kids as possible, while their rioting friends were trying to set the hospital and everyone in it on fire.

You can imagine what was going on with my wife, Ettie, who was watching the latest news on TV and tried many times to call the hospital and reach me on the phone. When she did get through, she was told that I was missing.

Luckily, for all the wounded and injured inside Bara, the police, supported by the Anti-Urban Terrorism Unit, and firefighting squad arrived. The sound of army helicopters was heard above our heads and anti-riot vehicles down below, sirens and gunshots. They were able to gain control of the situation, unlike at many other public businesses and school buildings, police stations, and clinics that were set on fire. I found out later that a white doctor, who had dedicated his life to help the black population, was burned to death when his clinic was set on fire. He died while taking care of the injured people.

In order to protect medical personnel working at Bara, the security forces established a new route to the hospital to avoid any confrontation with the rioters. The road cut through the army camp. At last, after a very busy night where I had performed sixteen major surgeries and many other minor treatments I had lost count of, I made it home to my wife and children, who were very happy and relieved to see me alive.

The rioting spread from Soweto to Johannesburg, Witwatersrand, Pretoria, Durban and Cape Town, and developed into the largest outbreak of violence South Africa had experienced. It continued for the rest of 1976. Unlike the previous riots, the police were unable to quell the rioters, even with force. As soon as the upheavals were suppressed in one area, they flared up elsewhere.

For us, life slowly returned back to normal, but this normal was not what it used to be. I'd diagnose it as a bit "abnormal normal." While we all stood witness, the black continent was waking up, and there was absolutely no doubt that the black majority would gain control; if not right away, then very soon. The South African example spread out to the rest of the continent. Recently, Mozambique had received its independence from the Portuguese, and a lot of white refugees were coming to South Africa. Only three countries in Africa were still under the rule of white minorities: Rhodesia, South Africa, and South West Africa /Namibia. The order in which the countries would be gaining their independence was very clear: Rhodesia was going to be the first. It was a beautiful country, rich in resources and very fertile. In fact, it supplied food to many other countries in Africa. It was also one of the major tobacco growing countries, but had no access to the sea. All exports and imports had to go through South Africa.

The second one in line for independence was Namibia. It was also a beautiful country, very rich in minerals and diamonds. In Namibia, most of the white population was of German origin – the ones who had settled in Namibia after World War II; finally, South Africa. It was the last country on the black continent to break free from white minority rule. It was the richest and one of the most developed countries in the continent, with very fertile soil suitable for growing crops, vegetables and fruit. It was rich in minerals and abundant in precious metals like gold and platinum. No doubt the governments of these countries that held on to their former ex-colonies exploited their resources and their people. While the former colonists lived like kings, the natives were suppressed and lived under terrible conditions.

The year 1976 was marked by several wars all over the world – the South African army was fighting terrorists in Angola. There were many simultaneous civil wars going on in the various countries in the southern part of the African continent. There was the much talk about the Cold War between the United States and USSR, and the Middle East. Amidst all of these wars, I, the screwed one, was fleeing one country in a state of constant never ending war to find yet another war zone. The questions that I had asked myself the day I landed in South Africa still remained unanswered: *"Where is this peace that I am looking for? Does the real meaning of the word exist in our lives, or is it just another dictionary term?"*

Chapter 20

A Different Medicine

After the student uprising was over the hospital returned to its routine; life returned to its track. The ICUs were less full, the usual sickness incidence was back to normal. Unfortunately, the rapport between the white doctors and the black nurses was never the same. Bara was the hospital for the colored people entirely run by the whites. The white doctors were doing their best to help the black population. The nurses were stealing food, blankets, linens, towels, sometimes even medical equipment and then selling it in Soweto. Being a humanitarian, I feel that somewhere, somehow, perhaps due to a collective white history of colonialism, we were accountable for their poverty as well. We all held a fair share in their misery.

Being a physician, however, does not let me forgive or forget a particularly gruesome case of negligence and utmost ignorance on behalf of a nurse, regardless of her skin color. One afternoon, a wounded person in very critical condition arrived at Bara hospital. An orthopedic surgeon, Freddy, and myself had been operating on him for sixteen hours. By the end of the surgery I could not get our patient into the intensive care unit because it was full. There was no other option but to send him back to the general ward. I was concerned that he might not get the required care there, so I stayed with him for about two hours, instructing the nurses on how to take care of him. I was very unsure about the nurses there – that's why I laid out precise directions of what to do and was very specific requesting they check his blood pressure, pulse and breathing every ten minutes. They were told to let me know of any changes in his condition.

Early in the morning, after I was done with the patients, I went to sleep for a few hours, only to be awakened about two hours later by the same nurse telling me that the patient was not doing so well. When I asked what was wrong, she retorted, "He's not breathing well." I had a feeling she'd screwed-up already, so I asked her to elaborate on this news, and what came out of that woman was simply astounding.

"There are long intervals between his breathing," she said.

I was pretty sure that that was not the whole story, so I asked, "When was the last time he was breathing?"

"His last breath was about half an hour ago." Her reply made me gasp for air, and want to pull the hair off the stupid nurse's head.

I rushed to the ward and found the patient dead. I touched him. He was cold. It was very clear that he had died a few hours ago. I still do not know what stopped me from pulling her hair out. I guess the reasoning is that it would not have helped my patient. After having operated for hours on someone, spending hours trying to get into her head exactly what to do and how to do it, I got to hear – no doubt, several hours after the patient had died – "He breathed half an hour ago." I tell you, after what I'd heard it was difficult to control myself and behave professionally.

Overall, though, we had a really high standard of medicine, but the cases we had to deal with were far too different from those in other developed countries. I encountered so many bizarre examples that I could write many a book about them, but I will bring only a few to your attention.

Let's start with a young girl. She arrived with a severe intestinal obstruction. It was clear to me that the cause of this obstruction was nothing else but the worms in her digestive system. Without wasting time I moved her to the operating room where she underwent immediate surgery. You would not believe it, but I removed two buckets full of worms from her intestine – rather sick but true – which was another grisly testimony to the lifestyle of poor South Africans. Over there, worms were a very commonplace problem, and this case was just one of them.

The second case was rather uncommon for me, but, undeniably, very, very sickening as well. While I was in the emergency room, one of the interns asked me to look at a patient who was waiting for me, sitting on a bench. As I peeped out to take a look at the new patient, I saw an elderly black man with short white hair. From a distance I had not noticed anything special, or anything abnormal. What followed made my stomach churn. The intern insisted that I took another look at his hair. As I did, I could hardly manage to get outside before I started vomiting. It was something that I had never ever seen before. What looked to me like white hair were maggots eating the necrotic tissue of his scalp. It was sick! It was very sick, but, as a doctor and a healer, I had to see many such cases from time to time.

One particular day, the emergency room was full of patients. Many of them were drunks, while others – a very common sight – had all kinds of stab wounds. Because there were not enough beds, most of them were lying on stretchers. There was hardly any space to move in between. While I was busy with other patients, a young female was brought in on a stretcher. She had a total of forty-two stab wounds to her body. Some wounds were in the chest, and it looked like one of the stabs had penetrated her heart. As soon as she was rolled in she went into cardiac arrest. We immediately started resuscitation. During her surgery, I found two stab wounds in the heart. I immediately repaired them. The patient's condition was critical. With a lot of effort, we finally succeeded in getting her heart beating again. She started breathing.

As I have already mentioned, the ER was exceptionally full that day, and the patients lay side by side. As I was about to close the chest incision of the woman, a drunken patient who lay on the stretcher next to her leaned over and vomited into the open chest. Everyone was shocked. We immediately cleaned the chest with antibiotic solutions (all this time her heart was beating normally). I quickly closed the chest and transferred her to the intensive care unit. A few days later she was discharged, healthy and happy, with no trace of any infection or other complication.

It's a well-known fact that most post-operative infections develop due to the presence of germs that are resistant to many antibiotics. This type of infection is rising continuously, largely because of overuse of antibiotics. In Africa, most of the black population grows up in very difficult conditions; people are very often undernourished, and in my time, there was no electricity or even running water. People in South Africa developed a natural resistance to many infections, so if, by any chance they do get one, most of the time it will clear up without the use of any antibiotics. Due to this strong immune system, the post-surgery infections at Bara were very rare. The simple reason was that those who had survived the tough living conditions, where children's mortality was very high, were the ones with a highly developed immune system, and those people were resistant to all sorts of diseases bacteria and germs.

In the township of Soweto, a big city with about two million people, most had no electricity, running water, or even the elementary sanitary conditions; most of the inhabitants lived in shacks made out of wood, metal sheets, clay, cardboards, blankets, and any other material that could be found. Despite these atrocious squatter camp-like quarters of Soweto, it was a town of traditional healers that would treat their patients with herbs and all sorts of local concoctions they made themselves. A short drive away – and a lifetime away – from Soweto, which was envisioned by apartheid's architects as a vast dorm for black workers, lay the exclusive, whites-only luxurious neighborhood of Johannesburg with beautiful houses, (some of them resembling European castles), lush green gardens, parks and fountains.

Going back to "Soweto doctors," whatever they put in their witch's brew was not so bad until they started using the horns of different animals. Every week we received numerous patients who were poisoned. Many of them died as a result of kidney or liver failure or because their bowels were perforated by the horns that were used to give enemas. I cannot tell you about the so-called "success stories" of the horn treatment, as I did not hear of them, or perhaps they did not come to our attention. It was funny when some patients came to us with a referral letter from the witch doctors. The letter usually started with: "Dear colleague…"

*

Once I operated on a man who had a bowel obstruction. It was not a complicated operation, and he recovered quickly. One day he came to see me again in the outpatient clinic. He pulled out a document and asked for my help. The document said that my patient was sued for 400 South African Rands. He was being sued by one of my "dear colleagues," a witch doctor that had treated my patient before he came to see me. The witch doctor claimed that he was the one who had cured him. My patient had come to ask me to testify in the trial, and explain that I operated and cured him.

I was called many times to testify in murders and assault trials that took place in local courts in Soweto. It was a very unsafe place for white people, and to get in and out I would have to get a police escort. During one particular case I received a letter from a well-known Mafioso who warned me that if I dared to testify against his son, who had murdered another person, my family's and my own life would be in jeopardy. I had no other option but to report him to the police, and the trial was canceled.

*

Many times my interns came to me and asked me to sign their diagnosis. One such intern asked me to sign a document claiming that a certain patient was mentally ill. In order to make such a claim, he needed signatures from three doctors. He did get it from two of them. When he approached me with the same request, I asked to see the patient before signing any paperwork. The patient was an old man lying in bed with a towel wrapped around his head. I couldn't speak to him in English, so I asked one of the nurses to translate. I asked him what was wrong. He replied that he kept hearing voices all the time. I asked what kind of voices.

He confessed that they were voices of different people looking for doctors, calling nurses and asking for help. It was not very hard to guess that they those were different hospital announcements addressed to physicians and nurses that he had been hearing throughout the day – and he was to be certified as mentally ill, not only by the intern but also by two other physicians. I wonder when we will learn to treat sickness the way it should be treated rather than making our own assumptions.

While working at the hospital I was usually very busy with no sense of time whatsoever. Before I knew it, the year came to an end, and then came the holidays —the only time, perhaps, when I saw the whole city joyful and happy. Like any other major cosmopolitan city, Johannesburg, the largest city in South Africa, was festive and cheerful, beautifully decorated for Christmas. There's one thing that no other city in the country can offer like Johannesburg does: shopping. Especially now, Christmas shoppers were flocking the Carlton Centre, Sandton Shopping Centre, the fun Oriental Plaza and not-to-be-missed Rosebank Flea Market. Other than all the festivities, there was only one thing missing, and it was a bit strange for me and the children because we had associated Christmas with snow. Being in the southern hemisphere meant that typical Christmas weather came in summer. So, there was no white Christmas for us.

Meanwhile, things at the hospital were going well. I was happy with my salary at the hospital. It was good enough for us to live a nice life. But renting a house, furnishing it well as per our needs, and buying two cars put us in big debt. On top of that we were expecting my parents to visit us during the holiday season. They had sent me money to buy their tickets, but I used the money to cover some of my debt and bought their tickets on a credit card.

That day, I promised myself that never again was I going to buy anything on credit (except a house mortgage because it is easier that way). Even today, many decades later, I have kept that promise. Today, in the United States, I only buy things with cash. I have no credit history and my credit score is very low. This attitude of mine has kept my nights peaceful, but it also led me to yet another screwed situation. When I wanted to get a contract on a cell phone or to get a mortgage on a house, I was denied because I had no credit history. Isn't it a screwed-up situation when a person who buys only with cash, owns a house and a car and has no debt, is scored much lower than people who owe thousands and thousands of dollars? I think it should be the opposite. Maybe this affinity for credit records has led to our recent great financial crisis.

Finally, the long anticipation of seeing my parents ended. They arrived in Johannesburg and were happily reunited with the rest of my family. It was Christmas vacation, and we decided it was a great chance for us to travel and see South Africa. It is a beautiful country. You can see many places of untouched nature. The prices are cheap, and at those times the crime rates were low. The only screwed thing was, it was ruled by the white minority. In this beautiful country, only the whites lived in luxury, while the suppressed and poor black majority was waiting for "the change."

The world was doing its part in helping the majority in their struggle against the white minority. The United Nations and many other countries instated sanctions against the white government of South Africa. The war in Angola continued, and the black majority in Rhodesia was about to take control of the country. As we watched the political movement in the neighboring states unfold and grew closer to South African borders, there was no doubt that the winds of change were blowing in our direction. It would only take a sparkle to ignite the flame of the anti-apartheid movement.

Chapter 21

Do Bad Things Really Happen for a Good Reason?

I was delighted at the low crime rate in South Africa until an incident led to a major change in my life. It was Friday morning. Ran, my son, came to my room and asked, "Daddy, Daddy, where is your car?" I was a little surprised, and replied, "It's in the garage."

"No, It is not!" he replied. I quickly went to the garage to see what he was talking about, only to find that my car was stolen. I had to get to the hospital. I was on duty that day, so I took my wife's car. As I drove towards Bara, my fate was waiting for me at the corner. There was a big traffic jam. There was nothing I could do about it, so I sat in the car listening to the radio.

Suddenly a car that was trying to bypass traffic hit me from behind. Bad fortune struck twice the same day. I wondered how screwed things could get within such a short time) I felt terrible pain in my neck, chest, around my right arm and shoulder. I somehow managed to get to the hospital and took some tablets to control the pain. I slept all night in the hospital. In the morning one of the nurses told me that she could not wake me up during the night when she wanted me to see a patient. It was probably the result of the painkillers.

My condition improved gradually, but the pain in my neck and the weakness in my right arm persisted. The pain didn't want to go away, which affected my work. I saw many doctors. All of them told me there was nothing they could do about it. Two weeks passed and the pain persisted. On one occasion, during surgery, I had such severe sharp pain my neck that I had to quit and ask my colleague to take over. While my condition remained the same day after day, I tried to avoid major surgeries. The problem of not being able to bend my neck and keep it in this position for many hours while working at the operating table forced me to get involved with consultations and training other doctors and medical students.

Not being able to do what I liked to do was a real pain in the neck! I kept wondering all the time how I got so screwed. I tried everything with no result. I saw many neck specialists. Some of them suggested surgery, but all agreed that it would only be a temporary solution. I took medication to reduce pain, but I was afraid of getting addicted to painkillers. I tried to avoid taking them as much as possible, but that meant missing work many times.

The problem that had started with Ran telling me my car was stolen now took the form of unbearable pain. Unfortunately, with all my experience and other doctors' advice, I was unable to find a realistic solution until a friend suggested I should see a Chinese doctor of acupuncture. I chuckled and told him, "I may just as well go and see the witch doctor on the other side of the road."

I did not get any better. The pain was there all the time. My friend Marco kept nagging me with his Chinese acupuncturist. Eventually I yielded to his persistence and decided to go and see the Chinese man. His room was nothing like the hospital where I worked. It wasn't clean. The so-called "clinic" from which he operated was in his house. I saw him taking out the needles from a very murky liquid that was supposed to be the sterilizing solution. I was scared to catch all sorts of infection, because my immune system was not as strong as that of the natives.

Backing off and running seemed like a good idea, but the China man promised me that he was going to use new sterilized needles. I gave up. What happened next was as good as a miracle. It took only six treatments to get me almost free of pain. I was back to work. I could function easily and operate without pain. It was clear to me that it had nothing to do with psychology or the placebo effect, because I had never believed in the effectiveness of acupuncture. So, the miracle had something to do with the treatment itself.

Was Western medicine that I studied and practiced the only way to relieve pain and help others, or was there something else too, that we in the West refused to see and accept? As far as I remember, China started to open to the West right after President Nixon's visit. Acupuncture was still considered in the West a primitive "witchcraft" without any scientific base, precisely the reason I was so skeptical when my friend Marco mentioned Chinese acupuncture. But bear in mind that acupuncture has been practiced successfully in China for about five thousand years. That's a pretty long time, I must say. It has been with us many years before Western medicine even started.

Things got better again, and with some financial help from my friends we bought our first house in Johannesburg. My joy was boundless when in May of 1978 Ettie became pregnant again. We were expecting our third child. The new house and the news of a new arrival awaiting us was nothing more than a blessing. We were supposed to move in July and our new baby was expected at the beginning of September.

With all the good news came bad news. My mother was hospitalized with a bowel obstruction. To my relief her condition was good, except that she became severely depressed. Her depression was not new for us. She had suffered from it for many years now. Fortunately, she recovered quickly and was discharged from the hospital after a few days.

One morning I woke up and told Ettie that I had to go to Israel. I did not know why, but I had to go. It was very clear to my wife that I was indeed screwed (as if she had not seen the signs before). From her perspective, things looked this way: She was seven months pregnant, we were about to move into a new house in a few days, and I told her that I had to go to Israel for an unknown reason. But there was no way she could have seen how screwed I really was.

We moved our furniture and belongings into the new house and without even opening any boxes, the next day we were on our way to

Israel. Our families were very happy to see us. The day of our arrival passed happily, and we all enjoyed being reunited for a while. By evening, when we all had settled down, my mother called me to her room. She told me that there was something that she wanted me to see that worried her. She had not mentioned anything to my father, as she did not want him to know. She told me that she felt a lump in her left breast. The news came as a bolt of lightning.

My first reaction was to deny what I had just heard. I thought that it could not be serious. It was only two weeks ago that she was discharged from the hospital, and they did not find anything. When I examined her, the room started spinning around me. It felt even worse than my first experience at surgery. It felt worse than anything I had felt. I knew she had cancer. The next day I took her to the head of the surgical department, who was also a friend of mine, and asked him to check my mother out. He concurred with my diagnosis and scheduled a biopsy for the next day. What I was afraid of had come true. It was a cancer growth, and he performed a radical mastectomy.

My mother was told that it was a suspicious tumor and in order to reduce the risk, it would be wiser to remove the breast. She agreed. Radical mastectomy was the operation of choice at that time, where the breast with the underlying tissue, the muscles going down to the rib cage, and any suspicious lymphatic tissue under the armpit, had to be removed. The only ray of hope in that situation was the pathology examination showed that the cancer was not spreading.

Now it was time for the rumormongers to have some fun. The rumors spread quickly that a doctor's mother was in the hospital two weeks ago and was not diagnosed with breast cancer and was just operated on to remove the breast. It was very obvious that the cancer did not just start growing the last two weeks since she was released from the hospital.

So, an investigation started to find out what went wrong with my mother's treatment. When I looked at her hospital chart from the previous admissions, the doctor who examined her wrote that he did not find any masses in her breast. That made me furious and sad at the same time. I do not know what was so screwed up in this health system that a doctor did not even bother to examine a woman properly, but wrote that she was all right? Had I not been there with her that evening, I would have never been able to save my mother from cancer and this medical system. Meanwhile, my mother was recovering from the surgery. Her depression was augmenting, and it was not at all helping her case.

While my mother was at the hospital recovering, we went to visit Ettie's parents in the town of Dimona, where they moved after we had left Israel. While we were waiting at a bus stop, I noticed how ethnically diverse the people standing next to us were. Some of them were black. They must have been from the small black community of Dimona consisting of people who called themselves the black Hebrews from Chicago. At that time, Ran was about four years old and knew that in South Africa when he talked to us in Hebrew, no one would understand. To my shock and utter shame, he started yelling out in Hebrew, "I am not getting on this bus, not with these black people!" This was a bus station in Israel, and everybody knew Hebrew. I could not tell how embarrassed I felt. Everybody was staring at us, as if we were some kind of racists who had taught their children to behave this way.

The worse thing was that our son, who was raised in South Africa, sounded like a racist, and I can assure you that he did not get it from us. Perhaps it was the neighborhood where we lived, where the screwed-up parents filled the minds of their children with all this hatred. Since that day I made sure that my children knew how other people live. I made sure they realized that everyone was equal. Pretty soon this little boy became a human rights activist, supporting the movement of South African blacks against apartheid.

The time of our departure had come and Ettie started having contractions. We rushed her to the hospital where she was admitted for observation and received medication to prevent the contractions. She was discharged in a couple days, and after a tearful goodbye from our parents, we were on our way back to Johannesburg.

Chapter 22

Welcome, Ori

Finally, the expected delivery came, and on September 5th, 1978, I found myself screaming "Mazel tov!" again. Our son Ori (meaning "my light" in English) was born. Unlike his brother and sister, he was born during the day with a very short delivery time and no complications. He was a perfectly healthy and screaming baby.

There was a Jewish school in the neighborhood where we lived. In my opinion that school was for rich Jewish spoiled children, but I was forced to give in to the pressure from my wife and parents and agreed to send our children to that school. All of my children were kept busy. Ravit started going to elementary school. Ran was in kindergarten, and the maid was taking very good care of Ori. She used to tie him with a blanket on her back while she did the housework, just like Anna who babysat Ran. As she worked, baby Ori slept happily on her back, relaxed and at peace.

Overall, bringing up children in South Africa was so much easier than in Israel. The children were taken care of, the household chores were done, and a babysitter was available so we were free in the evenings, knowing that our children were in safe hands. These were the benefits of living a pleasant, comfortable life style of the whites in a screwed racist country.

My mother recovered from surgery. We tried to convince her that she did not have cancer anymore, but she refused to believe the good news, and her depression grew worse every day. She believed that she would die soon. Her depression was getting a solid grip on her, so I convinced my parents to move to Johannesburg to be closer to us and enjoy their grandchildren. Finally, they arrived. We all were very happy and excited that day. The children were happy, jumping up and down, kissing and hugging their grandparents. I was relieved to have my parents with us.

Chapter 23

The Art of Acupuncture

The real voyage of discovery consists not in seeking new landscapes, but in having new eyes.

--Marcel Proust

Blessings often come in disguise. The theft of my car and the car accident that led to months and months of agonizing pain led me to the discovery of miraculous acupuncture. Not only did it relieve me of the neck pain, but offered a new direction in my life.

Like an inquisitive child astounded by something immensely great and unexplainable, I wanted to know how it actually worked, what were the constituent parts of this miracle machine. I wanted to study them and explore the hidden medical secrets hidden from Westerners. I was sure that besides acupuncture, there were some other forms of alternative or "primitive" medicine that were also considered a joke by the modern medical community. Is our society so screwed as not to accept a remedy that is drug-free and so effective, or simply afraid of the unknown?

After having been stunned by this mind-boggling acupuncture, it was clear to me that I had to study the subject further. I had to know what the philosophy behind this treatment was. I came to a decision, and in December 1979, Ettie and I were going to Hong Kong. We made an arrangement for her to join me for ten days until I settled down. After that she would return home while I stayed there to study the art of acupuncture.

There were many reasons for choosing Hong Kong over mainland China. It was easier to communicate there because it was a British Colony – most of the people spoke English. Hong Kong, in fact, was a major cosmopolitan city back then, and still is. It has always been the place where East meets West. In Hong Kong we found a different world. It was a beautiful city, full of colors and life, always busy. The streets were always full of cars and pedestrians. People seemed happier and more polite. It was not only a great city for the ones who lived there, but also a paradise for shoppers, because it was tax-free.

Even the food was different and so delicious! We learned pretty quickly not to inquire about what we were eating – we didn't want to get shocked. Though food was very tasty, everything that could be eaten was being eaten in Hong Kong. We could never be quite sure if we were eating a snake or some other creature. The city's potential was fully utilized by its residents. Every inch of the land was used for development. There were shops upon shops of every kind everywhere: under staircases, in small building, on the streets and in the malls, including many designer high-class boutiques. The prices were low and the service was very good.

Meanwhile, I looked for a suitable place to learn acupuncture. There were many Chinese medicine and acupuncture clinics, a lot of options to make my choice from. Finally I found an English-speaking Chinese doctor who was very well-educated and even published a book on acupuncture in English. Since he was going to give a course in acupuncture for foreign doctors, I decided to join it. During the course we visited many clinics and hospitals. We witnessed a number of operations, even the major ones, which were performed under acupuncture with no general anesthesia.

It was even more astonishing than the last time when I witnessed the surgery that was performed under hypnosis. Here, things were radically different. The patients were fully awake and experienced no pain. You could even communicate with them during the surgery. I witnessed a major chest surgery and the painless removal of the thyroid gland done with no general anesthesia. I visited a place where patients were recovering after a stroke. It appeared to me that the recovery was much faster and way better than what I had seen in other countries. I specifically looked into the mechanism of pain-management and various treatments in case of arteriosclerotic vascular disease.

After having successfully finished the course on the technique of acupuncture and its miraculous benefits, there was no doubt in my mind that what I had learned so far would be just the foundation for my continuing studies of this beautiful and ancient medical tradition. Before my departure, I bought many needles made out of silver and an electrical instrument that you attach to the needles during treatments to magnify the effect of the therapy.

I returned to Johannesburg and my family. Everybody was very happy to see me, especially Ravit, Ran and Ori – they got so many gifts from Hong Kong. I still remember little Ori, who at that time was just one-and-a-half years old, jumping on the couch screaming, "DADDY! DADDY! DADDY!"

When I returned to work, I tried to find a way to combine what I had learned from the East with Western medicine. I knew there was much more to medicine than the way we had been treating our patients. Too many medications were being prescribed and too many surgeries performed. As I worked to find a solution, I hoped that I would be able to apply it someday soon. While I was working to find harmony between the two, my colleges were absolutely sure that I got screwed in Hong Kong, as if after having worked with me for three years, they had not known that already. It appeared to them that I definitely had a screw loose after visiting Hong Kong. I was a madman who was trying to introduce Chinese "witchcraft" to Western medicine. As a joke, my colleagues hung up a dartboard in the doctor's dining room so I could practice throwing my Chinese needles at it.

One day I was called to the intensive care unit where a lady in her fifties waited. She weighed over four hundred pounds. Her situation was very complicated. She had had a severe heart attack the same day, and started bleeding from her stomach as well. Everything the other doctors had done failed to stop the bleeding. She needed immediate surgery. Being so overweight in such a critical condition was not helping at all. Administering a general anesthetic was not an option because she had just had a massive heart attack. I knew I wouldn't be able to use any local anesthetic without overdosing the patient – that would have been fatal in her case, but I had to operate, otherwise, there was no chance to save her life.

She was so huge that we had no operating table large enough to support her size. In order to operate on her we had to put two operating tables together. My only prayer was that the woman knew some English to be able to give her consent for letting me do acupuncture versus anesthesia. Luckily, she did have enough knowledge to understand me and agree to my offer. I tried to combine hypnosis, acupuncture, and a bit of local anesthetics. Her life depended on the success of my technique.

The first problem I faced was that my Chinese needles lay comfortably in a box at my home, and I had to substitute injection needles for them. I mean, needles are needles, right? As I proceeded with this experiment, I noticed that the operating room started to fill up with other doctors who were watching the screwed doctor perform something weird that they had never seen before. To begin with, I had to remove about two thirds of the lady's stomach. I was a bit anxious about the outcome, but my patient was relaxed. The experiment was working. The combination of hypnosis, acupuncture and anesthesia did not let her feel any pain. While I performed the operation, all the anesthesiologist had to do was to give her oxygen, fluids, medication to keep her stabilized, monitor her pulse and blood pressure. The result was that the surgery ended successfully. My patient did not feel even a moment of pain. We were able to stop the bleeding, and her condition stabilized.

Throughout the whole procedure the so-called critics and spectators, who were not only sure of my failure, but also were talking about me being screwed, were watching me. The real screwed part was that they did not ask me a single question about how I did it without anesthesia. All they did was watch it in disbelief, and then ignore it. A few days later, the lady got better, and in no time recovered from her heart attack and surgery and returned home, fat and happy.

*

It was time to renew my medical license, take an exam and update its status from "restricted" to "unrestricted." After I passed the exam I was able to open my private practice. I opened a small clinic in the neighborhood where we lived. This clinic became the first place where I could, without any worries and suspicious spectators, treat my patients the way I felt was the best for them. I could use modern medicine, acupuncture, hypnosis, or a combination of them. This new clinic had proved itself to be a gift and I was very happy to have received it.

As more and more people learned about my unorthodox methods, rumors spread too. There was talk about how a crazy doctor had opened a clinic and was treating people with needles. These rumors have certainly never posed a problem to me, but had a negative effect on my patients. As a result, they avoided being seen and very often came after dark. It was only sometime later that I started to understand why. They did not want to be seen at the crazy doctor's, but were not ashamed to be treated and cured of their pain.

One of my visitors after dark was the South African international boxing champion. He had been suffering from severe pain in his shoulder and was told that he would need surgery to solve the problem that would have prevented him from boxing for at least six months. So one night he came to see me, asking for my help. Treating such a person was an honor in itself. After a few treatments he was free of pain and was boxing again.

While working at my clinic, I was learning more and more myself. I found out that the needle therapy was very effective for all sorts of backache, neck pain, and joint pain. Once, even the Professor of surgery referred his nephew to me, suffering from severe neck pain. When the patient got better, the professor's wife came to see me too – naturally, after dark.

Then a surprise followed. As my practice gained reputation, I received a letter from the South African Medical Council. The letter said that it had come to their attention that I was treating patients with unacceptable methods. They warned me to stop my practice immediately or my medical license would be revoked. It was very unclear to me why I had to practice only methods acceptable by Western medicine practitioners or stand to lose my license. In fact, the method proved to be very humane – it treated within a record fast time the cause of pain with no medication, surgery or side effects. Obviously, as with everything, there were a few exceptions.

One Friday night the phone rang in my house and a man on the other end told me that his son was having acute appendicitis. I tried to calm him down because he was panicking. Since I first had to confirm the diagnosis, I told him that I would meet him at the hospital, and if the diagnosis was correct, I would be ready to operate on his son. To my surprise, the father wanted me to treat his son with acupuncture. I tried to explain to him that acute appendicitis is a medical emergency that generally requires prompt removal of the appendix to prevent life-threatening complications such as ruptured appendix and peritonitis.

The following Sunday, in the *Sunday Times of South Africa*, a national newspaper, there was a big article about the acupuncture treatments. The guy who had called me to treat his son had written the article in which he criticized me for refusing to treat his son with acupuncture. After the article was published, he contacted me in order to see what my reaction was.

Even though I supported alternative forms of medicine, I did not intend to get away from the Western medicine that I had grown up with. I knew that there were many good things about it. I was practicing surgery, and I loved it. However, deep inside I felt that integration of all forms of Western and Eastern medicine was a key to success. As a result I had to look for ways of applying what I had learned in Hong Kong without losing my medical license.

Injections are a routine procedure in hospitals all over the world. So, why not use a syringe and needles as an acceptable tool in Western medicine and inject a certain drug-free solution to acupuncture points? Would I get similar results? To validate my theory, I tried different kinds of solutions including distilled water, physiologic solutions, vitamins, etc., and finally concluded that Vitamin B solution presented, so far, the best choice.

Not only was it good for the body, but also gave continuous, long-lasting stimulation at the point of injection. The treatment was faster and even better than using acupuncture needles. It had proven to be so effective that the duration and effectiveness of one such treatment equaled the results of six acupuncture sessions. Because I was using the standard medical syringe and needles, it was acceptable to the medical community as well. I had finally done it!

It was almost like a medical miracle to see a hunched-over patient with backache being able to gain normal posture and walk straight with no pain within two minutes after the injections. As my popularity increased, I was interviewed by one of the South African TV stations. Very soon the program was broadcast all over South Africa. As a result I received a lot of calls from many parts of the country, but alas, the medical community remained deaf to my innovative methods.

One of the most stubborn of the modern medical practitioners was Mark, a very close friend of mine. When he had returned with his family from a summer vacation in the United States, he came over to see me. He told me that during the trip he had suffered from severe abdominal pain. Because he did not want to disturb his family's vacation, he did not consult a physician. When I examined him, I found that his abdomen was full of masses. My friend had a very advanced stage of cancer. After I made the diagnosis, I think I might have turned pale.

He was shivering when he asked, "What did you find?" I told him that I would like another physician to examine him, and called a surgeon-friend to see him. Unfortunately, there was a consensus. I then referred him to a well-known gastroenterologist, and a few days later, he came back with a smile on his face telling me that the gastroenterologist had diagnosed a stomach ulcer and prescribed treatment. Not only was I surprised, but also truthfully stunned. I did not believe this diagnosis, but I hoped I was wrong.

Unfortunately, I was right and the gastroenterologist was wrong. My friend's condition soon deteriorated. I called the gastroenterologist and told him that I was positive it was advanced cancer. He did not accept it and called another surgeon to get a different opinion. I happened to overhear him telling the surgeon, "There is this screwed surgeon diagnosing advanced cancer, while I think it is just an ulcer."

The next day my friend went to see the surgeon, and an emergency laparotomy revealed metastatic cancer, probably of pancreatic origin. A few days later my friend passed away. The gastroenterologist was too stubborn to admit that he had screwed-up the diagnosis. To this day I don't understand how a very experienced gastroenterologist did not diagnose the cancer or could not reconsider his opinion for the sake of the patient.

Chapter 24

New York, N.Y.

*Inside yourself or outside, you never have to change what you see,
only the way you see it.*

--Thaddeus Golas

S oon after my friend's death, I visited the U.S. and China to expand
my knowledge about acupuncture. I gained many insights and shared
many of my own findings. In July 1982, I returned from New York to
Johannesburg having no clue that my time in Johannesburg would soon
be cut short. Nothing screwed happened. In fact, what led me to another
visit to the United States has turned out to be one of the best learning
experiences of my life.

A few days after my return, I was reading a magazine about
acupuncture. While I was flipping through the pages, I happened to come
across an article advertising a two-week advanced acupuncture course
given in Roscoe, New York in September for physicians and other health
practitioners.

The teacher who conducted the course was Dr. Ralph Dale from
Florida. He was known as one of the greatest teachers in the Western world
on this subject. It was an opportunity I could not have missed. After a brief

evaluation of the situation, I decided to give it a shot. But my reputation did not let me have things the easy way. When my wife heard about it, she was furious. Well, she had the right to be furious. She screamed at me, "You have just returned from the trip! And now, you want to go on another trip? And during the high Jewish holidays..." For the next three weeks I got the silent treatment until I finally left for New York.

When I arrived at Roscoe I was swept away by its beauty. It was a pristine place located in the mountains of upstate New York overlooking a lake that magnified its beauty many times. The maple and oak trees covering the rolling hills of the Appalachians started to turn yellow, orange and red making a striking contrast with pine trees and firs. The air was crisp and fresh.

The course was to be conducted in a resort. It had small cottages by the lake to accommodate the guests, while in the main house there were dining rooms, lecture rooms, an indoor swimming pool and recreation area. About twenty people signed up for the course. There were many physicians, chiropractors and dentists, mostly from the United States, and two others – a lady physician from South America and myself, from South Africa.

It was a time of sharing, learning and growing; indeed, a life-changing experience. While I was there, I again encountered another case of gross negligence by doctors. One evening, the lady physician from South America and I were sitting by the lake. After talking briefly, I asked her why she came all the way from South America to learn about acupuncture. She told me the main reason for her visit was to find a way to treat her inoperable brain cancer. On hearing the words cancer I was taken back a bit. To me, she did not look like a cancer patient. She looked healthy and cheerful. It was hard to imagine there was a tumor in her brain. I asked her to show me her X-rays. She did, and during our conversation I found out that she had a head injury as a child, and had many episodes of convulsions and severe headaches. After hearing this part of the story, I grew very suspicious.

It was clear to me she had been misdiagnosed. There was actually no tumor in her brain. She had a scar in her brain as the result of a head injury, not inoperable brain cancer. I was sure of that. I recommended she get a second opinion from a neurosurgeon in New York City. Within a few days, I received a phone call from her. She sounded cheerful. Who wouldn't be if they were told they weren't really dying? She told me I was correct and she did not have cancer, it was just a scar tissue. She was not going to die from brain cancer. This news gave her a new life, a new energy, a new happiness.

After the episode with this woman, I still can't figure it out who was more screwed, the physicians who diagnosed brain cancer or my friend who accepted the diagnosis.

*

At the camp, everybody was impressed by the way I treated pain. I was asked to give demonstrations. For me, these demonstrations were easy. There was no shortage of patients, because many people from the little town and the surrounding areas were coming to see us to be treated by acupuncture. Having had a lot of practice, I had learned to sense precisely where to inject the Vitamin B solution into the patient's body. To my surprise, the others who practiced with me could not do it. The odd thing was that some of those points were the actual acupuncture points. All my teachers of acupuncture told me that only I could sense them myself – no one else could guide me. I mean, how come a screwed guy like me could have that perception while the rest in the group struggled with it?

In Roscoe, I had met my screwed twin brother. That was exciting – someone else like me! His name was Joel. He was a young chiropractor from California, and he was the guy who had the same gut feeling about acupuncture points, and much more than that! He could locate the problem just by "looking" at the patient. He would scan the patients with his eyes, recognizing the areas where the flow of energy was obstructed – or this was what he said that he did.

I knew that Chinese acupuncture is based on restoring uninterrupted flow of energy to the body in certain energy channels called meridians. So Joel said that many people could sense where the flow of energy was blocked. On hearing this theory, I was skeptical. It seemed to me that he was screwed and, at times, even more screwed than I was.

Sensing my skepticism, Joel gave us a simple test. It was called "the muscle resistance test." Using this test he could tell if a patient is allergic to a certain drug or any other substance, and what would be the correct doses of such medication. He also believed that different colors of clothes affected the body in different ways, e.g., the color pink depletes energy from the body while red gives a lot of energy to the body. He suggested that while wearing pink would be a good choice for a hyperactive person, the color red, on the other hand, would boost the energy levels, if depleted. To freak me out completely, he even demonstrated communication with a person by channeling, by simply asking a question in his mind and getting the correct answer from the patient using muscle testing.

I was stunned when he told me my date of birth, how many years I had been married and how many children I had. Later, he confessed that all that information was based on kinesiology. It was the basic science of chiropractic medicine.

When I asked for the science or for a more plausible explanation, he replied, "Every living organism functions by a flow of energy, so if there is any blockage and interruption to the free flow of energy, it will short-circuit the energy circle."

I still was not convinced, so I asked him to tell me more. He said, "Today we know that there are electrical impulses in the human body, and electromagnetic fields as well. We know about the transmission of electrical pulses from nerves to muscles, about the transmission from nerves to blood vessels that causes constrictions and dilatations, electrical signals from the heart can be recorded as ECG, signals from brain as EEG; and that we could record EMG from the muscles. While the healthy human body has uninterrupted flow of energy, diseases, pain, allergy and other symptoms are manifestations of partial or complete blockage to the free flow of energy, just like no electricity flows in a circuit if there is a fault. These faults can be easily diagnosed by testing muscle's resistance and some other simple ways."

On hearing this, even I, the screwed skeptical one, saw common sense in it. After I saw the demonstration, I turned into a believer. But it was a new concept – something not easily accepted by the brainwashed Western physicians. Even today, many people will not believe what I say, and think that I am totally screwed. But if you try to think about what I have said and have an open mind, you will see that I am talking about something that actually makes sense.

*

I would like to share one of our demonstrations, so that you could see how effective Joel was as a healer. There was a young guy who was lying dressed in his clothes on the examination table. He was a local who lived nearby. He came asking for help with some of his medical issues. We met him for the first time. We did not know anything about this person, nor about his medical history. We had never talked to him in the past. So while he lay there, Joel scanned him with his eyes, and a minute later he pointed to areas of his body: the right lower abdomen, chest and right knee.

Then he came up with his diagnosis. "Knee pain from shoes that were not giving him proper support, lower abdominal pain due to spasm of sphincter in the cecum (the location where digested food moves from the small to the large intestine), which was caused by sensitivity to gluten and bronchial asthma that was triggered by emotional factors" – all that without even touching the patient!

That was something truly wonderful. We all were mystified by his diagnosis. The greater shock came when the patient confirmed that these were the problems that had made him come to see us. Now, to solve these issues, Joel recommended getting proper supporting shoes, modifying his diet and avoiding gluten. The session ended with Joel showing a few relaxation techniques to overcome anxiety and stress.

A few days later the patient returned to thank us all – especially Joel – for helping him so much. He told us that he was felling very good, happy and healthy. The pain in his abdomen and knee areas went away. There were no more asthma attacks, and all this was without any prescription medicine. Pretty baffling, isn't it?

While the patient was cheered up, I was not. The reason was simple. In all the years of studying and practicing medicine, I hadn't been taught any of this – a clairvoyant chiropractor who gives an accurate diagnosis prescribing the right shoes, diet and yoga breathing. I wondered why they didn't teach this stuff at med school. We, the physicians, do not know anything about it. I was sure that, as usual, something was screwed. While there were people curing others without the use of medications, Western medicine referred to all of this as alternative medicine, primitive medicine, placebo effect, and sometimes even witchcraft and magician tricks. Some even hung dartboards in the dining room, to make fun of this branch of healing.

Like all good things, this course too came to an end. Sunday morning, a day before we left, Joel invited me to join him and two other physicians, Mark from New York and Bob from Alaska, to go on a trip to Manhattan. Joel was driving his large American car, while Mark and Bob were in the backseat. As I was getting into the car, I glanced at the Sunday *New York Times*, a writing pad and a pen that was lying between the front seats. As I looked out of the window, I saw that the highway was busy. In the middle of our conversation Joel suddenly asked, "Have you guys ever heard about the automatic writing and about the many things a man can do at once?" This sudden question came as a surprise, and what followed was more of a deliberate attempt to give all of us a heart attack.

We did not understand what he was talking about. I mean how many times have you heard a driver suddenly start talking about automatic writing?

"It is when your hand is writing without you consciously knowing what it has written," he explained while covering the steering wheel with the Sunday *Times*; then he reached out for the pen with his right hand and begins writing down something on the pad comfortably arranged between the seats. I was shocked to the extent that I couldn't say anything. I was sure that this was the end of my life. It appeared as if the car was driving by itself in between of all this traffic. My heart must have stopped for a moment. I was panting, gasping for air, expecting a terrible accident. I was so scared that I thought I needed double resuscitation – one to make me breathe again and another one to validate that I was not dreaming. It was really happening. Joel was going to kill us all.

I turned my head to check on Bob and Mark. They were still alive, very pale, but nevertheless conscious. After this drive to hell we got back to the resort, I asked Joel what he wrote about. "Take it. It's for you," was his answer. He folded the paper and stuck it in my pocket to read it later.

The following day was time to say goodbye. I was tearful and emotional. We had become a family, but we knew it was only a matter of time before we would meet again. As we were about to depart, Ralph, our great teacher, asked me to keep in touch with him and invited me to visit him in Florida. He also told me that my place was in the United States, because we had to work together to build the foundation for integrative medicine.

When I returned to New York City – which was more like returning from a different planet – I took a few days to digest all that had happened to me in Roscoe. I spent hours in my hotel room recuperating and sleeping, enjoyed my leisure time walking on the streets of New York and shopping for my children and family in Johannesburg – the normal routine vacation that helped me to get back to the real world.

Then I flew to Johannesburg. While on board the airplane I read for the first time what Joel had written for me. "We all are a small part of the large universe. Being part of the universe gives us access to infinite knowledge. There is no question in this world that cannot be answered; no problem in this world that cannot be solved. We can find the answers and solutions to every question and problem as long as we are open and willing to listen, willing to learn and accept. We all are immortal; we were never born; we will never die. We only change the physical body in different lifetimes. Our body, mind and soul are one. Any attempt to separate them will bring diseases, pain and suffering, physical and mental." A profoundly beautiful description of my friend's life philosophy.

*

Back home in Johannesburg, life was normal. For a few days I couldn't even tell my wife and friends about out-of-this-world experience that had happened to me in Roscoe. I was afraid I wouldn't be understood. Alas, when I finally spoke, I realized that was the case. Indeed, everyone was convinced that during the last few weeks I had lost the little bit of sanity that I still had, and that I was beyond any help.

What can I say? I recognized that I became a different person and was willing to accept the shift that had taken place in me. Those changes were profound, but I could not yet verbalize them. A change begins with many small changes. I began thinking differently; I began solving the problems differently.

I used to treat many patients suffering from duodenal and stomach ulcers. The conventional recommended treatment was diet, and when that failed, in order to reduce acidity in the stomach, the patient was encouraged to undergo surgery to remove a large part of the stomach and a part of the vagus nerve.

Acidity in the stomach is believed to be the cause of ulcers. Of course, one can ask if I have a screw loose, and why have I changed the subject so abruptly and started talking about ulcers. Well, I somehow "sensed" that while everybody else treated ulcers with diet and eventual surgery, being "screwed" somehow made me recognize the true reason for ulcers —microorganisms. Therefore, I started to treat my patients with combination of Pepto-Bismol and Flagyl. I had a 70% success rate with it without surgery or even a diet.

As usual, many of my novelties were objected to by my fellow colleagues. The treatment of ulcers was no exception. I can't tell you if that was due to the old conservative mind-set, or simply due to financial reasons. After all, the treatment that I proposed was very inexpensive versus a complicated diet plan and then an expensive surgery. Two years later an Australian physician wrote an article confirming that peptic ulcers were a bacterial infection. I am just wondering if his discovery had earned him a reputation of a Loose Screw Physician like myself? Today it is a well-known fact that a type of bacteria called *Helicobacter pylori* is the main cause of ulcers, and its treatment is done with antibiotics.

In fact I knew that my professional life had to change. I could no longer practice only conventional medicine knowing there was so much more that I could do to help people. If I hadn't done that, it would have been like turning my face away from the world and letting it burn. Another contributing factor was the volatile nature of the country. Since the riots in Soweto, many white people were emigrating from South Africa. We all knew that the days of the white minority government were numbered. Meanwhile, there was still a war in Angola where the South African army was fighting terrorists as well as Cuban mercenaries. Rumors were spreading that the Afrikaners would divide the country so that the blacks and the whites would live in different states. The chief concern was the rising violence between the two races. Again, I, who was born during a war, who had been brought up during many wars, who left Israel for South Africa looking for peace, found my family and myself in between the war again.

*

During one of my visits to New York, I was invited to dinner at a friend's house. There, I met many well-known people. One of the guests was an official who held a high position in the U.S. federal government, in the Department of Education under President Ronald Reagan. After dinner, we got along well and he asked me, "Why don't you come to live in the United States?" Well, for me there were many reasons to not to go to U.S. – the main one being that I didn't like the American system of education. On hearing this, he was very surprised and asked me to explain why. I told him that I found the system incapable of teaching students to think – they are taught to follow directions and act like robots.

The funny thing was that he agreed. Not only it was true, according to him, but it was deliberately designed to function that way, where ninety percent of the population would have to act like what I called robots, getting up every morning, having breakfast, going to work, coming home for dinner, watching TV and going to bed, then waking up at the same time the next morning to do the same thing, having barbecue on the weekends, going to visit friends and family, and going on vacation once a year. This was necessary to ensure that they did not interfere with the rest of the ten percent of the population (like himself, I suppose) who were the ones who learned how to think on their own. They were the so-called "leaders" in every field, i.e., medicine, education, finance, research – "the true leaders" of the future. "It is because of these 10% that we, the USA, are leading the world today. Can't you see?" he asked.

As I said, I couldn't believe my ears. The hardest thing to understand was that this was coming from a high official in the Department of Education. He was telling me that only ten percent of the population of the most advanced country in the world would be the ones to learn and be able to think. Many parents, who wanted to see their children in this ten percent category, would have to send their children to private schools. This time I learned something. Just like during the time of my father's sickness, I had learned that there were two types of medicine, one for the rich and the other for the poor. Similarly, there was this American education – one for the poor and another, a different education, for the rich.

Soon after this conversation I was on my way to visit Florida, namely my friend and teacher Ralph, and some other friends and their families. There, everybody tried to convince me that it was about time I left South Africa and came to the United States. Ralph even arranged my meeting with physicians and other healthcare providers. Some of them were so impressed by my work that they offered me a temporary job until I got my medical license.

The next problem was to get a license in the United States, I would have to take a test in medicine which was very difficult, designed to prevent doctors from other countries coming and taking jobs from the American physicians (and only ten percent of them, according to the Washington official, actually learned how to think on their own). The good news was that while they did not want any new doctors from outside the system, nurses were in big demand. They were even given a preferential status by the immigration authorities. Fortunately, my wife was a nurse.

While in the USA. at a medical conference I met two great surgeons, Dr. Michael E. De Bakey, "The Tornado" from Texas, and Dr. Denton Cooley. Both of them were from Houston, Texas. They were the greatest in their respective fields of heart and vascular surgery. I knew that it was very difficult – and, certainly a privilege – to get to work with them. There were many surgeons from around the world that wanted to be part of their successful teams. Good fortune struck, and after a brief interview, I was offered a new and exciting position in Houston working with them.

Chapter 25

Home, Sweet Home

Good Friday, April 1st, 1983. After my night duty in the hospital, I was very excited. My family and I were going to board a flight to Florida. The prospect of going to a new country had gotten the children all excited. While I was working late at night, Ettie had left early to prepare for the exam required to be a licensed nurse. We got our tourist visas and were all ready to begin a new life, this time in the U.S. Once Ettie passed her test, we would apply for a permanent resident status with help from an immigration attorney, so that we would be able to stay and work in the U.S. legally. That was our theory. Little did we know what lay ahead of us.

After reaching the U.S, we started looking for a place to stay. Because it was going to be a long visit we rented an apartment in a hotel in Fort Lauderdale. Within a few days Ettie took her test while I was exploring ways to prepare for my own certification test. We were looking forward to moving to a house.

One evening I received a phone call from my brother in Israel. He called to let us know that my mother was severely depressed, and Ettie's father was very sick. To add to the sudden depression that I had gone into after hearing this news, he said, "If you care about our parents, you should immediately return to Israel."

The news came as a lightning bolt from the clear blue sky. We cancelled all our plans, and started planning for our return to Israel. While Ettie, Ori and I stayed back, Ravit and Ran were the first to fly to Israel. For those little children it was the first time they had to go alone anywhere. Two weeks later Ettie, Ori and I joined them in Israel.

To be frank, while I was preparing to return to Israel there was only one question that echoed in my mind. "Is this really meant to be, us going home? Are we returning to our home for good?"

As soon as we reached Israel we checked up on our parents' medical condition. It was not as bad as we were told. Not that I was disappointed in any way to see my parents healthy (I loved them so much), but somehow I felt cheated. It seemed as if this was a cheap trick to bring us back to Israel. Well, trick or not, this was not a joke – we were back in Israel.

After a few days I realized that it was going to be a bumpy ride. We rented a house in Hertzelia, outside Tel Aviv, and sent the children to a nearby school where they had to communicate, read and write in Hebrew. We spoke Hebrew at home, so they grew up with this language, but they had been going to an English-speaking school in Johannesburg. It was very difficult for them. As far as getting a job was concerned, I was very confident that with my experience in surgery, it would be a piece of cake.

*

When I arrived at the Department of Immigration around 8:00 a.m. the next day, the time when all the government offices open in Israel, there was no one there. Finally, around 9:00 a.m., a lady shows up, sits down at her desk, takes out a sandwich from her bag, gets a cup of coffee, and starts eating. I thought maybe she was late today, so I asked her if I could come in. "Don't you see I'm having a tea break?" she snapped. My first instinct was to throw her sandwich out the window, but I reluctantly gained control of myself and stepped outside, letting her finish having her breakfast. Finally, when the break was over I was called in. I presented our paperwork and told her everything about my work in Johannesburg and the trips to the U.S. "Why would you even come back with South African citizenship and a pending American Green Card? Do you have a picture of yourself?" she asked. I didn't.

I contacted a few hospitals and met with some Heads of Departments of Surgery – all of them promised to contact me soon, but no one did. I had to get a job. Without a job things would get really ugly for my family. That day I lost all hope. I went to see the Vice CEO of the Ministry of Health. We had studied together in medical school. He was friendly, but explained that it was up to the Heads of the Departments of Surgery to hire surgeons.

The time has come to collect unemployment benefits. There was a huge crowd in the basement office of the Department of Unemployment in downtown Tel Aviv. People were sitting on the floor and some were standing. I stood in line behind two young physicians who lost their jobs as soon as the internship was over. Neither of them could see a future ahead of them. After having left the clerk's office, they told me that they had been offered a job in the computer industry. I listened with disbelief that after six years of med school, a young physician would be asked to work with computers. I had to help them out. That night I called a friend in Johannesburg and asked him to arrange for these two young Israelis to have a phone interview. Insofar as my own interview, I was told that due to the economic situation in Israel it could be a long time until I found a suitable offer.

It was true. The economic situation was bad. Shares of the major banks had collapsed, there was uncontrolled inflation, and it was so high that the prices of goods changed hourly. Once I wanted to buy shoes for Ran. I chose a pair that I liked and told the salesman that I would be back with Ran after school. The salesman, however, did not warn me about inflation, and two hours later when we got back to the shop, the price of the shoes had increased substantially.

With things getting costlier every moment, I needed a job to support my family – even getting a regular job in the medical field was hard to do. I scheduled a meeting with the Head of the largest healthcare provider in Israel, who was impressed by my experience and promised to do his best to get me a job. As soon as I left his office, he chased after me – to stay off the record – and begged me to go back to the United States or South Africa, because no Head of any Department of Surgery in Israel would employ me. "Why wouldn't they? Don't they need experienced people to work for them?" I wondered. "This is the real problem," he confessed. "You have too much experience and you're a threat to them." What can I say? That was a pretty fine kettle of fish.

A few weeks later it was parents' day at Ran's school. I asked his teacher how Ran was doing, particularly in reading and writing Hebrew. She could not understand my question replying that she didn't realize Ran couldn't read or write in Hebrew. He'd been in her class for about six weeks. Was the education system in Israel screwed-up as well? Were they making robots here as well? The teacher who taught the children did not know how her students were performing. Things did change in Israel, but not for the better.

That day we went to sleep early. At midnight the phone rang and woke us up. The first thought that came to my mind was somebody died, or there was another war. The voice on the phone announced that we were live on the air. It was an Israeli radio show called "Coming Home" sponsored by the Israeli Vice Prime Minister. The intention of the program was to bring back the ex-Israelis, especially the professionals. He told me that my brother had called to say that a physician and his wife who was a nurse were about to leave Israel with their three young children, because they could not find any work. The Israeli Vice Prime Minister was online, and asked me what it this was all about. It was about time for him to know the truth. When I told him I was a qualified surgeon with a lot of experience, but I couldn't find a job because I was overqualified. He was surprised and promised to attend to it. He gave me his secretary's phone number and asked me to call him in the morning. When the producer of the program asked why Dr. Goldstein should get special preference, the Vice Prime Minister replied that the family's situation had touched his heart.

The following morning, during my phone conversation with his secretary, I was informed that due to the current economic situation in Israel, the Vice Prime Minister's office was not able to assist me with my work placement. What a real screw-up after all! Dishonest, to say the least!

Telling people one thing on the air and then stabbing them from behind...
What a bunch of hypocrites!

Apart from this screw-up, my family was very happy to have us back
home. We would visit my parents, my brother and his family, my in-laws.
Ettie's mother loved playing with her grandchildren. She came to visit us
many times by herself while Herbert, her husband, whose stomach ulcers
no longer bothered him, stayed home, unhappy to share his wife with
the grandchildren. One evening they came together – his wife's nagging
worked. That night Herbert made it very clear that it would be the last
time he came for a visit. Shortly after, he developed a severe kidney failure
and needed abdominal dialyses. Since then he had his wife's attention all
to himself. When I heard of Herbert's sickness, I remembered the words
of his attending physician, who years ago had told me that people like my
father-in-law needed to be sick, and if we removed the ulcer, he might
develop something else, and who knows, it might be a more severe ailment
than the previous one.

Meanwhile, I still had no job. The situation in Israel was quickly
deteriorating. Matters were getting worse. The economy was collapsing.
There was spiraling inflation. Things that used to cost a few Israeli Liras
now skyrocketed to a million Liras. The Israeli Lira was then replaced
by the Shekel. After the Shekel lost its value, it was replaced by the New
Shekel. Changing the currency was not helping to solve the problem;
instead, things should have been done to generate employment.

To add to our problems, in northern Israel people were getting killed
and injured by terrorist rockets coming from Lebanon. There was despair,
sadness and problems. This time Israel was in a new war called "The
Peace of Galilee." During this war Israel had invaded Lebanon to destroy
terrorists camps and arms, and stop them from shooting rockets at Israel.
As if the war was not bad enough, its name was a sad oxymoron in itself.

The outcome of this situation was that I was unable to find work
– overqualified, bad economy, a new so-called Peaceful War, my son's
teacher did not know whether her student could read and write, Vice Prime
Minister's secretary telling us to stay in Israel so that we can suffer with
the rest of the Israelis.

I was starting to lose faith. There was a minority Orthodox Jewish community that forced the government to close public transportation on Saturdays. They allowed only religious marriage to take place in Israel. If someone did not want to get married by a Rabbi, they would have to go to another country. This minority group dictated who was Jewish and who wasn't. If, according to them, you were not "Jewish enough," then you could not get married or even get buried in the common cemetery.

It was our own people harassing our own people. Even the students were discriminated against on the basis of religion. The students in Yeshiva, which was a very religious school, did not have to serve in the army and got paid to study. This minority religious group had forced their beliefs on the rest of the population, and we had no other option but to follow them in order to survive, or even get buried in the same cemetery. And all of it in the name of God. God was brought in to justify all the wrongdoings. The same God, but with a different name, Allah, was, according to imams, sending suicide bombers [called martyrs] to Paradise with seventy-two virgins if they explode themselves and innocent Israeli women and children.

One Saturday night while sitting at the dinner table with all my family members, the phone rang. It was Ettie's aunt. She told us that her application for a work permit was finally approved. Upon hearing this miraculously wonderful news, my mother started crying. She knew that it was time for us to leave home.

Chapter 26

❧

Land of the Free

I t was the end of the summer, 1983, when we arrived in Florida. The school year was about to start. Before we found a suitable house to live in, we temporarily rented an apartment at a hotel in Fort Lauderdale. Though it was a comfortable place to stay, we had to find a house in a good neighborhood with good schools nearby.

By now you can understand my skepticism about a good school for my children. We wanted to send our children to a school that would teach them how to think and not to be like robots. I found work as a physiotherapist's assistant. It not only provided me with income, but also gave me enough time to study for my medical certification test. It was really interesting to be on the other side of this field. All these years I had been referring patients to physiotherapists, giving them instruction about what to do, and now I was the one getting instructions.

To get to work I traveled to West Palm Beach, which was about an hour drive. Occasionally, on my way back, I would stop and visit Coney. Who is Coney? She was a wonderful and a very spiritual lady. She was also known to be psychic, but I, the Screw–Loose Physician, could not find the courage to believe much in her abilities at the time. Once I told Coney that we were looking to buy a second car for Ettie. As soon as she heard that, she looked carefully at my car, as if she was examining it to find some fault with it and then said, "This car is not safe for you..."

I shrugged it off as one of her typical psychic false alarms. Within a few days we found a nice car for Ettie. I told the salesman to get the car ready because I would be picking it up the next day. The next day, while sitting at the intersection waiting for the light to change, I looked at the rearview mirror and saw a truck in the same lane I was in, approaching at very fast speed. I sensed that it would not be able to stop. Before I had any time to react and get myself out of the car the truck hit me from behind, smashing my car into the car in front of me.

Everything went numb. I blacked out for a few moments. The next thing I heard was police and ambulance sirens. They pulled me out of the car. My face was bleeding and there was severe pain in my neck and back. The rescue team stabilized my neck and back, and I was transferred to a nearby hospital. While I lay there, I managed to move my fingers and toes, so I was relieved to find I was not paralyzed. I was in excruciating pain and was examined by the trauma surgeon, who ordered X-rays of my neck, my back, my chest and skull. The X-ray technician refused to take my neck X-rays because I was wearing a gold necklace. That was a ridiculous thing to say. I asked him to remove the thing, but he refused.

"Sir, we are not allowed to touch patient's jewelry."

"If you free my hands, I'll take it off myself," I offered.

"Sir, I will need the physician's orders to free your hands."

"Well, then why don't you stick the darned necklace in my mouth?"

He obliged and stuck my jewelry in my mouth and took the X-rays of my neck. From the image on the screen, I could see fractures in my lower back and lower neck, but because the areas of the fractures looked stabilized, I did not worry about movements that could endanger the spinal cord.

There was a young doctor on duty. When he was called to see the result of my X-rays, he reported that it looked good to him, and could not see any fractures. Since I wanted to go home as soon as possible, that was good news for me. If he had seen those fractures, I definitely would have had to stay. They treated my wounds, advised me to see an orthopedic surgeon, and released me. I called Ettie right away and told her what had happened. I also asked her to call the salesman who sold us the car yesterday and ask him to bring the car to the hospital so that I could give him a check.

Minutes later, Ettie called back. It turned out that the salesman, while taking the car for service, had an accident as well, and now that car was gone too. An hour or so later a policeman arrived in the emergency room to take my statement about the accident. He told me that, first, no one else was injured in the accident; second, my car was totaled; and third, sadly, the two watermelons on the backseat of my car did not survive the accident. I asked about the truck. Why didn't it stop before hitting me? I did not get an answer – strange behavior on behalf of the law-enforcing agent. There was no point in pursuing it any further.

As soon as I arrived in the hotel, the phone rang. It was Coney. She had called me earlier when I already left to warn me to be more careful while driving. If this warning had come earlier, would I have been able to avoid the accident? I told her it was too late. She was not surprised. Perhaps there were some powers in her that either I was not aware of or did not want to accept.

The next day I found myself in excruciating pain in the neck and back area. We rented a car and Ettie drove me to the orthopedic surgeon who did see fractures in my lower neck and back. He confessed that there was nothing much that could be done at that stage. As a result of the accident, my right arm was weak. I kept taking painkillers to control the pain, hoping that it would soon get better, but it didn't. The pain persisted, and the symptoms got worse. I was in so much pain that I could not even go back to work.

School was about to start soon. We finally rented a house in Boca Raton. The house was in a good neighborhood, and to our relief, it had very good schools nearby. One day, Dr. Ralph Dale, a friend and one of the greatest acupuncturists in the western world, came with his wife to visit us. Ralph gave me treatments to ease the pain in my back and neck.

After the treatment, while we were sitting at the table having a conversation, Ori, our youngest son, who was about to start his first year in school, joined us. At that time, Ori didn't know how to read yet, and had never opened any book, other than the storybooks that Ettie and I had read to him. While we sat there chatting, he started explaining to us about the electromagnetic fields in the human body. It took me a moment to believe it was our little Ori speaking. We were all stunned. How many times have you heard a six-year-old child, who does not even know how to read or write, give a scientific explanation of electromagnetic fields in the human body?

Ralph was so amazed that he went to his home and came back shortly (his home was about an hour's drive away, so it was not that short of a trip for him). He returned with a book on electromagnetic fields that concurred with the way Ori had explained it to us. Ralph really thought that Ori knew it from his past life. The concept of past lives was something I could not have accepted at that time. Therefore, I did not believe in that explanation, but today I do think so.

The school year started. The children loved their school, especially the teachers and their friends. The standard of education was very high. It was something I had always expected my children to have. Life was almost back to normal, except for my inability to work due to severe pain in my neck and back. I tried physiotherapy, but did not help much. Medical bills were skyrocketing, and we did not have medical insurance. Someone advised me to get a lawyer and sue the company of the truck that hit me. I did so and hired an attorney who reassured me that he would get me some compensation or at least would get my medical bills paid.

My days of pain turned to weeks, and the weeks turned to months. My condition was not improving. Medical bills were piling up and I had no way to pay them. I felt depressed, used and hopeless. Though my medical insurance had expired, I still had my life insurance in South Africa – I was worth much more dead than alive. I had sunk into such a deep depression that I decided to put an end to my life and my misery. I prepared audiocassettes for Ettie and the children, called my family in Israel on the phone and talked to them. In the late evening, before Ettie, Ravit and Ran went to sleep, I said my final goodbye to them, and was grateful they did not suspect anything.

After the three of them went to sleep, only little Ori and I were awake. He was sitting on my lap. As I looked at his face, tears started flowing from my eyes and I had a lump in my throat. Seeing me cry, Ori said, "Daddy... I am so happy and lucky! There is this child in my class who lost his father... since then, he is miserable and sad... You know, Daddy... he can't even stop crying, he is sad because he can't even hug him anymore." After saying these words he looked up to me and said, "I know... that you are in pain and can't work, but you are here with us. I am so happy and lucky to have you." Saying this, he started hugging and kissing me. I burst out crying, hugging and kissing him back.

At that moment, I felt like someone had turned on the switch in my head. The pain, painkillers, and unemployment must have had an effect on my psyche. I instantly realized that I was terribly wrong and selfish to consider suicide. I had to fight. The pain had made me weak, but when I thought about what Ori had told me, I was filled with sadness over my life and the possible harm I could have done to my children. Seeing me cry, Ori started crying too. He hugged me and kissed me good night. Before leaving, he uttered, "I love you very much" and then went to bed. I could not talk at all. I wanted to tell him how much I loved him. I wanted to tell him that he had given a new life to his father, but I could not.

After Ori left, I wept throughout the night. It felt as if a valve had opened inside me, releasing all the pressure that had been building up since the accident. In the morning I called Ralph and asked him for another treatment. He arrived in the afternoon with his wife and another woman. While giving me my treatment in another room, he asked, "What do you think about the lady that has come with us?"

I said that she seemed to be very nice. Hearing this, Ralph chuckled, "I mean, how old do you think she is?"

"In her fifties, I suppose," I said.

He took her picture from his pocket, gave it to me and told me she was sixty-five years old. When I looked at the picture, the difference was striking. That was a picture of her older sister or even her mother – wrinkled and old, not at all the same face that I saw five minutes ago.

Ralph explained to me that the picture I was looking at was taken only two weeks ago, and since then, she had her nonsurgical facelift done by a physician in Florida. I could not believe it. The lady looked almost twenty years younger than her actual age. I quickly asked the lady if she would mind giving me her physician's name and phone number, and she did.

The next morning, without making any appointment, I went to see this doctor. Only after I had told his secretary that I was an M.D. myself did she let me in. When I met Dr. Ron, I told him how much I was impressed by his work. He let me see the photo album demonstrating his work. The pictures were taken before and after the treatment. I had never seen anything like it! I was very excited about this new technique and asked him if he would teach it to me. He refused politely with a smile on his face, explaining that he was in a partnership with another businessman, and together they were teaching it to American physicians. He added that this type of "plastic treatment" cost tens of thousands of dollars. I persisted, saying that I was not American, but was licensed to practice medicine in Israel and South Africa. He refused again. It seemed that Dr. Ron was determined not to reveal his know-how.

Being stubborn by nature, I did not back down. I knew that I had to learn it. That was it: I told him that starting the next morning, I'd be sitting outside his office – without disturbing anybody – day after day after day until he taught me. He laughed. I almost cried. For the next ten days, I sat outside his office. Every morning, when he arrived, we greeted each other and then late in the afternoon said goodbye to each other. After seeing me there every day, he still did not want to teach me. But I had made up my mind that I had to learn this thing.

It was day number 11. Dr. Ron called me in to tell me that I was wasting my time. Even if he agreed to teach me, he explained, I would not be able to afford it. I offered him $15,000 in cash and promised that I would return the balance by working for him. He gave up and agreed. Wow! I was so happy. I had managed to get his agreement, but the screwed part there was that I had absolutely no idea where to get those $15,000. As I was driving home, however, I felt more optimistic and hoped that things would work out after all.

When I told Ettie the good news, she came to a conclusion that, besides being a Loose-Screw Person, I had become much worse in the long run; probably as a result of being on painkillers for such a long time. Ettie was not irritated by my decision to learn something new. All she asked was where I was supposed to get $15,000? My answer was rather screwed, but true: "I have no idea, but I know I will." As you can imagine, this kind of answer did not make her feel any better.

In the evening I received an unexpected phone call from Bob. I had not seen or heard from him since the course in Roscoe, N.Y. To my surprise, Bob was in Florida visiting his father. When we met, I told him about the nonsurgical facelift. Bob, excited, agreed to give me $15,000 on condition that after I learned the technique I would teach it to him. My life was turning around after all, and I started to see the light at the end of the tunnel.

The next morning I was at Dr. Ron's. I had a certified check for $15,000. He could not believe it and neither could I. The next week I started my training with five other American doctors, training that would be incredibly beneficial to my professional career.

*

I arrived early at Dr. Ron's office where I met five doctors that were just as fascinated by the results as I was. Dr. Ron introduced us to a female patient and explained that during the initial stages of this course we would be strictly observing him. First, Dr. Ron left the room and returned a few minutes later holding a glass filled with special solution. As he walked towards us, he suddenly tripped and the solution spilled on the carpet. Within a few seconds there was a big hole in the carpet. Seeing this, the patient turned white, and I suppose we followed her example, too. The thick carpet had a hole in it, and Dr. Ron would be applying that solution to the patient's face – anybody would be scared!

"Doctor, is this ... is this the solution that you will be applying to my face?" asked the brave woman. This was the same question that had crossed my mind – I am not sure I would have had the guts she had to agree to this sort of rejuvenation miracle if I were wearing her shoes. His answer was affirmative. "Just remember that your face is not made out of synthetic material like the carpet, so this solution will react differently in your case."

That was reassuring, wasn't it? I don't think anybody would be at peace after having seen the condition of the carpet, but we carried on. Dr. Ron prepared more solution and we stepped into the treatment room.

The patient lying on the bed was given general anesthesia and connected to an IV line. Dr. Ron cleaned her face and applied the "carpet dissolving" solution in a very precise and delicate way with an applicator. When he was done, he covered her face with a mask made from small pieces of medical tape. It was strange – the patient's face looked like an Egyptian mummy. The whole treatment took about an hour. She was then transferred to a limousine that took her to a nearby hotel where she was supposed to stay for eight days (that would be the duration of her treatment). It was a small hotel by the beach. The lady who ran it took care of the patients and provided them with a special light diet and any necessary assistance. This is how we observed the first treatment. Initially the patient was all wrinkled, and in eight days the face would tighten up and all the wrinkles disappeared.

The next morning we joined Dr. Ron to see the patient in her hotel room. On entering her room, we saw something that we had not expected at all, at least not me and the other students, and we were shocked. The patient lay in her bed. As we took a look at her face, it was abnormally swollen, about three times the normal size. The mask that was white and clean yesterday was all wet and brown. Parts of it looked as if they were coming apart. The lady's eyes bulged, and she couldn't even open them. I'd say it was a severe infection.

We quickly took a look at our teacher, Dr. Ron. He was the only one smiling. "This is what she should look like one day after the treatment. There is no need to worry. It is normal," he reassured us. I was still worried. I had never seen a person's face so swollen, and I had never seen someone apply a "carpet dissolving solution" to someone's face. Meanwhile, Dr. Ron cleaned the patient's eyes using Q-tips and she could see again. Fortunately, there was no mirror in the room so the patient couldn't see herself. I am sure if she had seen her face right then, she would have freaked out totally. The woman looked all relaxed and comfortable. There was no pain or even a burning sensation, only slight discomfort.

When we returned to the office Dr. Ron performed one more treatment. The treatment looked very simple and easy to do. The mask was the tricky part. We practiced on a doll using small pieces of medical tape. A lot of experience I had gained while working at Baragwaneth Hospital performing many surgeries and dressings a day made the task seem very simple and natural for me. My mask looked pretty good. Dr. Ron even complimented me and asked me to assist the others.

By the end of the day, when we were practicing making the masks, Ron called me to his room and told me that he was very happy to have me with him. He said, "I have been looking for a long time for someone talent, and with good hands." From that day, I started paying my debts by helping other students.

After all, it looked like being screwed with a lot of surgical experience was not that bad, at least not there, while it was more of a curse back home in Israel. The third morning of our course we went to see the patients in the hotel. The faces of both of them were still very swollen. The mask of the first patient was falling apart, and murky fluids were leaking from it. Again, we all felt skeptical, and looked at Ron for some explanation. He perhaps sensed what we felt and explained that what we saw was the old skin dissolving. It left the masks soiled.

Back at the office, Ron performed another treatment. The next day, about forty-eight hours after the initial treatment, the first patient's mask was supposed to be removed. To make the mask come off easily, she had to take a hot bath. What was hidden underneath the mask resembled a scene from a horror movie – there was no skin left. Ron applied her face with a special antibacterial powder, which together with the secretion from the skin would form the second mask. This second mask would be removed on the eighth day.

The swelling finally subsided, and the patients were comfortable and happy. During the entire course, we observed six treatments and became quite experienced at making the masks. On the night of the seventh day, Vaseline was applied to the patient's face and, finally, the next morning the mask was peeled off. The results were amazing: simply – WOW! She looked fantastic and all her wrinkles were gone. We were truly amazed. The skin on her face was so delicate and smooth it looked and felt just like a baby's skin. The lady looked at least twenty years younger in just eight days.

A mirror was given to the patient for the first time. Her reaction was the best testimony to a more than a brilliant result: tears rolled down her cheeks. She was speechless. I have seen this type of happiness only in maternity wards when new babies are born. After a very emotional goodbye, with lots of hugs and kisses, our happy patient was on her way home to enjoy her new face. Our course was over too. We all got our certificates of graduation, a bottle of treatment solution, the formula for how to prepare the solution in a sealed envelope, the powder for the second mask along with some advertising and promotional materials, and a menu of a proper diet for the patients. I was very happy and excited. Thankfully I had found something that I could do despite my pain and disability.

*

A week later I was on my way to Israel. Not only did I want to see my family, but also find the practical application of this new nonsurgical facelift in Israel. A teacher volunteered to be my first patient. Bob, who had given me the money, was also flying in for his training. I picked him up at the airport. While driving to Beer Sheba, Bob looked out the window and suddenly looked at me and said, "I have been here before, I think … I think I know this place very well." He'd never been to Israel, I can assure you. He felt like it was a déjà vu, something from his past life. I was then sure that Bob was screwed as well as I was. That déjà vu thing from his previous life was a proof of that.

While Bob was practicing his déjà vu instinct, I was meditating about my first facelift procedure. The watch. Yes, my first watch that I got as a gift. No matter how many times I took it apart and then put it together again while leaving some parts out, it still functioned. Even with missing parts, it worked just fine. Here we go… That's the answer. First, it is not necessary to do the entire treatment under general anesthesia. Why? There's acupuncture and hypnosis plus painkillers – if necessary – together they will take care of the burning sensation that lasts for up to six hours. That will eliminate the need for a general anesthesia.

D-Day arrived. I asked the patient for permission to have several students observing this new procedure, and she agreed. Using hypnosis, I suggested to her that when I cleaned her face, it would become numb, and she would not have any discomfort or pain.

Meanwhile, Bob was monitoring the patient's pulse and blood pressure. I began. First, I cleaned hear face, applied the solution and the mask. During the entire treatment, the patient was very comfortable and kept talking to us. Finally, in less than an hour the treatment was over. The mask was very well done. I am sure my teacher would have been very proud of me.

Eight days later, when the second mask was removed, the results where amazing. Everyone watched the stunning metamorphosis that had occurred underneath the mask with disbelief.

The news about this new treatment spread all over Israel like wildfire. I decided that it was about time I opened a clinic in Israel. I planned for my father to run it, and when there were a certain number of patients, I'd fly in from Florida to do the facelifts. My friend Bob had a plan to do the same in Alaska where he lived – sign up at least four patients and then fly me in.

One day after my return to Florida, Dr. Ron and I were in a coffee shop in Fort Lauderdale. I was telling him about my Israeli experience, and about doing the treatment under hypnosis. I showed him the pictures, and told him about the tremendous success that I had had. Suddenly a stranger came to our table, looked at us and said, "I know you guys. You were fixing heads in Atlantis and then left." I thought he was crazy – I had never worked together with Dr. Ron who had a different interpretation of what we had heard from the stranger. "We *have* worked together before, and it was not a coincidence that we are back together." I asked him, " If that is so, then why did you give me such a bad time before agreeing to train me?" He did not answer.

Chapter 27

On Spiritualism

The body is mortal, but the person dwelling in the body is immortal and immeasurable.

--Bhagavad Gita

Ettie and I were among fifteen people attending a weekend seminar on Extra Sensory Perception (ESP) given by Coney, the psychic. Coney's house was more of a retreat offering peace and relaxation. She had a beautiful garden with a whirlpool, and you could hear the sounds of soothing music in the background. I felt undisturbed by the troubles of the world, and my own troubles seemed to disappear.

Ettie was very skeptical about the whole thing while, I was intrigued by the world of the unknown, that paranormal kingdom where there are no boundaries between life and death. It was described by Connie as "communication with the world of spirits" who, if we leave our judgment and limitations, can become our guides and teachers.

"We all have the ability to communicate with this other side," she started. "We all can see the past and the future... Sadly though, we all are influenced by our parents, our teachers, our friends; by the religious people and others around us; and it is due to their influence that over time we suppress and ignore and even block this ability."

She went on saying that, "We are afraid to do so, just because we do not want to look like freaks, [or screwed in my case]. We all have had this experience with our parents, when our parents can feel that sometimes something has happened to us, or it is going to happen to a loved one, without even talking to them. Then there was the experience where we suddenly think about a certain person from whom we had not heard from for a long time, and suddenly that person calls. The phone rings and we know who is calling before we answer," and she went on giving many such examples.

When Coney talked about it I remembered immediately the feeling that I once had when I wanted to go to Israel from Johannesburg, and when I got there, I found out that my mother had breast cancer. My going there not only helped diagnose her, but saved her life.

Coney said that we are an integration of body, mind and soul. The physical body, as we know it, is a vehicle we use in our lifetime. It gives us the ability to function and do all we need to do, and holds in it the mind and the soul. The mind itself is the computer, controlling the physical body and making it functional. The mind consists of conscious and unconscious parts. The conscious mind is our ego. We use this part most of the time when we are awake, while on the other hand the unconscious mind represents the real us. This is the part of us that has no limits and knows no boundaries. It is the part that knows all and can do all. We can all access this mind during deep relaxation, hypnosis and meditation. While most of us find it difficult to access the subconscious, those of us who did not suppress the "real" us are the enlightened ones. They can access it most of the time.

While the soul is the immortal part of us, it is given to us by God. So it is a part of God. The soul is indestructible: It was never born and will never die. Our souls come to this world to experience and evolve to a higher level, and they are given free choice to do whatever they want to do. Our choices and the resulting consequences determine the way our life will turn.

Everything that our body does first starts in our mind. It is then converted to thoughts, and they lead to words and actions. Everything we experience, be it happiness, love, wealth, successes or failure, arises from our mind. So is the state of being healthy or sick. Getting sick and healing again starts in our mind. We are all loved and the fear that grips us is the enemy of love.

That day I learned there were no coincidences in life. Everything happened to us for a reason. At times we may not know the reason, but sooner or later we all see that it happened for the best, which made me jump up from my seat and ask, "Did all the patients I treated want to be sick? What about my car accident? When the accident happened, I wasn't even driving. I was stationary at the time, waiting for the traffic lights to turn green. How did I make that accident happen? And why would I even want myself to be in pain?"

After listening to this, Coney replied with a smile on her face. "Yes. Most sick people don't know consciously that they need to be sick, but they do. It can be for many reasons, like getting attention, guilt complex, self-punishment, teaching or learning a lesson, or to bring change in their lives like lifestyle, work, and habits."

She then looked at me and continued, "Your accident too happened for a reason.

It happened so you will have to change things in your life, or work that needed to be changed." When she said those words, I immediately remembered the physician telling me that my father-in-law needed to be sick, and if we cured him of his ulcer, then he would get sick again, and that it might be more serious, which actually happened years later.

The most surprising thing was that if I believed what she had said, it meant that all my patients wanted to be sick. And if all of us had the ability to heal ourselves, then why did we need physicians? Was I not the only one "screwed" in that room? How was it even possible that I had attracted the accident that was about to happen, when I was not even driving? And how could Coney know about it a day before? Only years later would I be able to follow the path of those mysteries and truly grasp their metaphysical meaning.

*

We can easily forgive a child who is afraid of the dark; the real tragedy of life is when men are afraid of the light.

--Plato

*

Chapter 28

Anguilla

After I started working with Dr. Ron, I got a license to perform face treatments. Prescribing medications had to be done by a certified physician.

It was almost summer. Ettie and the children would be going to Israel to visit our families, but I would be staying in Florida, partly because I had started working recently, and there was a lot of debt to be paid back.

One morning Ron invited me to his office and announced that his partner and himself were going to open a health resort on the island of Anguilla in the Caribbean that is only about four-hour flight from Miami. It is a small island near St. Martin. The place that Ron had bought was being renovated and was supposed to be ready by July. The resort was planning to provide holistic and cosmetic treatments to patients from around the world, mainly from the United States. (With alternative medicine becoming more and more popular, this kind of a venture could have given huge returns.) Ron showed me some pictures. It looked more like a beautiful beach resort than a clinic. Ron offered me the opportunity to be the medical director. Along with the job, I was offered a very attractive salary, and my family could join me during the school holidays. All of this sounded very attractive. In fact, it was so attractive that I found it too good to be true. I still had to deliver the news to Ettie, who agreed with me.

The next day I told Ron that I would accept the position and applied for the required license to practice medicine on the island. As soon as all the paperwork was done, Ron asked me to leave for Anguilla as soon as possible and make sure that the medical facilities would be ready before the grand opening that was supposed to be attended by many celebrities and representatives of the media.

I left for the Caribbean. Ettie and our trio left for Israel, and we agreed to reunite on Anguilla. When I was supposed to depart for the resort, a beautiful big limousine came to pick me up to take me to the Miami airport, from where I flew to St. Martin, and then a private plane took me to Anguilla.

A handsome young man named Edie picked me up at the Anguilla airport. Edie had escaped from Iran after the fall of the monarchy and the beginning of the Khomeini Islamic Republic. He was the administrator in charge of the center.

The island, small and secluded, warm and welcoming, is part of the British Commonwealth. At that time its population consisted of about 6,000 people. Blessed by tropical trade winds, surrounded by tranquil turquoise seas, it is a Caribbean paradise frequently visited by American and European tourists. I found the Anguillans to be genuinely gentle and gracious, friendly and joyous, predominantly Christian. There is one church for every two square miles. With zero crime or violence, it was a custom to park the car and leave your keys in it. I felt that I had finally found peace and tranquility on this little island untouched by sorrow and grief. Anguilla – and a lot of people that have been there will agree with me – has some of the most beautiful beaches in the world, even compared to Thailand and the Greek Isles. The powdery white beaches, more than thirty, were aqua blue to all shades of turquoise, with placid waters and incredible sunsets – images that come to my mind today when I think about that quiet little Caribbean paradise.

The Anguilla Health Resort was located on a beautiful beach and consisted of a main building along with a clinic, dining facilities, a lecture room and an entertainment area. Around the main building there were small, beautiful oceanfront bungalows to accommodate patients and guests. Each bungalow had a small kitchen, a living room and a bedroom. All this offered patients privacy and relaxation in the Caribbean resort by the sea.

When I arrived I was introduced to all the members of the center, and soon dinner prepared by a Swiss chef was served. The sun was setting in the ocean, coloring the sea and the sky with all shades of opaque pink to lavender blue…

*

The next morning I was busy organizing the clinic for the grand opening. The people working in the center were very friendly and highly professional in their respective fields.

Time passed very quickly working at the resort, and soon Ettie and the children arrived. Absence of TV and friends turned out to be a blessing. The kids spent a lot of time exploring and playing on the beach, swimming and hunting shells. The first guests arrived, including some celebrities, media reporters, and a well-known researcher from California, John Jonson, who specialized in the immune system.

During our talks at the dinner table, John told us that sharks have the best immune system among all living creatures, which explains why they never get cancer. He said that if we could specifically identify that gene in sharks, we might be able to copy it to boost our own immune system. That could be extremely beneficial in combating HIV, cancer and other diseases. Locating and studying that gene was a goal of John's life until one day a squad team from the FDA, fully armed with machine guns, raided his house and confiscated all that he had researched. I guess anyone in the U.S. who's looking for an alternative cure for cancer without drugs or chemotherapy presents a real danger to the gigantic profits of pharmaceutical corporations and is sooner or later doomed to follow his path, i.e., quit your research or go to jail. What a screwed-up system!

According to John, the pharmaceutical industry controls health systems all over the world and is capable of doing everything possible to prevent cheaper and more effective alternative treatments without drug side effects that are linked to heart attacks, strokes, gastrointestinal bleeding or hemorrhaging, severe ulcers, thrombotic thrombocytopenic purpora, and death. It looks to me like a pretty screwed state of affairs in the department of human health and wellbeing. Is medicine all about power, position, greed, control, lust for power and money? These people are making their fortune off our health. What happened to education and preventative medicine to control the very cause of these ailments?

During the inauguration, Jim, a reporter from Los Angeles, California wanted to interview me. I agreed. We discussed many issues related to health, and also examined how some things were still screwed in the healthcare system. During the interview I noticed that Jim was having difficulty in moving one of his shoulders. Looking at his face, I knew he was in pain whenever he had to move his shoulder. He told me that for the past six years there had been agonizing pain in his shoulder, and because of that he could only perform very limited movements, a condition known as a "frozen shoulder." I found out that Jim had had numerous treatments and consulted many physicians, but all failed to help him. He was dependent on drugs as a way to ease the pain.

After telling him about my experience with pain management, I told him that he would not require any medications, and there would be instant relief. For a moment he hesitated, I am sure he was thinking that I was totally screwed. (Who wouldn't be? I am sure he had tried everything, and my claim was rather radical). When Jim agreed to leave his shoulder pain behind, I injected a vitamin solution at certain points – you won't believe it – and within a few minutes the pain was gone. I gave him three more consecutive sessions. The result? For the first time in six years, Jim's shoulder felt as good as new.

A few days later there was the article in a Los Angeles magazines written by Jim. He wrote about his visit to Anguilla Health Resort. The article was all about how impressive the place was. He noticed, however, that his impression was that most of the people working in the Center were not in touch with reality, except for, according to him, a certain doctor who also happened to be the medical director, i.e., Dr. Amnon Goldstein. He praised me a lot, saying that I was highly professional, knowledgeable and made sense, the only person who had both feet on the ground. I was elated over this article, but the funny thing was, he called me "the only one having both feet on the ground and a person who made sense." That day I received my first treatment in positive thinking and good self-esteem from Jim, a Los Angeles reporter.

One evening Ron came to my room asking for help. Both of his feet were sore, swollen, and edematous. I examined him and asked, "Why do you, an experienced physician, need my help?"

He replied, "I am only a face physician and have no idea about any other form of medicine."

I did not understand what he meant by being "just" a face doctor, because there are no "just something" doctors – we have a general idea about the human body and illnesses. What he said sounded suspicious to me, but who cares, I am the screwed one, anyway.

After the grand opening was over, within a few days the summer vacation was almost over, too. Ettie and the children went back to Florida – leaving the island was very difficult for Ravit, Ran and Ori. They said it was the best vacation of their life, even without TV.

My family left and the number of patients coming to the island declined. There was not much business anymore, and, within a few weeks Ron asked me to return to Florida. It looked like the center was having some financial problems, and it was going to be closed until things improved for the better.

When I was back in Florida, I was in charge of all the facelifts and training other physicians. I managed to pay back a lot of my debts. (I keep calling those debts "my debts", because no one else knew about them – not even my wife. I am sure that after she reads this book, she will find out about them). My reasons are not hard to understand. I did not want her to worry.

For all the time I was there, Ron did not show up once. We communicated only on the phone. It was very strange for me not to see him in the office. As per the rumors that were spreading, he had moved out of state. There was an ongoing investigation about him being an M.D. I can say in his defense that he let a qualified physician prescribe all the medications, administer anesthesia, or offer any necessary medical assistance with any of the clients at the clinic. All the face treatments that he performed were of the highest professional standard.

One of the consultants who had worked with Dr. Ron for over twenty years was a sixty-five years old lady, Elie. She was one of his first facelift patients back in California when he started, and she looked fantastic for her age. Nevertheless, she told me that she was due for another facelift and asked me to do it for her. When I did, she complimented me, saying the treatment was much easier that time, with no anesthesia, shorter and with better results. After a few days, Ron's office in Florida was closed down, and, meanwhile, Elie and I continued to work together using a dermatologist's office, waiting for something new to come up.

Chapter 29

On Human Values

The non-surgical facelifts drew a lot of attention in Israel. I had become pretty famous back there. My father, who had retired by then, remained the administrator of my office, while I returned to Israel over regular periods to perform treatments and visit my family. During those days my mother got a viral brain infection, and her condition was getting worse. The infection was serious. Her attending physician and even I doubted that she would ever recover. It was a life-threatening condition, but against all odds my mother's will to live took over, and she survived. Along with the infection, the depression that she suffered from for many years disappeared. The sad part was that her ability to function diminished considerably.

Looking back at the way my mother was, I see a woman who used to hold three different jobs to support her family and raise her children: "the kitchen wizard" who could handle any number of guests during a party, and the high society lady. That lady could hardly function by herself anymore. The house duties and taking care of my mother became the responsibility of my father, and he did it lovingly, with the utmost dedication and compassion. I had always known that my father loved my mother more than anyone else, but during those days, I could see the love for real. Work is a manifestation of love.

Because taking care of my mother took all of my father's time, I had to look for someone else to run my office. You remember Dr. Eger, the Head of the Department of Surgery, who was also my teacher, mentor, friend and a second father. He was the one who had died at the age of forty-two from lung cancer. He was one of the few people that I had admired most in my life. A few days before he died he had asked me to take care of his son. At that time Avi, his son, was twelve years old. But now, in his twenties, married, a doting father of two children, he was very unhappy with his job. My mother helped Avi's mother get a position as a manager of a prestigious hotel in Beer Sheba when her husband passed away, and now it was my time to keep the promise I had made to his father years ago. I arranged to meet with him and offered to let him to run my office as a partner. After having seen some of my facelifts, he got excitedly accepted my offer.

No time was lost, and we began at once. The first round of facelifts took place in a prestigious hotel in Beer Sheba where his mother worked. As I have said, due to the increasing popularity of the "Floridian Facelift," I received a sort of celebrity status in Israel where people, mostly women, lined up for Dr. Goldstein's miracle rejuvenating non-surgical facelift. This time I had about forty. After leaving my clinic, the patients stayed in the Beer Sheba hotel for a week, and the hotel provided all the required service and a special diet.

One of the patients was Dalia, a journalist from a leading women's magazine, and after having her facelift she wrote an article where she gave a great review of the treatment, including some colorful before-and-after photographs. Thanks to that, people got to know us better and could see the results for themselves. That was a good promotion for us. The number of patients leapt up high and so did the frequency of my trips to Israel.

One early morning, I woke to someone banging on the front door downstairs. My father came to my room and told me that there were some people who wanted to see me. Still in my pajamas, I went downstairs where I saw two policemen and a civilian. They told me they were from the Taxation Department Special Assignment Unit and were taking me to the police headquarters of Beer Sheba. They treated me like a criminal and would not let me put on my clothes without being escorted by one of them. At the police station I was interrogated about my clinic in Israel, the number of treatments I had done, how much we were getting paid, and all sorts of questions. I explained to them that I could give them all the information regarding the medical side of the business, but they would have to talk to my partner regarding the financial and administrative part of it. The then let me go without giving any explanation about what that fuss was all about.

At the Beer Sheba hotel, I found out that my patients had been questioned by the police and their rooms had been searched. Police raided my Tel Aviv office and my partner's house as well. Later on I found out that we had been accused of tax evasion. We had just started the office in Israel, and we hadn't filed any tax returns yet, so how could we be accused of evading taxes? We hired an attorney (another unpredictable legal expense), who informed us that the hotel raids and interrogation of my patients were illegal, since any place where patients were still receiving medical treatment was considered to be a clinic, and there are certain laws protecting the confidentiality and privacy of patients. They dropped the charges, but we never got an explanation or even an apology.

*

After the supposed tax evasion fiasco, I returned to Florida. Dr. Ron's business was shut down in Florida. There was not much work left to do. While I was away, there had been a lot of bad publicity when the news spread about Ron not being an M.D. I had no idea, what to do next. A few days later I was supposed to leave for Anchorage, Alaska, where Bob had finally been able to find potential clients. Bob was the friend who had given me the money to start my facelift training.

All this time Bob was practicing holistic medicine that is known to remove heavy metals and calcium deposits from the body, and by doing so, unclogs the arteries. It is used as a treatment for people who suffer from a partial or complete blockage in their arteries, including heart disease. One of his patients, a member of the government of Alaska, suffered from coronary artery blockage, and instead of having a bypass operation was treated with holistic medicine. After having accomplished his treatment at Bob's clinic, heart surgery was no longer needed – which was truly amazing – prompting this prominent government official to pass a bill with Congress forcing medical insurance companies to cover alternative medicine treatments.

I found it fascinating that there was a treatment to remove blockages from arteries without surgical intervention. The sad part was in a country where the number one killer was and still is heart disease, alternative medical treatment is not recognized by the medical board and insurance companies. Of course, these kinds of treatments do not bring a lot of revenue to hospitals, insurance and pharmaceutical companies as much as surgical bypasses and medications do.

The Alaskan treatments turned out to be a success and during my two weeks there, I also ignited my old love of traveling. I saw a part of the untouched wilderness of the state and even went salmon fishing.

After my return from Alaska, there was no income in Florida, so I had to fly quite often to Israel. What follows next is one of the biggest lessons of my life. A lesson that I learned late. I am not sure that have learned it yet, but whatever. It so happened that on one of my trips, my partner Avi came to the airport to pick me up. I noticed that Avi was driving a brand new luxury car. I didn't realize that we were making so much money that my partner could afford to buy a swanky new car.

Sami, a young French dermatologist from Paris married to an Israeli girl, joined our team at this time. After he heard about us and read all the publications in the media, he approached my partner and they signed a contract in which he would be trained to do the facelifts together with me. According to the established training routine, stage one consisted of just observing. Stage two consisted of him getting enough patients so that I could fly to Paris to assist him with launching his business.

It was a typically normal day. We were on schedule with our workload. The only thing different was that I was assisted by a new nurse. I was quite impressed by her interaction with patients. There was something fishy going on here, though, because at the end of the treatment course I did not get the expected results in some patients. I did not understand what was going on. After having performed so many treatments. I had not seen anything like this before. On investigating the case further, I found out that the new nurse stole some of the solution that I used for treatments and to hide it, diluted the solution with water. She was not only good at talking, but also good at stealing. I fired her immediately.

Since the nurse had screwed up, I had to offer a makeup facelift to some of the patients during my next visit to Israel. Before I left for Florida I approached my partner, Avi, and explained to him that I needed some money, mainly because there was no income in the U.S. He went pale and stuttered a bit. This guy who I cared for as though he was my younger brother was telling me that there was no money left in the bank account. I was really shocked! I mean who wouldn't be? I was expecting to get money back home, but my dear partner had used the money in the bank account to buy himself a new luxury car and withdrew the rest from the account authorizing the bank to keep that account only in his name so that I could not access it.

I was not hurt as much by the loss of money, but my feelings were hurt. Avi had always been like a little brother to me. I had kept my promise to his father to help him and this is how he had paid me back? He betrayed my trust and embezzled all the money. He still seemed like a brother to me, but he had to learn his lesson.

It was a hurtful process to initiate a lawsuit against him, but I had no other choice. Later on I found out that he was trying to do treatments with a student of mine from Las Vegas, and when that failed too, he escaped Israel and went to Hungary, the same country that his family had come from when he was a little child. He was such a coward that he left his wife and his two young children back in Israel with a lot of debt.

Was I so screwed that I was unable to distinguish between an honest person and a dishonest individual? Was it wrong in trusting someone whom you had cared for like your own family since he was a little child? I still haven't found the right answer.

After Avi screwed things up for me, I had to look for someone else to take care of my clinic. One of the patients, a cosmetologist, working as a volunteer in the Department of Plastic Surgery, offered to join me and manage my office in Israel, while my father would be responsible for the accounting. After having taken care of the mess, I returned back to Florida broken both financially and emotionally –more the latter– because I felt insecure trusting anyone anymore.

Chapter 30

❦

The Magic Formula

O ne particular morning a lady in her eighties entered my office and put an envelope full of cash on my desk. I was rather surprised by her odd way of asking for a facelift. You don't see people just coming in to your clinic and paying in advance without even saying what they are paying for! I asked how I could help her. The reason she had placed the envelope on my desk without any further questions was that she wanted to have her face done the next day.

I wondered why it was so urgent for a lady in her eighties to have the facelift the very next day. She explained that she had wanted to have it done for many years, but her husband kept telling her that she looked young and beautiful to him and was against it. I wonder what the husband's problem was. She said that whenever she looked in the mirror she saw a person looking back at her from the other side that made her feel like dying. The day before she came to see me was her 50th wedding anniversary, and her husband told her she could have any present she liked. It would not be very hard to guess what she had asked for.

We did not do the treatment the next day as she had demanded because there were tests that had to be done before the treatment. It was only a few days later that her facelift was performed. When she came for the follow-up, she said, "Doctor, since the day of my facelift... I... I...

cannot stop looking in the mirror. Before, every time I looked in mirror I wanted to die. But now, I can't even stop looking at myself." She was so happy that some nights she was afraid to go to sleep. She was afraid all this might disappear in the morning when she woke up.

*

Before I proceed with my next case, I would like to explain the procedure of the non-surgical facelift that I have been writing about for the last few chapters.

The first day of the treatment, a solution is applied to the face of the patient. The purpose of the solution is to dissolve the outer layers of the skin that have been damaged by sun, improper nutrition, aging, stress and other factors while stimulating the deeper layers to produce collagen and elastin. That gives the new skin a smoother appearance and restores the elasticity to the damaged skin. The final result would now be a new smooth, tighter, firmer and radiantly glowing skin. The new skin would be more like a baby's skin, obviously, because it has been re-grown. The immediate results of the treatment are very good. But as time goes on, they further improve, as it takes time for the skin to create more collagen and elastin in the deeper layers.

Technically, it is very similar to a chemical peel, but the big difference is in the formula I used. A chemical peel destroys many of the cells in the deeper layer that creates melanin, the substance that gives the color to our skin and protects us from sun radiation and skin cancer. People who have had a chemical peel look very pale and cannot expose themselves to the sun without sunblock. I was looking for ways to improve the treatments, and created a formula that dissolves only the outer layer of the skin to stimulate the production of collagen and elastin. It tightens the skin without causing any damage to the pigment of the skin. As a result of my innovation, it can be performed on any skin color, and after the recovery period the skin will return to its original color (plus you can always go out in the sun without soaking yourself in sunscreen lotion).

The solution that I had prepared was very sensitive to the acidity of the skin/pH because the pH of the outer layer of the skin is different from the pH in the deeper layers, so the solution dissolves only the outer layer and does not harm the deeper layers. When it gets to the deeper layers, the change of pH neutralizes the dissolving activity of the formula, and only the substance that stimulates the production of elastin and collagen continues to work. Therefore, there cannot be any damage to the deeper layers, and it will never form any scars.

The non-surgical facelift is performed with no general or local anesthesia. The burning sensation during the first few hours of the treatment can be easily treated with analgesic tablets. The treatment is always performed with all the equipment necessary for any emergency. Many of my patients are not very young, even though many younger people have had it, too just to get rid of their skin defects and scars. It is as effective for men as well as for women, but can be performed only to the facial area because treatment to other parts of the body will not give the same results due to difference of the pH of the skin. During the entire treatment course, the patients stay in a hotel or a private clinic where qualified nurses attend to them, and I see them at least twice a day. A week later, by the end of the treatment, the new skin is already formed, which for a short period of time might appear red, but the redness disappears very quickly.

I have been asked many times why do I not perform these treatments in a hospital. I think I have already told my readers about my views on infections in hospitals. Whenever someone asks me this question, my answer is always the same: "I like to avoid infections as much as I can." Many may be surprised by this answer, but after having worked for many years as a surgeon in different hospitals, it is very clear to me that hospitals carry a lot of infections, and some of those germs have become resistant to antibiotics. Overusing antibiotics is the chief reason why we are facing this problem. This problem is becoming increasingly more complex with each coming year as many hospital patients are getting sick or even dying from severe infections that can't be treated with antibiotics. That's why, to my mind, hospitals are for sick people. The facial treatment is for healthy people, which is done mainly for cosmetic reasons. There is no need to take unnecessary risks. One more thing I would like to share here is that I am very proud that after having treated more than 5,000 patients, I have never (yes, never ever) had any case of an infection or a scar.

Another FAQ is, "Do I need a treatment?" Well, for this question, my answer is, "If you look into the mirror and you are happy with what you see, then you do not need this treatment. Exceptions are some skin conditions like skin tumors that are malignant or may turn malignant because of sun damage. In this case, you should go for it.

Another question asked is, "How old do you think I am?" I don't know why it matters to my patients, but they still ask me as if my guessing their age is some kind of entertainment. I did fall into this trap a few times (that means I said they looked older or younger than they actually were) and since then I refused to answer this question.

During a trip to Israel I was going to treat about forty people in Dan Panorama, a luxurious seafront hotel in Tel Aviv. Luna, one of my patients, was an eighty-four-year-old woman. When she came to my office I noticed that all the fingers on her right hand were missing. I kept looking at her hand again and again, wondering what might have been the reason for that kind of amputation. When I finally decided to ask her about it, Luna told me that as a young girl during World War II she was in a Nazi concentration camp. One of the drunken German soldiers tortured her and amputated her fingers with a knife, leaving her to bleed to death. It was her friends in the concentration camp who took care of Luna and saved her life.

When the Allied forces freed the prisoners, she moved to Israel where she adopted twelve children who needed help. All these children were grown up; all of them had received higher education and had fine families. Luna told me that she is surrounded by young people all the time, so she, too, wants to look younger. She told her family she was going on a vacation to a beach resort in the southern part of Israel for a week and she wanted to surprise them with her new face. The facelift was a success. When I saw Luna for the follow-up, she told me that one of her kids told her she needed another vacation because there was still one little line left on her face.

I remember another lady, Dina, with a very wrinkled face. When I looked at her, I was really disturbed: she had numerous growths on her face, some of them already cancerous, and the rest were going to be cancerous soon. Dina's husband, who was a very well-known dentist in Israel, had insisted that she should have the treatment to get rid of the growth. It was a good idea. The patient had some other problems though, i.e., while lying on the treatment table she asked me to put some water on her face and tell her husband that she had the treatment done. I did Dina's facelift anyway. Her skin looked as young as a baby's skin. About six months later she came for the follow-up and asked if I could do something for a little line above her upper lip. I suppose she started to like the person facing her in the mirror every morning.

According to a small study that I conducted among my patients, the majority looked at themselves in the mirror standing about 3-4 feet away from it before the facial treatment. After the treatment, they would examine themselves for prolonged periods in the mirror at a distance of 3-4 inches, often using a magnifying glass to find imperfections.

Chapter 31

The Root of the Problem

The patients in this group were very friendly and interesting. During the week's stay in the hotel, we used to have daily meetings where we would discuss proper ways of taking care of one's skin after the treatment, nutrition, and other topics that they wanted to discuss. I showed them that by performing a muscle resistance test we could find out if a certain substance, medication, food or color was good or bad for you, and we could also engage in a two-way communication without uttering a word. All you have to do is have that question in your mind and then by performing the right muscle testing technique, you can receive an answer to it. My friend Joel, from California, first demonstrated it to me.

One of the ladies in the group asked me for a demo, so I decided to find out her birthday. To my surprise, I got two different dates for her birthday. She started weeping. It turned out to be that the first date was her birthday, which I had guessed correctly; the second one symbolized her resurrection from clinical death, which followed a serious brain infection that she had contracted as a girl. Resuscitation brought her back to life; she started breathing again; her heart started pumping blood again. That was the second date, which I had guessed correctly as well.

During one of those sessions I demonstrated to the group that the color pink depletes the body of energy. It is a good color for hyperactive people who are restless and very nervous. While going through the treatment course, the body needs all the energy to heal, and that's why I do not want any of my patients wearing pink, especially on the day of the treatment. I was very particular about that color.

Every time a patient wore pink something went wrong, i.e., being restless, having more burning sensation, having an unstable pulse and blood pressure, things that usually prolonged the treatment. That's why the nurse working with me was instructed to make sure that none of the patients wear pink. As an example, there was a case of a female patient being very restless and complaining about a burning sensation, and the whole treatment took longer than usual. I asked if the patient was wearing anything pink, and the nurse confessed that the woman had pink underwear, which she had covered with a blanket before the treatment so I could not see it.

I also demonstrated hypnosis because many patients requested it. One of the young ladies in the group told us that she was very scared whenever she heard a dog bark, especially when she couldn't see the dog. Whenever she heard barking she would start shivering and look for a place to hide. It was very embarrassing for her, especially when it happened during her work, or when others were around. She asked me to find the reason for this and agreed to undergo hypnosis in front of the group.

Under hypnosis I suggested to her that she was in a large room sitting in a very comfortable armchair. At that stage I asked her to go back to where her fear for the barking dogs had started. All of a sudden she turned pale, started trembling and talking in a different language that I could not understand. One of the ladies in the group said she was speaking Polish, and so I asked her to translate. The following is the exact translation. (Trust me, I am not making this up – all what I say here happened that afternoon.) *"She is describing a large room with many young children in it. It's very cold and they all are wearing torn clothes; all of them are hungry, thirsty and suffer from malnutrition. Some of them are very sick."*

Hearing this, we all became very curious, so I asked where this place was, and found out that she was referring to a concentration camp run by the Nazis in Poland. In that room were all the young children who were being taken away from their parents and were going to be sent to the death chambers. She tried to scream because a guard with dogs was walking outside. Those dogs were barking loudly, and it was just then that another girl covered her mouth to stop her from screaming. The dog barking was accompanied by the sound of gunshots.

It was, perhaps, because the dogs discovered a prisoner outside, and the German soldiers shot them. That is what happens under hypnosis: you can reprogram a patient and change her inner fears. That is what I did. When she woke up, the other lady tried to speak to her in Polish, but she did not understand even a single word. She only spoke Hebrew, and she was too young to be in a concentration camp, because she was born after the war. So it had to be a previous life (I had started believing in it lately) and her fears of a dog barking disappeared after the hypnosis session.

It was years before I read a book by Dr. Brian Weiss from Miami Mt. Sinai Hospital. Dr. Weiss narrated many accounts of his patients' previous lives that he had witnessed while conducting hypnosis. In medical hypnosis it is known as regression back to the time when the problems started, very often to their previous life.

During this time of sharing with a group of my patients [1987], we had been watching the four-hour ABC miniseries "Out on a Limb" adapted from an autobiographical book starring Shirley MacLaine (playing herself) where she described how she was introduced to the spiritual and mystical world. She was daring, sincere, and outspoken in her views on reincarnation, meditation, trans-channeling, and even UFOs. A courageous woman and a great actress that was straightforward and candid about her belief system. I loved every moment of that show and watched it several times. It really clicked with me in many ways. We were both walking the same path. Since my car accident in Florida I had attended many seminars by different people on subjects where spirituality, past life, kabala, and many other topics, related to the mind and soul, were discussed.

I became more positive, less skeptical, and eventually stopped doubting that we all had lived previous lives and were going to live many more lives in the future. Today I can hypnotize almost anyone and take him or her back to the previous life, proving that we did live before in different places, talked different languages, and had a different gender. And it is possible that many of our fears had undoubtedly originated in our previous life.

Another patient once asked me for help with her daughter, who was twenty-five years old and had a severe stuttering problem since she was three. She stuttered was so badly that she could neither get a job nor have a relationship. Under hypnosis I regressed her back to the place and time where the stuttering started. She described the dining room in the house when she was just three-years-old and her father came home very drunk. He started yelling and violently abusing her mother. The little girl became so terrified seeing her mother's face covered with blood that she became hysterical, crying and screaming. When her father heard her screaming, he told her to shut up or he'd kill her. Scared, hiding under the table, the girl covered her mouth to stop screaming, which led to the twenty-two years of stuttering. We solved the problem, the stuttering disappeared, and the woman gained her normal life.

Most cases of stuttering are due to an emotional problem and can be treated easily. Stuttering is usually a result of some kind of trauma that took place earlier in life, when someone wanted to scream or say something, but could not do so because of fear or any other reason. For me, it was very screwed that thousands of people who stuttered went through many long treatments without results. Most of these patients needed emotional treatment instead.

A prominent psychiatrist once called me to congratulate me with my swift success in achieving extraordinary good results with one of his patients within a very short period. He confessed that he had been trying to treat that young woman for years without any seemingly noticeable results. The patient suffered from severe scars and pigmentation marks on her face. She refused to look at herself in the mirror and she had a very low self-image. After she had undergone my non-surgical facial treatment, she could not get away from the mirror and had fallen in love with herself. Not only did she look better, but her attitude towards life changed.

One old and very sick-looking lady wanted to have a facelift. To me, she looked as if she could die any time. When I inquired more about her, she explained that she had very advanced cancer and her life expectancy was very short, therefore she wanted the treatment as soon as possible. I was rather puzzled by it. I could not understand why someone who was going to die soon needed a cosmetic face treatment, so I asked her.

She said, "Doctor, I have always been the black sheep in my family. My mother and sister both were beautiful and I was very ugly, but when my Mom and sister died they were very wrinkled and aged, this treatment would be my revenge. I want to have a smooth skin when I die." Of course, I refused to fix her face, but it showed me how screwed-up we could be. I mean, how does it matter to those who are already dead whether they have wrinkled skin or smooth?

The cosmetic industry has become one of the largest in the world. To me, it seems to be an industry of illusions. It is no different than the tricks performed by a magician on stage just to fool us and keep us entertained. When we get older, we search for our youth, and desperately run after it, trying to get it back, trying to preserve those last grains of youthfulness that will soon be gone with the wind. The even more screwed thing here is that when we were very young, we wanted to look older and took our appearance for granted. I remember my grandfather used to say, "We should have been born as old people and die as young. This way, with all the experience and knowledge that we have accumulated throughout our lives we could appreciate our youth in a better way." And as always, I think the same way my grandfather did.

As far as vanity is concerned, I would like to touch upon one other anecdote. In medical school one of my fellow students played a dirty trick on me – or shall I say a potentially deadly prank – by putting rat poison in my food. Though it didn't kill me, obviously, it made me very sick, and I lost all the hair on my body – and I mean, all of it. When I recovered, the hair on my body grew back, except on my head. I'd have preferred it to be the other way round – but whatever. So there I was, bald at twenty-one.

Getting bald (forcefully!) did bother me for many years, and when I used to look at myself I saw a 230-pound bald surgeon and a father of three. I didn't like what I saw, so I decided to change my life. I went on a severe diet and in three months lost 70 pounds, bought a hairpiece for my shiny, bald head that I am wearing even as I write these pages. I notice that today, many men are bald, and it is okay, but the trauma that I had as a young man prevents me even now from accepting it, and I still wear the hairpiece even though sometimes it looks rather ridiculous. It is pretty screwed, but nobody has seen me without my hairpiece, except for my wife.

Chapter 32

Dr. Alex

After all my adventures in Israel, when I returned back to Florida Dr. Ralph Dale called me. He excitedly told me that one of the greatest physicians in the Western world, specializing in the field of acupuncture, was coming to Florida and he wanted to learn the non-surgical facelift. The request came as a surprise to me. I was not ready. It was the holiday season and that meant I couldn't find any patients to work with.

I looked all over for a suitable patient. One night I was sitting at home wondering what to do, when Ettie walked in and started talking. As I looked at my wife I saw the perfect patient, and told her that I think she should have her face done. At that time Ettie was thirty-eight years old, but somehow her face looked much older than her age. (After reading this she is sure going to get mad at me!) I think it was probably hereditary from her mother who was much wrinkled. Ettie agreed.

Dr. Alex, the physician who wanted to learn about my treatment, was from Madrid, Spain. Soon after his arrival we had a meeting. He seemed to be a very nice man with a lot of knowledge in traditional medicine as well as alternative treatments. He had great credentials. For many years he was hired as a doctor to the royal family in one the Arab countries. I told him that I would be performing a facelift on my wife. He was very touched by the fact that I was going to choose my wife as a model to demonstrate to him the beauty of this non-surgical technique.

The treatment was done in our bedroom. As expected, the results were stunning. Ettie looked like a movie star in her twenties, and I was the lucky husband of that gorgeous lady. She received a lot of compliments. Her uncle was celebrating his seventieth birthday. When we arrived to the party, everybody was amazed by the way Ettie looked. For days I could not believe that she was my Ettie. Everyone in her family wanted to look younger. Her aunt and her sister immediately asked for their facelift – and some other women, as well.

During Alex's stay in Florida we became close friends. We used to chat and discuss different forms of medicine until early in the morning. When we talked about my method of treating pain, I was surprised to find out that Alex also was tuning into the patient and locating the areas where the energy flow obstructed the problem spots – so that made two of us.

Before he returned to Spain, I invited him to join me for treatments in Israel where he could watch, and learn the treatment. Forty patients were better than just one, who also happened to be my wife. We also agreed that later on I would join him in Madrid where he could perform his first non-surgical facelift.

A few weeks later Dr. Alex joined me in Israel. Soon afterwards Ettie and I traveled to Madrid where Alex was going to perform two face treatments, one for his mother and the other one for a well-known Spanish celebrity. Dr. Alex was considered to be like royalty in Spain, and when my wife and I arrived at Madrid airport, we were supposed to receive a red carpet welcome. But the porters went on strike and it was a chaotic situation at the airport. Seeing this, Alex was disappointed, but Ettie and I were relieved.

Alex arranged for our luxurious accommodations in the center of Madrid. The service was excellent. While we stayed there we met his wife and three children, whom we found to be very warm, friendly and well educated. They spoke fluent English and could easily hold a conversation. Alex's children went to private schools. His youngest son attended a very high-society private school in London.

Alex resided in a mansion outside Madrid. It was one of the most beautiful residences I had ever seen. Alex had two servants, a couple from Portugal, who did the housework chores and cooked. During the entire dinner a servant dressed in uniform and wearing white gloves waited on us. Standing aside by the table, he magically appeared at the right time behind our backs to supply or replace any item on the table. Alex's house looked more like a museum and boasted all the gifts received during his service in the Middle East. It was all very impressive.

Alex's routine was as follows: he woke up every morning at 5:00 a.m. to practice Kenpō, a form of Japanese martial art, in which he held a black belt. After breakfast he went to his office where he worked until late at night, attending to all of his patients. One might ask why a person who had so much going in his life cared about non-surgical facelifts? He hoped that it would generate more income and he would have more free time to spend with his family.

Alex was not only a great family man, he was a great host, too. I mentioned once that I liked music, especially Spanish guitar music. Guess what Alex did the next day? He invited us to join him for dinner in a private club listening to Spanish guitar musicians. Early evening, Alex and his wife picked us up from the hotel and we went to the club. When we arrived at a very large, luxurious establishment in the center of Madrid, it looked all deserted to me, a very unlikely place for a club. It seemed strange that there were no people there – but only one table set up for four close to the stage. It was then that Alex told me that he had reserved the whole place for just the four of us to have dinner and enjoy Spanish music. That was definitely one of the best dinners I have ever had, accompanied by the two Spanish guitarists on stage who presented us with the cassettes of their program that night.

During our stay in Madrid we performed two face treatments and spent a beautiful time with Alex and his family. Back on the plane to Florida the flight attendant came to us with two champagne glasses and informed us that according to Alex's request, we would be given special service during the flight.

Alex and I stayed friends. A few months later, I found out that he could not perform non-surgical facelifts in Spain. The reason was that all the high-society husbands would not allow their wives to spend time alone in a hotel room, not even for a medical treatment. It was, and still is, hard for me to understand or accept, but perhaps that is part of Spanish culture. Is it due to lack of trust, fear or something else?

January 1986, the New Year had begun. My parents came to visit us in Florida. One night we had been invited for dinner with friends. We finished our desserts and were in the middle of a conversation when suddenly Ettie's face turned white. It looked like she was going to faint. She looked as pale as a ghost. I asked her what was wrong and she told me that she wanted to go home. As soon as we got home, the phone rang – it was Ettie's mother. Ettie's father had passed away. He died at the same time Ettie started feeling bad after the dinner. While my parents stayed with the children in Florida, Ettie and I went to Israel to attend her father's funeral. It was only a week later that we returned to Florida, this time with Ettie's mother.

What happened was terribly sad. But what amazes me is that when a person dies, someone who is thousands of miles away can sense that something bad has happened. It may sound rather supernatural, but I am sure that during our lifetime we have all had similar experiences. How can we explain it? And if we can't, then what is the force behind this connection with the ones we love?

Chapter 33

On the Road Again

Back in Florida, things slowly returned to normal, although we could never bring back Ettie's father. The whole family was with her during that hard time. Since the shutdown of Ron's center, we did not have much business left in Florida, so I had more time to spend with my wife. While work was drying up, Elie, Ron's assistant, was trying to convince me to move to California where she knew many people who could help us establish a lucrative and successful clinic.

I was not sure if I wanted to leave Florida, but there was no harm in exploring other possibilities. Within a few days we arrived to Los Angeles and from there we drove to San Diego. It was not my first visit to San Diego, but during that time I really fell in love with the city. San Diego is known to have the best weather in the U.S. Located in the southern part of San Diego County, the city is constantly cooled by the ocean breeze. Is a perfect place to raise your children – is has the best zoo in the country, Sea World, Wild Animal Park, Scripps Institution of Oceanography at La Jolla, San Marcos racetrack and its annual County Fair that brings a lot of families to that area. San Diego School District is well known for its high level of academic achievement, and my kids' education has always been on top of my list of priorities.

When I returned to Florida, interesting news awaited me. It was the lawyer who was handling my lawsuit against the company whose truck had hit me. Originally he had assured me that I would be compensated for all the misery and pain I had to endure for months after the accident. When I saw him this time it was a different story. He tried to convince me to drop my charges. When I refused, he practically threatened me by saying that he would use his influence and make it impossible for me to get my American citizenship. Eventually I dropped the charges, and he informed me he would send me a bill for his expenses. A few weeks later I hired another lawyer to work on the three-year-old case. After performing all the required investigations, the new lawyer did not see any reason why I should have dropped my charges. He was of the opinion that the first attorney had been paid off by the company involved in the accident. When the original lawyer found out that I had hired a new lawyer, he did not send me a bill for his "services." This small incident kept me wondering (again!) whatever happened to the principles of justice that the fathers of this nation laid so proudly.

Shortly after all this legal trouble I was supposed to leave for Paris. There, Sami, who started working with us on a contract thanks to Avi, was going to perform his first Floridian Facelift. Since the agreement between Sami and myself was signed by my previous partner, Avi, I refused to go unless I was paid by him. (I sure did learn a thing or two from Avi). In Paris we treated two women. The very first time I saw Sami perform the facelift, I sensed that he was not competent enough to do this type of treatment, even though he was a dermatologist. It seemed to me that his main motivation was financial gain, and his medical knowledge was very superficial. He did not want to heal – he just wanted to put money in the bank.

Back in Florida we were preparing to move to California. The children were not very happy leaving their school and friends. During our stay in Florida the children had really started to love their school. Their school was one of the best in our area. The education standards in Boca Raton were very high. The teachers took care of every student and monitored their progress. The teachers also knew the students by their first name; they supported the students, took care of their special needs and were actually teaching the children to think. Besides the school curriculum, the after-school programs were very enriching. While Ran was learning to play bassoon, Ori, who was only six years old, was learning computers that had just hit the home market. The relationship between student, teachers and parents was so close and friendly that parents took part in all the decision-making and problem-solving.

But in September 1986 the decision had been made: we rented a house and were moving to Southern California. My aunt and her two children from South Africa, who had been living with us for a while, were also coming along with us to San Diego. All our belongings were being packed and moved while the seven of us, three adults, five kids and a parrot, were driving across the country from east to west. The journey is said to be the best part of reaching a destination. That trip was interesting for me as well as for the children. We visited beautiful New Orleans and several other places. Ran, who has a phobia of heights, used to lie down on the bottom of the car every time we crossed a high bridge.

When we reached Texas a tornado brought heavy rains and high winds. All of this ruined our plans to move forward. We were trying to find a place to stay so we could be safe. The wicked weather changed fast – along with the storm came the midsummer heat of Texas, Arizona, and California. The temperatures soared, and all of us were panting. The parrot was the one who suffered the most. Ran had to spray his parrot with water every few minutes to keep him cool. We all took a deep breath when we arrived to San Diego. There, the climate was awesome, as always.

*

In San Diego we opened a beautiful office and we hired a sales representative who promised to bring us a lot of patients. Since Elie knew a lot of people in California, we thought that we would be able to get a lot of referrals. The sales representative promised to establish our steady clientele. Nothing of the sort happened. There was no flood of people pouring into our clinic.

One day Sami called me from Paris. He sounded quite alarmed. After a face treatment something had gone wrong. The problem was that he didn't even know what was wrong, so he had no idea what to do. When

I questioned him about the details, it did not seem to be very serious. I promised him that on my way to Tel Aviv the coming week, I would stop by in Paris and see what the problem was.

In Paris I met Sami and the lady who had received a facelift. I did not observe any problem. It was better to ask the patient herself. The woman told me that after the initial treatment her face swelled and when she saw Sami was panicked by it, she got scared too. My fears became a reality. Sami was not a proper candidate to perform this treatment, and I told him so. I wonder if he took my advice or ignored it completely, but I have not heard from him since.

*

In Tel Aviv a large group of patients waited for me. I enjoyed my work and loved getting to know each and every one of my patients. The time that I spent with them after the face treatments was very meaningful. It gave me a chance to connect to each patient personally and to explore my own ideas of hypnosis and past life.

This group of patients knew that I had performed hypnosis with my other groups, and they asked me to do it with them as well. One of the patients, a young hairdresser who was openly gay, asked to find out under hypnosis what the reasons for his sexual orientation were. He agreed to do it in front of the group. Under hypnosis, when I regressed him to where it had started, I expected him to go back to his childhood, but to my surprise he described altogether a new thing. He talked about an amphitheater in ancient Rome where gladiators fought. He was one of the gladiators and he described in great detail how he killed his opponents. In one of his fights he was killed and he described all the events that led to his death. It was unclear to us what all this bloodshed and killings had to do with his sexual preference in this life. We all were very curious, so when I asked him under hypnosis what the reasons were for his sexual orientation, his answer was that in the past life he had to kill men, so in this lifetime he had to learn to love them.

This might have sounded rather screwed, but when I repeatedly investigated other gay men under hypnosis, in many of them I found similar circumstances. Though they not all gladiators, most of them had issues like hating men or killing them in a previous life. Maybe it's not so screwed after all. The soul has a way to pay back all our wrong deeds. In this life, we learn and correct what we did in previous lifetimes.

*

Now, back to the story that took place in San Diego. The school year had started, and the five children were returning to school. I had inquired a lot about the school and the responses were really amazing. We had a lot of expectations for the school system in the area where we lived. I was pretty sure after hearing so many positive reports about San Diego schools that it would be similar to what we had back in Boca Raton, Florida.

Very soon I was proved wrong. We soon realized that this school was not the same as the one we had just left behind. My cousin came back from school beat up and bleeding. She looked like she had been in an accident. When we inquired what happened, she told us that some black kids in school found out that she was from South Africa, where there was apartheid, and they beat her up. This was in a high school in San Diego!

I was afraid things might be even more serious than we knew. We discovered that there were many types of gangs in the school. Some of them were blacks, some were Hispanics or whites; some were mixed, and they terrorized the rest of normal students. Ori, who was only eight years old, said that he was afraid to use the restrooms at school because members of different gangs who dealt drugs were attacking kids there. It was the first time that we had to face the problem of drugs in school. Before that our children had never even heard about drug dealers at schools.

As if that hadn't been enough, Ori's teacher called us for a parent's conference and told us that Ori was disturbing the class by talking to his friend. She had to change his seating and move him to the back of the class. His performance in school was not up to standards, and it seemed to her that he was going to fail. This revelation from Ori's teacher came as a shock to us. Ori was a very good student back in Florida. He had always performed way above the average. I tried to explain to the teacher that

Ori was disturbing the class because he was bored and not because he was unable to cope with the material. I tried to reason with her, but she had made up her mind about Ori and refused to accept that.

Only two weeks later a survey was conducted in school among bilingual students. The students were called for a special interview and their skills and IQ were tested as well. It was intended mainly for bilingual students who spoke English and Spanish. Ori joined them because he could speak both English and Hebrew. After this survey, we were called in for a second conference with the teachers. This time they said that Ori was highly gifted and talented and asked for our permission to promote him to a different class, a AAA (Advanced Accelerated Achievement) class where some of the instructors and teachers would be from the UCSD (University of California at San Diego). Naturally we gave our consent and Ori started the new class, where he again became an excellent student.

While little Ori became the gifted student, Ravit, our eldest child, started her driving education and she, of course, planned to drive our car. It was not an issue with me. We were happy to share our family car with her, and I became Ravit's first driving instructor. She learned to drive quite well except for one particular power pole that disturbed her. That pole kept disturbing her for years to come whenever she tried to drive past it.

Overall, driving schools in the U.S. are very good. However, it's rather strange that no one teaches car maintenance and mechanics. In many other countries drivers are required to pass a written test about mechanics and maintenance. My son, Ran, years after getting his driver's license, called me up when he was on the road asking what to do because his car was overheated. When I suggested he should check the water in the radiator he had no idea where the radiator was – all this in a country where the ratio of cars to families is the highest in the world.

*

Our new San Diego office was very beautiful: modern furniture, artwork and green plants. It was located downtown. We tried to oversee every possible detail when we opened it, but the biggest downside turned out to be the hotel rates, which were huge. Our patients had to spend a week recovering after their facelift under my strict supervision, and had to follow a special light diet. Luckily, our solution was only twenty minutes away from our office. Tijuana, on the other side of the border, offered a luxurious hotel with full service included for a fraction of the price we would have to pay in San Diego.

One of the first patients to receive our non-surgical facelift was our sales representative's sister-in-law. As expected, the outcome was so good that even Jerry's mother asked for the treatment. The reason I am telling this story is that after the face treatment had been done and all went well, we didn't get paid. Sounds screwed, and yes it was, perhaps, even more screwed than it sounds. We approached Jerry, the sales rep, and his sister-in-law, asking for payment. A few days later we received a letter from her husband who said that if we insisted on getting paid he would sue us for negligence and harming his wife's face. The cost of the legal expenses would have been so high that it would have actually been cheaper for us to cover the expenses. After this lesson I did not offer another free treatment to Jerry. Once bitten, twice shy.

The whole American healthcare system was screwed. What happened to us was just an example. Lawsuits against physicians for malpractice, negligence and damages were becoming quite frequent. Some physicians, in order to avoid malpractice lawsuits, dropped their charges, and sometimes paid the patient to avoid high legal expense and negative publicity. In one of the newspapers there was an article about a woman who was injured in a car accident and was suing her doctors. The reason for the lawsuit was that she had had a brain scan that supposedly affected her psychic abilities. The jury granted her $750,000.

Insurance malpractice was becoming so outrageously expensive that physicians had to pay $100,000 or more a year. Those who could not afford it were forced to close their practice.

Especially susceptible to lawsuits were obstetricians. The law stated that up to the age of sixteen, a child could sue the doctor who had delivered him for damages. Many hospitals closed their maternity ward, forcing women to travel long distances to get to a hospital and have a baby. As a result, more and more women started natural delivery at home with the help of a midwife.

It was obvious that patients were eventually going to pay for all of this, and due to their actions the cost of health care in the U.S. today is the highest in the world. Many cases could be told and retold about patients who ripped off hospitals and doctors. A woman from Los Angeles told us that she had witnessed a car accident and was so scared that she dropped one of her contact lenses. She initiated a claim for contact lenses, as well as requested compensation for being scared to drive after she had witnessed the accident. The insurance company settled her case for a large sum of money. After receiving the settlement, she was very happy.

The school year was coming to the end and we made plans to drive up the coast to Northern California: San Francisco, Reno, and the Yosemite Park.

The scenery was beautiful. The only problem we encountered was that in many sections of the road, there were cliffs and sharp turns – Ran and I have a problem with heights. Whatever fear of heights I may have had, it never prevented me from driving, but Ran would lie below the seat on the bottom of the car with his eyes closed every time we drove over a bridge, or when the serpentine of Highway 101 was too close to the vertical cliffs overlooking the blue Pacific.

In San Francisco Ran spent more time on the bottom of the car than sitting in his seat. When in Lake Tahoe – a mountain paradise for avid hikers and skiers in winter – we admired the serene beauty of the crystal lake, the pine tree forests covering the mountains, the varied granite rock formations emerging from the waters of the lake creating bizarre motifs and scenes. Being there made one's imagination run wild, stupefied and speechless by the majestic grandeur of Mother Nature. While I admired the divine granite silhouettes in the distance, a voice interrupted my chain of thought: "Why did we have to drive so far to see some water? We could have filled our bath tab at home with water." I thought my children would have enjoyed the nature, but, perhaps, I was wrong.

*

When we reached Reno it was a different story. As soon as the kids saw the casinos their eyes started to pop out with excitement. Even though they were under age to enter the casinos, they found a way in and loved it – the little children who still couldn't appreciate the beauty of the nature were trying their best to get in the casinos.

Soon we headed for Yosemite Park, a world famous treasure of the world located about 9,000 feet above sea level. It was getting dark and I found myself driving towards the entrance following the road signs and fighting my fear of heights every turn of the road. At the end of this trial we found out that it was past closing hours already, and now, at dusk, we had to drive down the mountain just to repeat the same torture the very next morning.

I don't regret doing it, however, because what we had discovered the morning after far exceeded any expectations of a well-planned family vacation. While winding our way through the park, in one section of it there was a fire and some roads were closed. I was not particularly happy driving down the hill again, and knowing there was a fire nearby didn't help. When we eventually got safely to the bottom of the hill, we all took a deep breath of relief and enjoyed the scenery.

Back in San Diego we met a family from Johannesburg who lived nearby. Manny and Adele lived in the same neighborhood as we did and their children attended the same school district as our kids. We had a lot in common and became very close. While their children studied in a private Jewish school, our children went to a public school. Manny and Adele had lost most of their money due to a failed business venture with one of their relatives. Their house was foreclosed and they had to rent a house nearby. Adele's parents were still in Johannesburg and her mother suffered from Alzheimer's. She was confined to an institution and hardly recognized her own family.

*

In April 1987 we celebrated Ran's Bar Mitzvah with our friends and family. As a present, I offered Ran to join me on my next trip to Israel. The trip started with the flight to Tel Aviv. Ran let everyone on board know about his weird sense of humor by screaming that the wings of the plane were on fire. Many passengers got scared and the flight attendant politely told him to shut up. Since he was asked to do so, he decided to lie down on the floor and fall asleep.

My office in Israel was in the center of Tel Aviv in a nice apartment complex and had many rooms. I lived and worked there. Very soon Ran became friendly with all the staff members. His ability to make connections and become friendly with people older than him was really amazing, and he is still that way.

*

It was summer and there was a large group of patients. During their week's stay in the hotel, Ran became a central figure in that group. He was helping everyone he could, from taking care of the patients by serving them food, to talking to them, which helped to keep their minds off things. He did everything. Overnight, he had become a star. Many patients cried when they had to say goodbye to him.

When I returned back from that trip to Israel, I was invited to a lecture given by a minister in San Diego. The title of that lecture was: "Living With A Life-Threatening Disease." A young minister introduced himself as an AIDS sufferer. He looked very healthy. Then he started telling us his story. According to him, his condition had deteriorated very much. He was suffering from pneumonia, was losing weight rapidly, and contracted other opportunistic infections that are common with advanced stages of AIDS. He was spending more time in the hospital than outside. During one of his stays in the hospital, he grew very sick and ran a high fever. It was then that he had a vision. It was very clear to him that he saw Jesus, who told him that he was not going to die then. Jesus said to him that there were more things that he still had to do in this lifetime. Jesus instructed him about proper nutrition, to take supplements, and he would become better. The next morning he felt much better and was released from hospital.

After that vision, he started to live by the guidance he was given. In a very short period of time, he recovered fully. All the symptoms of the disease disappeared. He was functioning as well as he had before he got sick. He started implementing all the things that he was instructed to do while he was sick. Four years since that day, he looked very healthy. Having done everything he was supposed to do, he was expecting death and was ready for it. Knowing clearly that soon he was going to get ill again and die from AIDS, he returned to his previous lifestyle, eating everything that he was not supposed to eat. That was the first time I met someone with AIDS.

I don't know if that young man actually saw Jesus in his vision or not – that doesn't really matter. What matters is once he started believing that in order to recover he had to drop his bad eating habits and lead a healthy lifestyle, his AIDS went into remission. This was before there were anti-AIDS medications. We all have a free choice, and he had clearly made his.

*

My aunt, who was staying with us along with her two children, decided to go on a trip by bus from San Diego to Las Vegas. On her way back a young man was sitting next to her. They started chatting and then he made a very funny observation – that she looked older than the way she was behaving. A rather "screwed" compliment to give to a woman. Later, when she got back, she started examining herself in the mirror and asked me to fix her face. I had to abide by her wish. She had to look the age she acted. Just before Halloween, I did her face.

This treatment had its own hilarious moments. Like every normal Halloween, children were trick or treating from door to door. My aunt was still wearing a mask on her face. When she went to get the door, all we heard was a bunch of kids screaming and running away from our house. After a short time my aunt and her kids left for South Africa. When they left, she looked about twenty years younger.

Toward the end of the year I decided to visit Johannesburg on my way from Tel Aviv. I was flying to South Africa on New Year's Eve in 1987. It had been five years since we left South Africa, and it was time to see if things had changed there. Before I left, Adele, our close friend, asked me to see her mother, who was suffering from Alzheimer's. I said I would. A few days before my flight Adele called and told me that she would be in Johannesburg, too. We decided to meet in Johannesburg and go together to see her mother who stayed in a special institution.

Chapter 34

The New Year in Johannesburg

January 1st, 1988, I landed in Johannesburg. I stayed in a hotel and contacted my aunt and some friends who were still living in South Africa. Since I had promised Adele that I would go with her to see her mother, I made an appointment with her but requested that the meeting should take place at home and not at the institution where her mother was located.

Adele's mother was a fragile, petite lady. She looked as if she were wandering in space, not aware of who she was or where she was. I had a feeling that I could help her. The first thing that came to my mind was an old lesson given to me by a teacher, so I put my hand on her little hand and made a connection with her. I explained to her that her family loved her very much and was concerned about her health. I told her that we all wanted to see her healthy and happy at home and offered her help to get well. To my utter surprise, her eyes filled up with tears as she gazed at me, " Will you … will you … really … help me to get well?"

"Yes." I said it out loud. We started talking. It became very clear to me that she was not suffering from Alzheimer's. I explained to her what treatment was required: a very strict diet for the first two weeks and after that we would add more food. She would also have to take supplements and vitamins in order to get her stronger and better. Her answer was that she would do anything possible to make herself better, and be able to stay at home with her family and loved ones as long as she will not have to return to the institution.

At this point, I asked her family to join us. They were shocked, crying and sobbing, amazed at the transformation that took place. But who would not be? They had lost all faith and hope of her living a full life again, and there she was on the brink of a new beginning. While the whole family was crying, overwhelmed with love, the only one who was very joyful was her little dog who had not seen her for six years. The dog was jumping all over her. She quickly recognized all her family and spoke to each one of them. I told the family that, in my opinion, it was a wrong diagnosis, and it was not a case of Alzheimer's. I announced that I would treat her under one condition, that she stayed home with them. Without hesitating they all agreed.

I instructed the maid what food to prepare for her and how to take care of her. I stopped most of the medications that she was on. As I had expected, she recovered within a short period of time. Her memory was functioning well. She did not show any signs of Alzheimer's. She never went back to the institution.

After her mother was fit as a fiddle, Adele left for the U.S. How ironic it was that she flew in preparing to say goodbye to her mom, but instead she was saying, "I will see you soon!" The family, the doctors and other members of the institution where she was staying for the past six years thought that it was a medical miracle. I am not sure if miracle is the correct term. I do not see myself as a miracle worker. I am a physician, and more so, I am a healer. All I do is to devote my time and efforts to my patients, and do all that I can to find out everything about them before I make a diagnosis.

But then again I am only a human being, so I do make mistakes as well. But all this experience made me wonder. It seemed like things had more depth to them than what we expected them to be. I had no doubt that if Adele's mother's attending doctor had taken time to connect and spend more time just asking questions of the poor woman, he would have recognized that she was just brokenhearted and struck by grief of separation from her loved ones, and wouldn't have to spend six years of her life in a medical facility for Alzheimer's patients. The worst part is that once there is a diagnosis sticker on a patient, it is obvious that most other people will treat them accordingly. Patients who are locked up in an institution without connecting to the outside world or family will deteriorate with time and would soon be ready to die, as was clear from Adele's mother's case. The reality is that patients are still willing to be helped if help is offered to them.

Many patients who are diagnosed with terminal illness, provided they really want to get well and receive the right help, will show remarkable signs of improvement, and there is a chance that they even could be healed.

When we ask a person that is ill if he or she really wants to get well, most of the time, the answer is, "Of course I do." But do they really want to? This part is a bit tricky. It is easy to find the right answer by talking to the patients, to get to know them and sometimes use hypnosis to get to their subconscious mind, where the real person is, not the one behind the mask.

Many patients – you might remember one of them happened to be my father-in-law – need to be sick for different reasons. Some are sick in order to avoid doing things; some get sick to get more attention; some for self-punishment; some to learn or to teach a lesson, and so on.

All the years I have spent practicing medicine, everybody knew that in order to switch me to a high gear, or to make me find solutions, I need to be challenged. The best way to get me going is to say that a certain patient is untreatable or that he could not be helped or has no hope.

When I get the patient's cooperation, most of the time we find the right solution and treatment – some other times we don't – but we never fail to explore, we never fail to give our best in treating the patient. When you give everything you have for what you believe in, you are bound many times to get backlashes professionally and emotionally. As Hilary Clinton puts it, "I have the scars to prove it."

*

Lisa was another one of my patients in Johannesburg. When we met she confessed to me that one of her girlfriends told her she looked much better from a distance. Honest, wasn't she? Anyway, when Lisa heard about my facelifts and saw some of the photos, she got excited and asked me to do her face.

She assured me that she would advertise it to her friends and to the media. I agreed and did the treatment at her home. As expected, she looked beautiful. Immediately after the treatment, she contacted the *South African Sunday Times*. A reporter interviewed her and me. There was a large article published with colorful photos about the treatment. The title of the article was "The miracle of medical cosmetics without a knife arrives to South Africa." Too long for a title, but it was sure an honor.

At Lisa's house I met one of her friends who told me that her son was involved in a car accident about two years ago. He was in coma for three months, and when he came out of it he did not remember most of his past. He was confined to his home and avoided any social activity. The boy's state of mind was so bad that she asked for help. When I met John, I saw a guy in his early twenties with severe mental and emotional issues due to the accident. The most prominent problem was his inability to concentrate and to remember things from the past. I explained to his parents that I could not promise anything. I did not know how much of it was due to brain damage, and how much was a result of post-traumatic emotional damage.

I assured them that if he would come to San Diego where I lived, I would be happy to assess his state of mind and then assist him. His parents thoroughly checked my background and, once convinced that I was not going to kidnap their son, agreed to send him to San Diego.

*

During my New Year's vacation in Johannesburg there was another interesting case. A lawyer contacted me and told me that his young son, who was twenty-one years old, had turned mental. At first, I was pretty taken aback by his sudden diagnosis of his son, and I did not understand what the meaning of "going mental" was. So I asked him to explain. He told me that his boy was a student at one of the universities. He was having trouble finding his place at home or in society. He did not study properly and after two failed relationships with girls of his age, all of a sudden decided he was gay and moved in with one of his lecturers at the university.

The case was interesting enough to call my attention. When I met the guy, I found him to be nice and intelligent. He was very bright. He could fluently speak two languages, Afrikaans and English, but seemed to be a bit confused. When he started talking, he would change the subject in the middle of the sentence. He had no goals in his life and told me that the guy he lived with was abusing him both mentally and emotionally.

I used hypnosis on him. Under hypnosis, I regressed him to the place and time where the problem started. He described a delivery room in a hospital in Cape Town, South Africa. He described it in full detail. There was a small step between the delivery room and the next room. There were doctors, a midwife, and a pediatrician. The description was so detailed that he even mentioned their names.

On the delivery table was a lady who was just about to give birth to her first child. All of a sudden he started talking in a different voice, laughing and crying at the same time. "No this is not my place," he kept saying. When I asked what it meant, he explained that, "I am a soul who is instructed to get into this baby, who was about to be delivered, but it was not the right body for me."

Then he started shivering like he was very cold and explained that when he was born it was very cold in the room. He started spitting, saying that the midwife put her finger into his mouth to clean it, and it tastes very salty. He continued to describe how he was cleaned and wrapped in diapers. The nurse, who was carrying him, almost tripped and dropped him when she stumbled on the small step at the entrance to the next room. While he said all this, I was very happy that he could not see my facial expressions. I was overwhelmed and confused, wondering if it was actually possible for a soul to enter a wrong body. Was this the reason why he was so confused about his life? Or is it possible that there were mistakes in the soul world, too?

The next morning I phoned the hospital in Cape Town and they confirmed what he described about the delivery room. I was very certain that since he was born, he had never been to that hospital again, and I knew that his family had moved from Cape Town to Johannesburg when he was a baby. There was no chance of him knowing about the hospital.

I usually recorded the sessions with my patients and gave them a copy of the cassette at the end of the session. This time I decided not to give it to him yet. The reason was simple: I did not want him to think that he was some "screwed" guy or a soul in a wrong body. During our next session, we decided to clarify his sexual orientation, and find out why he had changed from being heterosexual to homosexual. Under hypnosis he described the Swiss Alps where he and his girlfriend, a lovely, beautiful young lady, were about to get married. They are very much in love, happy, and were planning their future together. They were about to ski in the Alps.

He was the one skiing down first on a steep slope of the mountain. He told me that when he got to the bottom, he was waiting for his girlfriend to come down. A long time passed and she didn't arrive. After a while a rescue team came and told him that while his girlfriend was skiing, she fell into a hole, which triggered a loose snow avalanche that collapsed and killed her.

In another session, he described a different relationship with a young lady that ended when she was killed in a car accident. While he was still under hypnosis, he said that every girl he fell in love with died in an accident. It was then that he decided that he must stop entering into relations with females, and since then he had only relationships with men. I explained to him and showed him that in both cases it was not his fault. When he woke up, he asked me, "So, tell me Doctor, am I straight or gay?" My answer was, "The choice is yours! We all have a free choice."

*

While I was in South Africa I met some of my old friends. One of them was Paul, a patient of mine, and a very close friend. My children liked him very much. I told Paul that we might return to South Africa and I hoped that this time it would be much better. On hearing this, he asked me, "What wasn't good last time?" To this question of his I did not have an answer. But I was sure that he understood my feelings and what I meant.

My aunt, who had returned to South Africa from the U.S. after I treated her face, told me that because of her age, it was harder for her to find a job. One day she was interviewed for a job at one of the private hospitals, and on the application form, instead of writing the year 1934 (when she was actually born), she wrote 1943. Due to the face treatment, when they looked at her face they did not doubt her age and she got the job. This treatment not only made people look young and feel better, but it also elevated their self-esteem by helping them get jobs. Or to say it in a "screwed" way, to not get caught when they lied about their age.

Life in South Africa was very pleasant and tranquil, but it was clear to everyone that this was going to change soon. If one looked around, there were changes all over the globe. In Southern Africa, Rhodesia had turned to Zimbabwe when the black majority took over from the white minority. But their economic situation deteriorated very fast. The country that used to be a food barn to many countries in Africa now could hardly supply their own needs. The war in Angola was still ongoing; the South African soldiers fought terrorists and Cuban soldiers.

In South Africa everything seemed quiet and peaceful – on the surface, at least. In the streets of Johannesburg, one could see many policemen and soldiers. Crime in the white areas hardly existed, but it looked more like a war zone filled with policemen rather than a residential area. The economic sanctions that the United Nations and other countries had implemented against South Africa were still in effect. But it looked like the white regime was getting stronger from it, as it had started manufacturing everything locally from cars to arms, and even turning coal to liquid fuel. It looked like the sanctions against South Africa affected the sports primarily, taking away the right to participate in any international sport events. Sports in South Africa were very important, and were a favorite pastime of the black and white population.

Many of my friends tried to convince me we should return. When I left Johannesburg I felt happy knowing that the two ladies I had treated were well and happy. All the articles in the media about my non-surgical facelift would bring many more patients. All in all, it was a very good, productive and enjoyable trip.

Two days before I returned to San Diego, my wife called and asked me why I did not tell her that there was a child coming with me. I wonder what might have triggered her to say that. Later, I came to know that a rumor had spread in San Diego about John, who was coming for a treatment. According to his parents, he was still a child, even though he was twenty years old.

When John arrived we tried to make him feel at home as much as we could. He seemed to be a much-pampered kid. When he had arrived from Johannesburg, a lady who was supposed to take care of him accompanied him. Though all this love and care on behalf of his parents was fine, I didn't think that he needed special care, so we asked the lady not to stay with us.

During the six weeks of John's stay, we did everything possible to make him feel a part of our family. But his behavior was of a spoiled, rich child, which caused our children to resent him. He believed that everyone around him was supposed to serve him, while he didn't have to do anything in return.

When we started the treatment, I discovered that John had suffered from a very severe head injury in a car accident. He was in a deep coma for about three months. In the first session under hypnosis I regressed John to the time and scene of the accident. When he was back at the scene, he started describing what was going on around him. I was amazed at what I was hearing. He remembered every minute detail. He recalled how he had lost his consciousness in the car, and then he heard someone calling for help. The ambulance arrived, and he clearly stated that someone from the rescue team had said that he would not make it to the hospital. The ambulance raced with full sirens through the streets. John described what was going on outside the ambulance. He talked about things like traffic lights turning red one after another, the ambulance changing lanes and passing the cars that were staying in the left lane. On one side he saw a VW Beetle drive by, and on the other side he saw several other cars.

When they arrived at the emergency room he was wheeled in on a stretcher. While he was being taken into the operating room, people were moving aside, and one of the trauma surgeons looked at him and said, "There is not much work for us here. He will die soon." He was then transferred to the x-ray department, and then to surgery. A tube was inserted into his throat, and IV fluids and blood were given to him. At this stage, the surgeons told the anesthesiologist that in this case anesthesia would not be required, because John was already unconscious and did not feel any pain. All he had to do was to stabilize his condition.

John went on to describe how his wounds were cleaned and sutured. He did not feel any pain, and then was transferred to the intensive care unit. His kidneys were not functioning well, and every few minutes someone came to check how much urine he was excreting, as well as to take his blood pressure and pulse. John was so weak that his breathing had to be assisted by a respirator. After a few days, when he was still in a coma, he was transferred to the unit, where they took care of his head injuries.

He described every visitor and what she or he was talking about. He remembered seeing his mother crying, and everyone was concerned about the amount of fluid he was secreting. The attending surgeon told his parents that they did everything possible, but now all they had to do was wait and see. About three months later he opened his eyes – everyone was happy and welcomed him back to the land of the living (I'd say the land of the awake).

When I woke him up from the hypnosis, he did not remember any details of what he had just told me. My wife, when she heard all of this, couldn't believe it either. John was getting well very fast. His memory and general condition were improving, but the screwed thing was that the better he got, the less pleasant a person he became to everyone around him. It was very clear to us that part of John's problem was being rich, spoiled, and ungrateful. With all that had been done for him, we never heard him say, "Thank you," let alone the desire to express some kind of gratitude for the people that helped him out of the darkness he was in. "The child" believed that he didn't have to thank anyone. He took it for granted that everybody's job was to serve him and please him. The "sick John" was a much nicer person than the "normal John."

After John left, things got a bit easier, and we had more free time. One weekend there was a seminar in San Diego by a very well known professor of hypnosis. I decided to attend it and convince my wife to come with me. I did not regret that decision – neither did Ettie. By the end of that weekend my wife decided to advance her studies and get a Ph.D. in hypnosis.

*

Since I had treated Adele's mother, she kept informing us about the improvement in her mother's condition. She told us that her mother had fully recovered and was trying to make up for what she had missed in the past six years when she was confined to the institution. She stayed busy all the time, moved around very quickly, so that sometimes her family and even her husband could not catch up with her.

*

Then, there was this question of going back to South Africa. As Green Card holders, we did not have to remain in the U.S. the entire year. We were allowed to change residency as long as we were back for certain periods during the year. This law would change later, but then it helped us to make a decision to return to South Africa.

The financial situation of our friends was very bad. During our visit to South Africa, Adele's family was trying to convince her to return, and later they did return. Adele's father sent her the airline tickets for the whole family, and we offered to take a bigger container so we could ship their household together with ours. They could pay us later when they could afford to. We were all happy, especially the children.

Just before we were about to leave, a lady doctor from New York who had heard about my face treatments from her friends in Israel asked me to do her face before we left San Diego. There was only one problem. She was still recovering from hepatitis B. I asked her to take very extensive tests to make sure that she could have the treatment. Finally, when the results came in and were positive, I agreed to do it. She came from New York and stayed in our house during the treatment. While she stayed with us, she interacted wonderfully with everyone and soon became a very good friend.

After my Florida car accident, I was under a lot of debt. Now, leaving for South Africa, I was finally debt-free. I did not owe a single penny to anyone and promised myself that from now on I would never ever owe money again (with one exception: house mortgage). After we paid for airfare and our household shipping, we were left with $1,800.

Chapter 35

Back in the Southern Hemisphere

With three young children by our side and $1,800 in our pockets, we were on our way to South Africa. As per our plan, we decided that we would stop over in Israel, so we could visit our families and I could catch up on some treatments. This was in April of 1988.

On our way to Israel, we decided to stop in New York and spend a few days with Naomi, my patient from New York. It was a wonderful opportunity for the children to have a chance to visit the Big Apple for the first time. The visit to New York was great. Naomi did all that was possible to make our stay enjoyable and pleasant.

In Tel Aviv I was busy with my patients while Ettie and the children were enjoying the reunion with the family. My grandmother, who was about eighty-six years old, called me up and told me that she enjoyed seeing the whole family and said goodbye to everyone except me. What an odd thing to say! I did not understand why she had to say goodbye when she was very healthy and was doing very well.

My grandmother's intuition did not fail her. She died two days later. She died late at night from a heart attack. To show how much she loved us, she had cooked our favorite dishes and stuck them in the fridge so we could all enjoy them during the mourning period. I kept wondering how bizarre it was that so many people had a premonition about their death, and it turned out to be true.

*

After Ettie's father passed away, her mother, a very experienced nurse, started to work with me. I was very excited about it, because I knew I could completely trust her with my patients and, having received a facelift herself, she was surely a living testimonial of success. She would always carry a picture of herself before and didn't mind showing it to the clients. She was a highly qualified nurse and a very reliable person.

*

Our plane touched down in Johannesburg. Manny and Adele came to pick us up at the airport and take us to the same hotel where I was supposed to do six face treatments. I did not realize that my brief stint a few months ago had made me famous back in South Africa. The day I landed in Johannesburg I was asked to give an interview on national television. Naturally, I agreed.

On the second day of the treatments, something went terribly bad. I felt very sick – severe nausea, lack of appetite, fatigue, and in the evening I saw that my urine was very yellow. It didn't take me more than a few seconds to know what was wrong. I knew immediately that I was infected by hepatitis B by Naomi, the New York doctor. I also knew that I might have caught the infection when I did her face in San Diego about six weeks ago – exactly the right time for the incubation of the virus.

I arranged for the necessary blood work. My friend Buzy, who was also a surgeon, with whom I have worked for many years, came to visit me. When I told him that I was infected with hepatitis B, he gave me a puzzled look. He suggested a diagnosis of food poisoning or other more common conditions might make more sense. When the test results came back, it was obvious that I was right (I know for sure that I am not screwed in medicine). I had hepatitis B. It was a rather screwed thing to have happened to me. I was getting more and more yellow every day.

The other reason I felt so bad was I had scheduled six facelifts and was expecting a crew from South African TV to interview me. On top of it all, my wife was crying and screaming, telling me that I had to rest, or I'd screw myself even more –her fears were genuine. She had already had a hepatitis B infection when she was working as a nursing student and was hospitalized for a long time.

Finally, after being yelled at for some time, I reached an agreement with her. In six days I would be done with the treatments. If my test results did not show improved liver function, I would stop working and take it easy. However, I announced to everyone that within the next six days the infection would clear up and I would be fine. And as usual, after making such a big claim, they all thought that I was screwed out of my mind, but they did not make any comment.

When the TV crew arrived, I dressed in a suit and a tie, but was very yellow. I was not used to wearing ties, so it felt as though I was suffocating. I asked the cameraman to keep the best angle, so that my yellow color would not show. The interview went well. One of the questions asked (again) was: "Why don't you perform the treatments in hospitals? Why do you prefer a hotel?" And my answer (again) was, "To avoid any infection and contamination from hospitals." As usual, the people who were interviewing me were surprised. I explained to them that within a short time I would open my own clinic where I would accommodate the patients during the entire treatment process.

As I had proclaimed, on the sixth day my jaundice started to clear. The function of my liver was improving, and for me that was more proof that our mind is capable of controlling our body. Using its strength, we could heal or get sick. This was the fastest recovery from hepatitis B that I had ever seen. The good news was that I was not a carrier, so nobody could get infected. Yet again, for most people I was "screwed," but right.

*

Within a few weeks we rented a big house in a good area in Johannesburg. It was close to the schools that the kids were to be attending. Though the schools were all nice I was not happy about the fact that the kids would be going again to a Jewish school, that it was a school for rich, spoiled Jewish kids. But again, on this topic, I was in the minority, and I had to give up. The children were very happy to be back in the same school with their friends.

The interview taken when I was yellow was broadcast on TV. Most feedback was reaction from other doctors, including a prominent plastic surgeon that was serving as the Head of the Plastic Surgery Association of South Africa. I was really attacked badly. Many questions were raised. Questions like, how could I use a secret solution to do face treatments? How could I say that hospitals were a good place to get an infection? Many more questions were tossed at me. But sadly, none of those who had criticized me so harshly even bothered to contact me and ask for more details about the treatments.

On the other hand, I was happy by the interest of many viewers in the treatment. One of my friends who had listened to the attack launched on TV said, "You should be happy. If everyone were saying that you are good and doing the right thing, you should have packed and left. If everyone is attacking you, then this is a sign that you have something good going on, and they are scared that you will take away their patients." Then my friend encouraged me to carry on with my treatments.

The rather "screwed" thing for me was that so many doctors were against me because they were afraid to lose patients. A few days later, a representative of the Ministry of Health came and asked for a sample of my face solution, and they notified me later that it was approved for use on patients. After the interview I was flooded with offers from magazines and newspapers and other forms of media for interviews and advertisements of my non-surgical facelifts.

A few days later, I was invited to give a live radio interview in Cape Town and Durban. Several women's clubs invited me to deliver lectures on the technique. My phone rang off the hook, and the number of patients was growing rapidly. It looked good, but there was a problem in South Africa. Very few patients would tell others what kind of treatment they had. Most of them kept it a secret. When we first came to South Africa, one of the neighbors told my wife, "If you are invited for dinner and eat something good, don't ask for the recipe. Usually they drop key ingredients so you would not be able to prepare it as well as they did." I figured that the same was true about not letting your neighbor look as good as yourself.

*

Since everything was going well, we decided to take our Christmas vacation, which is a summer vacation in South Africa. We planed to travel with Manny, Adele and their family to Zimbabwe. The plan was to visit Victoria Falls. Adele's parents joined us, too. Her mother was surely making up for all the lost time. When all our stuff was packed, we left at night in two cars. It was very difficult for me to drive at night. By early morning we arrived at the border station between South Africa and Zimbabwe. When we crossed the border we decided to take a break at Bulawayo, which was the second largest city in Zimbabwe.

When we arrived there, the children were very thirsty and asked for cold drinks, so went to a supermarket. We were told that in order to get cold drinks, we would have to bring them empty bottles, otherwise we couldn't get the drinks. That was not an easy thing to do. We did find them eventually – the price for the empty bottles was higher than for full bottles. The reason for this is they couldn't manufacture bottles in Zimbabwe. Finally, after a treasure hunt, we kept the bottles like an actual treasure.

*

We decided to shop for gifts. The local shops hardly had any imported products. Most of the products were locally manufactured. Few areas of the city had electricity or running water. It was really surprising how in such a short period, after the black majority took control of the country, the country deteriorated. It was a result of mismanagement, rather than lack of resources. White farmers who worked in agriculture and supplied many countries in Africa were evicted from their farms, and the farms were given to black people who had no knowledge of agriculture and were unable to run the farms. The big question in my mind was whether the same thing would happen in South Africa.

We reached Victoria Falls eventually. The waterfalls are located on the Zambezi River between the countries of Zambia and Zimbabwe. The falls, some of the largest in the world [over 1.7 km and 108 m high], are one of the greatest natural wonders of the world. It was overwhelming to witness this mile-long curtain of falling water. The waterfalls, rainforests and unspoiled beauty are hard to describe. When you walk through these forests – Mosi-oa-Tunia and Victoria Falls National Park – you can see that all the trees are dripping water as if it's raining due to the humidity. A huge amount of spray, which shoots a thousand feet into the sky and can be seen 30 miles away, is generated by a large waterfall. Monkeys were jumping up in the trees, and mosquitoes carrying malaria were buzzing all around us. That was a malaria-prone area and visitors had to get anti-malaria medication, so they would not get sick.

Again my fear of heights came into play. Looking down from the altitude of 3,254 feet, hearing the grotesque rumble of the shooting wall of water was an unforgettable experience, but also provoked an extreme case of vertigo in my case. I was afraid that one of the kids would fall in. After descending from Victoria Falls, we went to visit the ruins of the Elephant Hills hotel, which had been destroyed by rockets from the other side of the border. There were wild pigs, baboons, monkeys, and other animals running wild among the ruins.

On one of the remaining walls somebody wrote, "You wanted it, you got it, look at what you've done with it." It is very sad that after such a long and devastating war to remove the white minority and to abolish apartheid, Zimbabwe came under a dictatorship, and the entire population was suppressed even worse than during white rule. Even today, thirty years later, after Zimbabwe had gained its independence, the situation is still deteriorating. Today I carry a bill from Zimbabwe in the amount of 30 billion Zimbabwe dollars – its real value is less than a dime.

*

On that trip we visited some very beautiful nature preserves, and on the demand of our gang of kids, went to a big casino hotel where they allowed children. Within an hour or so Ran and his friend came running, telling us they needed more money. They were on a winning streak and couldn't stop gambling. The hotel was surrounded by beautiful gardens, and many monkeys were around. The children were warned not to feed the monkeys, but of course they did, and after the monkeys had been fed, they started chasing the children, making funny faces, showing their teeth, gesticulating and making a lot of noise demanding more food. The children were so scared that they ran away and Ran tried to stop the monkeys by throwing my sunglasses at them. I should have handed him a less lethal and less expensive weapon.

On our way back to Johannesburg, we were rushing to get to the border before it closed. It was Christmas Eve and we had to reach South Africa on time. But something unpredictable happened. The quality of petrol in Zimbabwe was so bad that it caused my fuel pump to block. For the remaining part of the trip I had to be towed by Manny. We still managed to cross the Zimbabwe-South African border in time.

*

After a wonderful holiday, we arrived home early in the morning. After such a long journey our children were tired and were asleep in the back seat of the car. I got out of the car to open the house door. As soon as I opened the door, a thick cloud of fetid odor surrounded me. The smell was so bad that it was impossible to get into the house, unless you covered your face with a thick towel. I tried to switch on the lights, but the lights would not go on. It appeared to me that someone tried to break into the house and in order to disconnect the alarm system they switched the power off. But the alarm system that was connected to a battery probably did go off and the robbers disappeared without taking anything. The fact that there was no electricity and I could see the broken glass everywhere confirmed my suspicion. The stink bomb that exploded in my nose was a big turkey that was decomposing in the refrigerator as a result of the power outage.

*

The New Year was about to start and we were looking for a house where we would live and where I could also have my clinic. When I asked people for advice, many of my patients and friends explained to me that the house had to be in a very prestigious area, or otherwise many patients would not come. It sounded screwed to me. I thought all the time that the more important thing was the person who was giving the treatment, the way it was given, and what the outcomes were – not the location of the hospital or clinic.

Soon after our trip to Victoria Falls I made another trip to Israel. The lease on my office in Tel Aviv, which I was also using as an apartment, was about to expire. Since I had become more of a celebrity, the owner of one of the largest medical clinics in Tel Aviv offered to renew the lease on my office. He would employ my secretary and would take care of all the administration and advertising. All I had to do was to come to interview the patients, do the facelifts, and not worry about the management part of the business. However, there was a price to be paid. He was asking for fifty percent of the revenue. All of it didn't matter, and I agreed. The main reason that I agreed was the deteriorating health of my mother, which had prevented my father from taking proper care of my clinic. With this new arrangement I got more time with my mother and it was worth all the money. Within a few days I did another round of face treatments followed by the publication of more articles. I had become so ridiculously popular that people started recognizing me on the streets.

During that stay another strange thing happened. I'd rather say it was more of a good thing. One afternoon, while I was getting ready for my next treatments, a lady walked into my office holding two big binders filled with papers. She placed the binders on my desk and introduced herself. I took her for another lady who wanted the treatment done. When she found out that I did not know her real name, she told me that her husband was a high-ranking officer of the Israeli police force. I wondered what could she possibly want from me.

She said, "All the materials on your desk are research that I had conducted to find out who can give me the best facial treatment." According to her, I appeared to be number one in the world. I thanked her for such a big compliment. I had never bothered to check out who was the best or compare myself to others. Now I knew that I was "screwed" as well as number one in the world of facelifts. This was because I treated more patients than any other physician – with the best results and no complications.

Suddenly I had an urge to tell her something. It was as if I had received a message for her. I did not know what the source of the message was, nor had any idea what it meant. I explained to her that I was not completely crazy, and with her permission I delivered the message to her. At that point, her eyes filled up with tears, and she thanked me, saying that she knew the meaning of it and also knew where it was coming from. It was not the first time that I had become a receiver for messages meant for others. Similar things had happened to me in the past and many times I received messages for people I had never known. The strange thing was that most of the people who received the messages knew what they meant, and/or where they had come from. To my surprise, no one thought that I was crazy. Or I'd rather say that, at least, they did not say so. Within a few days, she had a facelift and during her week stay in the hotel, we became friends. During that week she told me what the message was that she had received from me. On a personal level, I was happy that I was able to deliver it to the recipient correctly.

*

When I returned to Johannesburg, my wife told me that she had found a house in the best neighborhood in the city, Hyde Park, and she liked it. We went to see it and I must say that Ettie had made a fantastic choice. It truly was a mansion by any stretch of the imagination – nine bedrooms and seven bathrooms split across four floors, sitting on an acre of garden-filled land with a tennis court and swimming pool to boot.

We bought it immediately. Actually, there were many factors: the price was fair (although a bit high), and, most importantly, it was big enough for the family and, given the layout, it even had a section I could use to house my clinic.

We had to take a big mortgage, but I was sure we would be able to pay it off sooner or later. But in order to get a mortgage, the bank required a life insurance policy for me. I was examined by the insurance physician, who didn't find any problems. Blood tests were sent in as well. The next morning the phone rang and a lab technician asked me if a sample of my blood for HIV had been sent? I panicked. The technician explained to me that the tube carrying my blood was broken, and wanted me to submit another sample. They ran the test, and everything was fine. I finally relaxed. During those days South Africa was number one in the world for the number of HIV infections. There was no treatment for this dangerous disease, and thousands were dying from AIDS.

Chapter 36

The Price for Success

Remember if people talk behind your back, it only means you're two steps ahead!

--Fannie Flagg

I was scheduled for another radio interview, and the person who was interviewing me mentioned the name of a famous Hollywood actress and asked whether I had treated her face. One of the main responsibilities of a doctor is not to give out the identity of his patients. As a result, my reaction was that because of medical confidentiality, I could neither confirm nor deny. It was agreed that no names should be mentioned.

Needless to say, after so many TV and radio interviews, the face treatment had become very popular. The number of patients kept on increasing. In fact, the number of interested people was so high that I started to make enemies – without knowing it, of course. One day I got a registered letter from South African Medical Council. The letter stated that the Plastic Surgery Association of South Africa filed a complaint against me, stating that I was advertising my medical services, which was against the law at that time in South Africa. They were also complaining that I was charging exuberant fees and was using a secret solution that could cause severe damage to the face. They further stated that the treatments were not performed in a suitably equipped clinic. An investigation was started and I was summoned to appear before a committee. My attorney would represent my case before the council.

To hire an attorney of this caliber was very expensive, as if I had a choice. I was so screwed over that my medical license was at stake. One thing was clear: for the rest of the year I could not let any other article or interview be released to the public. As I mentioned, my patients (mostly women) would never recommend me to their friends, a very South African tradition, and the number of patients was declining steadily.

The reality was that plastic surgeons did not know anything about my treatment, and, sadly, none of them contacted me to try to find out more details. It did not prevent them from lodging a complaint that I was endangering my patients. Was it their professional pride, fear, or just financial motivation?

My attorney, equipped with all the required documentation, and I entered the room that looked just like a courtroom in session. Many witnesses were called to testify. Since my lawyer was not a doctor and could not question the witnesses, I was allowed to ask the medical questions myself. It was not difficult to prove to the members of the committee that my skills and experience were well above the level of all the witnesses and the doctors that had accused me.

It became very obvious that what had happened to me was mainly because of professional jealousy and financial motivation. Eventually a verdict was made. The Head of the Committee announced that they did not find any ground for the accusations against me, and, in their opinion I had exhibited high professional standards along with reasonably priced treatments to my patients. The only thing that they could not ignore was that my name was advertised along with the non-surgical facelift by the South African media, which was against the law at the time. Many other doctors were doing the same, but that did not justify my doing it. Therefore, they kept me on probation for a year. If during that year I were to advertise again, my license would have been suspended.

It was all a pretty expensive screw-up. Professionally, I came out of it much stronger, but the number of patients kept diminishing very quickly –

and all of this was because of the professional jealousy of other physicians. A few years later the law had changed and doctors were allowed to advertise in South Africa, but it happened too late for me.

After the case was finalized, within a few weeks I was again traveling to Tel Aviv. When I entered my room, I found an envelope on my desk containing a letter that resembled the one I got in South Africa from the Medical Council. ("Oh God, not another lawsuit!" I thought). The letter was from the Plastic Surgery Association of Israel. It was a complaint against me to the Ministry of Health that I was advertising in Israel; and, as in South Africa, it was against Israeli law as well. Now, this is what I call déjà vu! But this time the complaint was only regarding advertising – not false accusations questioning my credibility.

A young attorney appointed to me by the insurance company seemed to be totally out of the loop about this business of mine. There was no other option. I had to defend myself in the hearing. I was presented with a list of all the articles and interviews by the Israeli media. In my defense, I had brought with me about twenty different magazines in which other physicians and plastic surgeons were advertising – the ones that had been pressing charges against me. I stated that there was not even one single magazine in Israel that did not have a medical column in which doctors were interviewed on different subjects and their names and contact information were published. All this attack and counter-attack did not help me – my medical license was suspended for three months. This was even a more royal screw-up than in South Africa. The scenario was such that I was not allowed to advertise, but the medical clinic that I was working for was allowed to advertise. The sum of it was that it was not the advertising that counted, but the person advertising.

During those days, a virus of an American origin was quickly spreading in Israel – many people were suing doctors and clinics. Most of the time there was no justification – the only true reason was the desire to make a quick buck. Malpractice insurance rates were skyrocketing, and the only stratum of society that was really screwed out of what was due were ordinary people who ended up paying for it.

I was sued once myself. There was as young patient with scars on her face that had her face done by me. Within a few weeks she claimed that my treatment had damaged her face. When we arrived at the court I showed the judge her pictures before the facelift. He saw the after-effects of my treatment in real life and the charges were dropped immediately. In fact, the judge complimented me on my work. Not all doctors had such a good stroke of luck. Some paid heavily, but in the end all the money was sucked from the pockets of the really sick people.

Chapter 37

~~

Tokyo, Japan

I was talking about various methods of surgery with my friends when I heard about a new method of eyelid surgery where the patient had the option if they did not like the results to revert it back. Sounds interesting? That's why I was interested. This technique originated in a Tokyo hospital. I had been intrigued by it so much that I started to inquire more about it. I contacted the hospital in Japan where this operation was being performed and was invited to come and learn it. I submitted a visa application to the Japanese consulate in Israel, but I was informed that a visitor's visa was usually not granted to Israelis because the Israeli mafia was growing rapidly in Japan; they had even managed to control the very lucrative market for paintings in Japan.

I applied for a Japanese visa using my South African passport – it was granted to me immediately. In August, I left for Japan. This was my first visit to Japan, and, as always, I was very excited to see the new country and experience their rich culture, not to mention their food.

Tokyo was a very modern and vibrant city. Everyone was in a hurry. It was rather strange, however, that except for a few public gardens, one could hardly see any greenery. I talked to the locals and they explained that the real estate in Tokyo was the most expensive in the world – developers used every square meter to make a profit building high-rises, hotels, gigantic malls, apartment complexes, restaurants, shops, boutiques, entertainments centers, night clubs, etc. The language barrier presented another gigantic problem. I always thought that English could be used in any part of the world, but few Japanese knew or agreed to speak English.

The city itself was very clean and when I entered the subway station I was amazed to see people standing in a line waiting for the train to come. When the train arrived, the doors opened exactly where the people stood in line. An even stranger thing was that you couldn't see any signs or markings where these lines were formed. It seemed like people somehow magically knew what to do. Even during the nighttime office buildings were lit up, and you could see the people coming in and leaving. Not only did the Japanese work for eight hours, but they also worked the whole day if they had to. They worked until they were finished with their projects, even if it took them twelve hours. With so much dedication to work, Japan was a country to be admired and its people a force to be reckoned with. They had a completely different work attitude from any other nation I had seen.

Prices of goods were very high and, at that time, Tokyo was considered to be the most expensive city in the world. Like everywhere else in the world, once you learned your way around you could find small restaurants and shops with good bargains. The menus in these restaurants were only in Japanese and the waiters did not know any English. Fortunately, there was a beautiful display in the window, a sort of plastic mold of all the dishes. All you had to do is ask the waiter to step outside with you and then point to one of the still life creations that in no time would materialize on your plate.

My first visit to the hospital where I was going to learn this new eyelid surgery left me very surprised. There was a very big operating room with ten operating tables in it, and between each of the two tables was a stand with a bowl to sanitize the hands before surgery with no running water. About ten operations were performed at once in the room. I had never seen anything like that in any other place of the world. I did not understand how it could be sterile.

Operations ran like a conveyer belt. The patient was on the table, and when done the next patient came straight away. The doctors told me that they hardly saw any infections and they would not use any antibiotics. I was assigned to a young doctor who was very experienced and who spoke a bit of English. Most of the surgeons were very young. Next door was a professor of plastic surgery who was readily available to assist the young doctors.

The atmosphere was very friendly and accommodating, and with such a large number of operations you could learn very quickly. The doctor who was assigned to me operated very fast and smoothly. He made over a million dollars a year. Every day he arrived at the hospital in a different luxury car, like a Bentley, Porsche, or Ferrari. He told me that he had seven cars – one for each day of the week.

After spending the morning and afternoon in the hospital, I liked going to the large electronic shops at night, where one could not only see the products, but also test them and play with them. It was a fun experience. I felt like a child in a toy store and enjoyed it a lot.

I decided to explore outside the city as well. There were many beautiful and very well maintained Japanese gardens, traditional homes, gorgeous Bonsai gardens, and, of course, the bullet train that took you very fast and anywhere you wanted to go. Overall, it was a very interesting visit, and I learned a lot.

Chapter 38

A Turn of the Screw

Upon my return to Johannesburg I hate to admit that the South African Association of Plastic Surgeons had achieved their goals. Though they had not won their case against me, the number of my patients was on the decline. The ladies would not tell their friends. I was not allowed to advertise. The situation was scary and, as usual, another turn of the screw.

Despite my strong opposition, the children were studying in the same Jewish school as the rich and spoiled Jewish kids. One day, Ori arrived home with a black eye. When I asked him what happened, he started crying and said, "One of the children from the senior class, who is in charge of the younger kids during morning prayers, hit me. I was not talking, but he won't listen. He thought that I was talking and hit me in my face with his fist."

I contacted the principal of the school immediately and he promised to investigate it. A few days later the principal called to inform me that he was not sure who was talking, but he agreed that the student had overreacted. His response surprised me. It seemed like he was trying to defend the older boy and was accusing Ori of talking. So, I told the principal that the student's job was to make sure there was no noise, and not to use force on younger children. I informed the principal that Ori was instructed that if he were attacked again, he was given my permission to strike back and use his extensive knowledge of Kung Fu. The principal's reply was, "If this is what you tell your children, I do not think they belong in this school." I was rather pleased to hear it from him and informed him immediately that it would be a great pleasure for me to send them to another school. And soon the three children were moved to another private school. Very soon they started flourishing and improved in every subject. Their circle of friends grew, and Ori became the best student in his class.

*

Then came the time of the Christmas holidays, and again we had summer vacations in South Africa. That yea, Ran decided to spend a week in Cape Town with some of his friends, a place where the Atlantic and Pacific Oceans meet. Cape Town is certainly one of the most beautiful cities in the world. Ran made his plans made in advance. He and his friends rented an apartment by the beach and were having a great time. When they returned back to Johannesburg, our son revealed to us that one night he was taking a stroll along the beach alone after dark. Two big black men approached him. One of them asked him for his possessions. Ran refused and the guy pulled out a knife and threatened him. He said that if Ran would not give him what he asked for, he was going to stab Ran. Lucky, our son had been learning and practicing Kung Fu with his younger brother since a very young age, and by then he had become very advanced.

Ran hates violence and always tries to find a way out without arguments and further violence, but that time he did not have much choice. What happened next was that within a few seconds, this big scary guy lay unconscious on the beach. When his buddy saw it, he pulled a knife and tried to attack Ran. Ran warned him that he would follow his buddy's fate. The guy ignored the warning, and, as expected, Ran took him down and screwed up his face really bad. Ran was overwhelmed by what had happened and was shivering. He went to the nearby road, stopped a cab and informed the driver that there were two dudes lying unconscious on the beach, and asked him to call for help. He then returned to his friends and told them what had happened. The next morning there was a big headline in Cape Town newspaper: "Two very well-known criminals were found lying unconscious and beat-up on the beach. They were transferred to a nearby hospital and from there will be moved to prison."

Of course, we were very happy that Ran wasn't hurt and managed to defend himself, but, suddenly I felt like there was a black void of space forming inside of me, and I was sinking into it. It was the worst nervous breakdown that I had ever had. I realized that Ran was at the same age as I was when I was raped. Doubts were rising in my head – was history repeating itself? I was afraid that all the turmoil I had to endure since I was raped, and all the horrors I had managed to suppress were coming to the surface again. With each day, I sank into a deeper and deeper depression. I could hardly function. I became a recluse and spent most of the days staring into empty space. Even simple things like eating, showering and shaving became a major task for me.

I encapsulated myself in a bubble. I became a prisoner in the glass ball of my sadness. All the attempts of my family and friends to help me were in vain. Every night before going to sleep I prayed not to wake up in the morning. When I would wake up alive, I started sinking lower and lower. It was like falling down into a deep dark hole, not knowing when the end would come. Life had once again lost all meaning, and all I wanted to do was to die. It seemed that death was the only way out. It turned out that what I managed to suppress all these years had become a giant monster that I could no longer conquer. All my personal and medical experience did not help. Everything looked meaningless.

After having been in this world of healing for years, I do not know of another disease when a human being is physically fit and totally aware of what's going on, yet feels so helpless. Even today, I can't comprehend what prevented me from committing suicide to escape this terrible suffering.

All the questions like: Why did it all happen? Why was I molested? Was it my fault? Could I have prevented it? Will it happen to my children? It was like running in a never-ending circle. You pass a point, and then you pass it again, and every time you see it, your pain increases. I could not answer them, could not find an answer. All my sexuality was in turmoil. Then the questions like "Did I repress homosexuality? Was this the reason that I was raped by a man?" kept dogging me during those days.

My emotional condition and financial issues created big problems in my family life. While the children were hurt to see their father in such a state, my wife Ettie silently endured all the suffering. Seeing me weak was not something that they were used to. I have always been positive in my thinking and acting. I had always been a very active physician who told his patients that there was always help available if you were just ready to accept it. I was the one who refused to accept that there was something like an untreatable disease because I knew that there was always a way out. I was trapped, for sure, and worse, refused to ask for help. The saying, "We are our own worst enemies," had become a reality. I had strained Ettie's patience to the limit. Our relationship was getting worse by the day – blocking all her attempts to help me or talk to me. I, the depressed one, saw her attempts to help me as an invasion of my privacy.

*

In January of 1991 I flew to Israel. A friend picked me up at the airport. I was surprised to see him. I had not told him that I was coming. It turned out that Ettie had contacted him and told him about my condition. She also told him that she was afraid that I might harm myself. I knew this friend from one of my previous visits to Israel. He was a doctor about my age who came to Israel from the U.S., grew up in a very religious family and was married and had three children. For many years he had known that he was more sexually attracted to men, but his religious family and society would not accept such a thing. So he suppressed it. He married and had a nice family. One day he just couldn't take it anymore. He left home after telling his wife and children that he was gay. His wife asked for a divorce. The two older children accepted him as gay, but his youngest daughter was too young to understand and resented him for leaving home. His religious parents refused to accept it, and even though they did not reject him fully, they had very little to do with him.

When I met his eighteen-year-old son, he told me that he understood his father and loved him very much. My friend came to the airport with a younger guy who was introduced to me as his boyfriend. To cheer me up, we went for a trip to the northern part of Israel. I know that I was not a good companion at the time, but I did feel a bit better. When I returned to my office my secretary noticed immediately that there was a big difference in me. She asked me what had happened. She was the first one to whom I told the whole story. The next day, she brought me an advertisement from a newspaper with information about an organization that helped rape victims, and she told me that she had made an appointment for me to see one of the counselors.

I reluctantly decided to go to meet the counselor. I told the counselor my story, and to my surprise, instead of trying to help me or cheer me up, he asked me to come and give a lecture to a group of people who were being trained to become counselors for rape victims. I agreed. There I was standing in front of the group of about twenty people and telling my story. Many of them cried, I had to stop from time to time and calm myself down. When I finished, the silence in the room continued for a long time, but I felt like a valve had opened up inside of me releasing a big part of the tension that had accumulated inside for so many years. When the time came for questions and answers, I was asked only one question: What is the best advice you can give to a rape victim? Without any hesitation, my answer was, "Talk about it. Do not suppress it inside, or else one day it will turn into a monster that you will find hard to fight."

It is obviously very difficult to talk about such a traumatic event, but the more we talk about it, the more healed you become, as the fears, pain, shame, misunderstanding, and self-guilt eventually subside. I do not think it will ever disappear, but it certainly is not going to control my life anymore. A few days later, there was an article in the newspaper about this meeting without mentioning my name. I was happy that the message got out to the public. I hoped that if my speech managed to help at least one person, it was worth doing.

Because there was a lot of volatility in the Middle East, Israel was on high alert. It was pretty obvious that a war was about to start in the

Persian Gulf to free Kuwait from Iraq. As if it was not enough, there was substantial evidence that Iraq would fire missiles at Israel. With all those problems in the country of my birth, I wanted to do something for it, as I had always done in wartime. I applied for volunteer work in a hospital, but I was told that no volunteers were needed. Since there was no need for me there, I returned to South Africa. It was only four days later that the first Gulf War started.

We were glued to the TV most of the day and night. One evening as I was talking with my parents on the phone, I heard on their end sirens warning everyone to get into shelters. Another missile was about to hit Israel. This war ended with the liberation of Kuwait. It looked like a temporary break – there were plenty of "hints" that the war would continue later on.

*

Ori, our son, turned thirteen years old. We planned on having his Bar Mitzvah party. Since we had not celebrated anything big with the rest of our family members, it was a good enough reason to do it in Israel. The plan was to combine it with my parents' 50th wedding anniversary. After the war was over I was anxious to see my parents. I knew that the war might not have affected them, but a son's heart ached to see his mother. My family and Ettie oversaw all the preparations. As expected, it was a beautiful party, but somewhere in my heart I had a feeling that it was one of the last times we would be able to celebrate anything with my mother. Even though her condition was stable, I sensed trouble. I have been very close to my mother all my life, so even the thought of a separation was bitter for me. I have seen my mother suffer so much in her life, but every time there was difficulty, she rose again to fight back. This mother of mine was ill. I could not bear to see her this way.

A few days after we came back from the celebration my father called and told me that my mother was in the hospital and her condition was critical. I lost no time and immediately flew back to Israel. When I saw my mother it was obvious to me what the problem was. She had an extensive brain hemorrhage. Her brain scans confirmed the diagnosis, and showed extensive brain damage. Her chances of survival were very slim. But her will to survive defeated all the odds. My mother lived. There was a high price to pay: half of her body was paralyzed. She could hardly speak and needed a very long and extensive rehabilitation. Even though the times were dark, I hoped that my mother would get well soon.

*

Since I am talking about the important women in my life, it is time I told you something about Ettie. As I mentioned, our financial problems and my depression had put a strain on our relationship. Things were not going well between us. The attack on Ran that had triggered the depression and confusion about my sexuality and other issues, had caused a rift between us. One evening I was on the floor by the sofa where she was sitting, and suddenly tears started tolling down my cheeks. I could not control myself and confessed to her that I was sexually attracted to men. To my surprise, her answer was that she knew about it for a very long time. I was very surprised. I'd say I was more than surprised – I was shocked. I asked her, "How could you know when I myself didn't?" Her answer was, "When we used to walk together, while other men looked at pretty women, you would look at pretty-looking men and nice cars passing by."

Her reply again brought me to a question. Was I really so screwed that I did not know, or was I just suppressing it because I could not accept it? And society was just as screwed-up as I was – where a relationship between people of the same sex was unacceptable and classified as a psychiatric disease, a sexual abnormality, and was looked down upon. In Israel, it was unacceptable and almost illegal; in South Africa, it was considered a criminal action. I wondered if it was the reason I had suppressed my feelings and had ignored them for so long.

With growing problems, our quarrels increased, too. One day Ettie and I had one such heated argument. After we were done arguing, I told her that I was leaving home. Her response was, "This is a nice present you are going to give to your youngest son for his Bar Mitzvah." Her statement hit the right spot.

I wonder if our Jewish mothers and wives get special training before they are even born, training to create a guilt complex in their children or husband, or was it hereditary? Anyway, I bowed to her statement and stayed home.

Chapter 39

The New Era

T hings in South Africa were changing quickly. In 1990 President De Klerk released Nelson Mandela from prison. It was a historic day. The majority of the population was celebrating, and among them were not only the blacks, but also most of the white population. We all had waited for it for many years. At last, the day had arrived.

During all of those years of working at Baragwaneth Hospital, we treated thousands of black patients and saved many lives. Now, we could all celebrate and be a part of history. We all knew that the big change was about to happen, and this was the end of apartheid. Soon a new country would be born and this time it would be ruled by its own people. With the new wave of reforms, most of the limitations on the blacks would be removed. They would not need special permission to get into white areas, post offices, shops, restaurants, and movie houses. Now they were free to go into any establishment. There were no more signs saying, "For Whites Only."

Things were changing in our neighborhood as well. Only few houses away from our home, a new neighbor was moving in. His name was Oliver Tambo and he was the president of the African National Congress. The ANC is the largest black party, and it is the party to which Nelson Mandela belonged. Soon after Mandela's release, negotiations started between the white government and the black parties to create a new constitution for the new South Africa. There was real buzz about preparing for the big day of free elections, when people of all races and colors would be voting for the new president and government. It was a very exciting time, but with all the cheer, there were many fears as well.

People feared that the transition to black government could involve bloodshed. Will the future of the new South Africa be like Zimbabwe, where dictatorship was established with destruction of all the economy, or will it be like Namibia?

Instead of apartheid against the blacks, will there be a regime against the whites? All these questions were topics of many a discussion. Among the white minority there were some groups forming with a Nazi type of ideology. They declared they would do anything to resist any transfer of government to the blacks.

We experienced a hint of the coming troubles ourselves. Ran, who studied Kung Fu for years that had saved his life during the incident in Cape Town, told us that the International Kung Fu Tournament was to take place in Johannesburg, but the Kung Fu Association was split into two: one side for the white people, and the other – for everybody with no discrimination. The white section had managed to block the issuing of visas that would allow black and colored participants to come to South Africa, extending the visa only to white people.

Ran who was eighteen years old at that time, was very disturbed and decided that he should visit our neighbor, Oliver Tambo, the president of the ANC, and tell him the problem. I did not believe that the guards outside his house would let him even close to the place, but Ran was determined to do so, and went on to see Oliver anyway.

More than three hours later Ran had not come back. We started worrying that something bad had happened. When Ran came back, he was radiating with happiness and joy. He was very excited and told us, "When I rang the doorbell, I introduced myself as a neighbor to Adele, the president's wife. She asked me to come in, and invited me to the president's office. I started telling him and his wife that the visas would not be issued for people who were not white to participate in the Kung Fu Tournament. While talking, we heard steps on the stairway, and, to my surprise, it was Nelson Mandela walking into the room. He joined us at the table."

Nelson Mandela was very polite and compassionate and took a lot of interest in Ran's concern. He stopped the conversation for a minute and made a phone call. At the end of the phone call, he gave Ran a phone number and the name of a person who was in charge of sports of the ANC and asked Ran to contact him soon.

When Ran later talked to this person, he told him that he had already made contact with the government, and it was already being evaluated. Next morning, our phone rang. Ettie answered and immediately hung up. She looked furious. When I asked what it was, she said that someone was playing a dirty trick on her by telling her that it was the secretary of the President of South Africa. A few minutes later the phone rang again and the same lady asked Ettie not to hang up, reassuring her that it really was the secretary who wanted to talk to Ran. Ran picked up the phone, and there was a big smile on his face. The President of South Africa, De Klerk, had promised him that within twenty-four hours visas would be issued to everyone who wanted to participate in this event.

Ran was a determined and righteous person, and nothing could stop him from doing whatever he thought was right and justified.

After the government's intervention, the international tournament took place, and Ran won one of the first-place awards in his category. Besides the medal, Swiss-Air airlines gave him as a gift a first-class ticket to Beijing and a two-week stay to be trained by a top Kung Fu master.

*

We were entering the new era in South Africa. The negotiations between the white and blacks were going well. Along with the progress came a lot of restlessness and uncertainty. Some people among the whites saw De Klerk as a traitor, but the majority knew that this was the right thing to do. It was the only solution for the future of South Africa.

All those years of apartheid had turned South Africa into one of the strongest and most established countries in the African continent.

Despite all the sanctions against South Africa, the country was prosperous and strong. The sanctions drove the government to look for alternate ways to get arms, petrol, and other products, resulting in much of it being manufactured in the country. The defense industry was almost independent, and the fear of not having enough petrol had created the largest petrol manufacturing plant in the world that was converting coal to liquid petrol – Sasol. Coal was almost unlimited in supply, and now was being turned into the liquid fuel, and with all its byproducts.

The restlessness was not limited only to the white minority, but had crept into the black majority as well. Many of them believed that as soon as the government changed, their economic situation would change too. They expected to get new homes, cars, and cash. Many white families said that their servants believed that once the changes took place, they would become the masters of the house and the whites would be the servants.

Fears and uncertainties apart, it was a very historic and exciting time. Right in front of our eyes history was being made and we were a part of it. Together hopes and fears formed one big question: What will happen? The blacks and whites looked into the outside world for other places to go to, where they could have peaceful and prosperous lives, places where the future was more certain. Many of the people who had foreign passports returned to their home countries while others were looking for other countries to go to. The top countries on the list were Canada, Australia, the U.S. and the U.K. Some of the Jews returned to Israel. Many of the refugees, who had come from Mozambique and Rhodesia after the change of government, were scared thinking that the same would happen in South Africa. Those who could leave were leaving.

Chapter 40

Leaving

Our friends and families told us that we had to return to the U.S. for the sake and security of our children. In 1993 we surrendered to the pressure and decided to move to Houston, Texas. I did not know why Houston. Maybe because for a long time I had wanted to work with Denton Cooley and Michael De Becky, with whom I was not able to work because of my car accident.

Ran had left for the U.S. to discover New York City by himself. There was, at the time, an economic recession. Many banks and business were closing and even in Manhattan luxury apartments were being auctioned.

Leaving South Africa involved selling our house – not an easy thing to do. The fact that it was a big and luxurious house in the best area did not help much. Fear of the unknown had created a big wave of emigration, and many more houses were for sale. This resulted in prices going down. Eventually we did manage to sell it for a very low price.

While I was not very sure of this new step we were going to take, our friends, Manny and Adele, encouraged us by saying that we were doing the right thing. They said that if they could they would have done it, too. There was also some bad news. Adele's father had died recently from lung cancer. The day before he died he thanked me for bringing his wife back to him after six years, and for giving him the best years of his life with her.

Adele's mother was healthy, but was very lonely after her husband died. Thanking me occasionally for curing her, sometimes she wondered if it was worth it, because she was all by herself again. The only thing she was sorry for was that she did not pass away before her husband.

*

In July 1993, after we had sold our house, Ettie and Ori flew to New York to meet Ran, and together they planned to drive to Houston, Texas, while Ravit and I stayed back to finalize some things and join them two weeks later. The most difficult part about leaving South Africa was the separation with our dogs. We had a beautiful German shepherd and a Rottweiler. They were so adorable and we all, especially the kids, loved them so much. Luckily, we found a good family that was to adopt both of them. The separation was emotional and devastating for us. My heart was broken after I left my two dogs, and I promised myself that I would never get a dog again, even though I love animals.

In August of 1993 we arrived to Houston. Ettie, Ran and Ori already did all the groundwork. They had already rented an apartment and had made all the arrangements to make an easy transfer for the rest of us. Ori had started school and Ettie had found a job as a nurse and had started to work already. One afternoon Ori returned from school and locked himself in his room. That was not like Ori at all. When we came up to his room, we heard him crying. We did not know what the problem was, but something was up. One day he opened up – the school was full of gangs that terrorized other kids, especially the newcomers. It was strange to see it happen in a city like Houston. Very soon the principal of the school invited us for a conference and told us that Ori's testing revealed that his level of education was much higher than the seniors' who graduate from high school. Ori's scores were very high, except American History. As soon as he completed the American History course, they wanted him to graduate from high school.

This surprised us. I expected Ori to continue in the same school for several more years. My only question was: "He is only fifteen years old.

What do you expect him to do after he is done with school?" The principal didn't have an answer.

Had the U.S.'s education level deteriorated even more since we left San Diego? Instead of getting better, had things gotten worse? That school was known to be one of the best in Houston.

In order to graduate from high school in South Africa and take matriculation exams, Ori would have had to study for two more years. It looked like the high official from the American Department of Education was right: 90 percent of the students would learn only to function as robots without thinking, while 10 percent of the population would learn to think. Perhaps this incompetence was one of the main reasons for the recession in America that followed several years later.

*

In the past we always had medical insurance. So we applied for health insurance and filled out all the required forms and even submitted our first payment. A nurse who had come to take blood and urine samples failed to take the blood from my veins four times. I told her that I would do it myself, and obviously I managed it the first try.

In the beginning of October 1993, I left for Israel. Besides the face treatments, I wanted to see my mother, who was very ill. She had had another brain stroke, and was even more restricted in her abilities. When I saw her, my mother was not functioning at all. I was touched to see my father take care of her with all the love he had. He not only took care of the woman he loved all his life, but also took care of the house. It was extremely difficult for him physically and emotionally, but he still found time to volunteer at a charity that gave medical instruments to people who needed them.

When I returned to Houston my worst nightmare was waiting for me. My wife informed me that she had received a call from the Health Department asking me to contact them as soon as I arrived. I felt again like the earth below my feet had vanished and a big hole in the ground had opened up and was swallowing me. Without knowing what awaited me, I immediately knew what was wrong. Even though I could not express it in words, I knew that something very bad was waiting for me the next day. I hoped it was a false alarm.

The next morning Ettie and I headed for the Health Department. The receptionist picked up a document with my name on it. Even though I was on the other side of the counter I could still see the words "HIV positive" written in bright red pen. I do not even remember what he said next. All I remember is that I was invited into a room. My wife was not allowed to come in with me.

What I heard next was not very clear to me, but I remember very clearly a question: "Are you feeling okay?" Well, who would feel okay after being diagnosed with HIV? I was scared and pale. I do not know what I said next. Then he told me that he got a report from the correctional services in Houston informing him that before I was released from prison I was found to be HIV positive. Prison? What did he just say? Is this a nightmare? Is this a screwed joke? I mean: living in prison? I had never even been inside a prison and where had this HIV come from? How could I get HIV? For a second I thought that I was completely screwed out of my mind and had started hallucinating.

I asked Ettie to come into the room. I needed someone next to me who knew me to reassure me that I was still sane. When she entered the room, she became very scared. I asked the counselor to tell her what he just told me, but he refused. According to him, he could only tell it to the patient. When I told her what he told me, she started laughing. Now it was certainly clear to me that this was not real (it was either a screwed joke, or I finally had a screw loose). I mean, I saw my wife hear that her husband was going to die from AIDS, and she was laughing? She said, "Don't you see? This is all a mistake. What do you have to do with a prison and HIV?" Hearing this, I cheered up a little and explained to the counselor that I had never been in prison and had no criminal background. He seemed confused, and asked us to repeat the test. But this time he asked both Ettie and I to take the test. Naturally, to be sure, we agreed. For me the next few days were a living nightmare. I knew that the diagnosis was right and the mistake was in the paperwork, but there was still a thin ray of hope. While we waited for results, I knew the longer it took, the worse the chances were. Standard procedure is that the first blood test results come the next day and, if positive, are sent for a second test to confirm, which may take up to two weeks.

Thanksgiving was approaching, and we were invited to Cincinnati, Ohio to be with friends. The children and I did not want to go, but Ettie and our friends convinced us and we bowed to their request. We drove from Houston to Cincinnati. Ori was about to get his driver's license and already had the learning permit, so he insisted that he should be allowed to drive as well. When we let him drive, he started to drive on the left side of the road like in South Africa. After about twenty-four hours we arrived in Cincinnati. It was definitely the worst Thanksgiving of my life. I tried to find something to be thankful for, but I came up empty handed, with only despair and uncertainty.

How could I have been infected with HIV? There was no other way except getting infected by one of the patients I was treating in South Africa, the same way I got hepatitis B. After all, South Africa was the number one country in the world as far as HIV was concerned. When we returned to Houston, there was a message on the answering machine asking me to contact the Health Department urgently. It was clear to me what the diagnosis was. My only hope now was that Ettie had not been infected, so at least the children would have one parent to take care of them.

At the health department the next day I was informed that the second test confirmed I was HIV positive. I was not surprised at all. Ettie had gone into the next room and few minutes later she came out crying. When I saw her cry, I almost collapsed. The thought of her being sick was too much for me to bear. She informed me that she did not have HIV. I asked her, "So, why you are crying instead of being happy?" She gave me the most unexpected answer. "I know that if I were infected, too, then you would have done everything possible in the world to find a cure for me, but because it is only you who are infected, you are not going to do a thing."

The next big problem was how to tell our children. After many hesitations on my behalf, we decided to tell the truth. First we told Ravit and Ran. Naturally they were shocked trying to control their emotions, and when they went back to their room we heard them crying. When Ori arrived from school we sat all together and I told him, too. His voice was trembling and he started crying. He said, "You will see, everything will be okay."

A few days later, I had more blood tests done to find out how my immune system was functioning and to see if I had any other diseases like tuberculosis or other STDs. In order to get the results I had to participate in a seminar for a few evenings. This seminar was conducted by the Houston Health Department and was designed to teach the people how to behave and what to do when they find out they are infected with HIV. When I received the test results, my CD4 cells were close to 500. The CD4 cells are the cells destroyed by the virus, and when they drop below 200, you are considered to have AIDS.

The rest of the test results were fine. At that time there was no effective treatment against the virus – the only medication was AZT in large doses. It was not a cure as such. It did not stop the virus, but rather slowed its progress. The sad part was that the side effects of the medicine would be even worse than the disease itself. I knew that for me it was a death sentence. The only question was when.

*

We met a lady who lived in the same apartment complex. She visited us often with her two little dogs and told us that her husband died from AIDS a few years earlier. She became very emotional telling us that it was a terrible and painfully prolonged death. After the death of her husband she was tested many times and was found HIV negative. Despite this, she could not get health insurance because she had been married to an AIDS patient. When I myself approached a health insurance company, I was told that there was no chance that my family or I would ever be able to get health insurance in the U.S.

I did not understand it. All this seemed so screwed to me. Does health insurance insure only people that are healthy? What if they get sick? Will the coverage be stopped? And what about their families? Does it mean that if one person is sick the whole family should get sick as well? The only way to get health insurance was through your workplace. This was the "screwed" situation in "the most advanced" society in the modern world.

It was obvious that without health insurance and with my condition we could not stay in the U.S. The only way out was to return to South Africa. So after four months in Houston, in December 1993, Ori and I returned to Johannesburg. The good thing was that Ori would start school soon. Ettie and Ravit followed us in a month. While we asked Ran to come with us, he decided to stay in the U.S. to find a cure for HIV.

Back in South Africa, our friends were both very happy and very surprised to see us back so soon. Since AIDS was a bit of a taboo at that time, and people were really scared of that disease, I did not tell most of our friends the reason for our return. I did tell my very good friend Bazy. Bazy was a surgeon. He and I had worked together for many years. I told him and his wife Melanie, not only because someone had to know. I had another reason of telling Bazy about it. I feared the impending suffering and I trusted him to relieve me of that.

The day I told him about my disease, I asked him to promise me that if my health deteriorated, and if I were unable to take care of myself, then he would help me end the suffering and misery. Perhaps he took my request as a last wish, or maybe not, but still, he agreed. Though AIDS was a new disease for me in terms of my medical and personal experience, it was ravaging Africa. In South Africa alone, thousands were dying and getting infected every day. South Africa had become the number one country in the world with more than 10 percent of the population infected by the deadly virus.

I was not scared of dying, and still I do not fear death. I had time and time again proven by hypnosis that we all have lived before and we would live again. We might change our physical body, and we might change sex, language and location, but our soul is eternal. It was never born and will never die. As a matter of fact, I see death as a graduation and going back home rather than a harsh punishment. I believe that when we have accomplished what we had come to do in this world, we are ready to return home to the soul world and prepare for our next life on earth.

I was more scared of being sick and miserable for a long time, making my family and friends suffer. I actually honor the Dutch people who provide euthanasia. I believe that every person has the right to die in dignity if this is his or her wish. And this is my wish: to die without pain and to not make my family suffer.

*

Very soon I made an appointment to see a physician who specialized in HIV. After having performed many tests, I was told that my CD4 number was around 500 as found in Houston, but a specific antigen to HIV, P24, was positive. Usually P24 is positive in the first stages of the infection and then becomes negative. If it gets positive again, then the HIV condition has deteriorated to AIDS. The viral load tests were not available at that time. The positive P24 could show that either I was still newly infected, or that my condition was deteriorating quickly towards AIDS. No one knew the answer.

As far as the CD4 number is concerned, when it's above 200, usually the infected person can live a normal life without any major risk of infections. When the number drops below 200, the risk of infection increases, especially for pneumonia and tuberculosis. At this stage, usually the patient gets antibiotics to prevent infections. When I met this specialist, he told me that I was not an exception in contracting HIV from a patient. He had met quite a few doctors and other healthcare providers who had been infected. Some of them were still under his treatment. According to him, all that could be done now was to live a normal life and see where it goes. I would have to repeat the blood tests every three months. Things did not look particularly bright for me, but I decided to give it a try. Before I left his office he smiled and said, "You have a good chance to live up to the year 2000." At that time, I did not believe him.

I had to move on with my life. There was no point sitting back and weeping over what was about to come. We rented a house and settled down. Ori was back to school and very happy to be with his friends again. As opposed to the U.S., there were no gangs in school, and the standard of education was very high. The most important thing was that the teachers cared about how the students were performing. They did everything possible to help and advance the students to the highest level of accomplishment. Our Ori was an outstanding student, and was talented in a lot of after-school activities. He was joining a special group for gifted children where they were challenged to think and create projects to foster their talents. Ori's education was well taken care of. It was for my kids' and Ettie's sake that I had to find the willpower to move on.

Chapter 41

Ran: The Sandwich
Child Syndrome

While Ravit was still in New York, Ran was traveling around the U.S. and Mexico to find a treatment for HIV. He left no stones unturned. Whenever he got a hint or a lead, he would plunge himself enthusiastically in that direction. By the beginning of 1994 he was in San Diego, California, when we heard the news about the big earthquake in that area. As a result, all the telephone lines were down, so he was unable to call for a while and we were very concerned. Our concerns for his wellbeing would not leave our minds. We remained glued to the TV set watching the news, hoping it would give us any reassurance that he was okay. Only a few days later he called and told us that he was fine and doing well. I wonder if he had even given it a thought about how his parents worried about him.

I believe his indifference was due to a strange syndrome that occurs in the middle children of the family. It is called the sandwich child syndrome, and as far as I know, Ran had always had it. For some reason he truly believed that his older sister and younger brother were getting more love and preferential treatment from his parents. I remember once when he got injured I wanted to give him a tetanus shot. I went with him to the pharmacy and bought the vaccination. As a doctor, I had a discount. A day after I injected him – and mind you, needles had always been a tricky thing with Ran, so the shot was difficult – he developed a local reaction. His upper arm turned red and swollen. And guess what? Who got all the blame? His parents. He said that this allergy was due the fact that he got the cheap injection, as he always did, because we didn't love him as much.

I wish to tell him every day how much we love him. If he only knew how much he is loved and how much we miss him, maybe he would feel better about being a sandwich boy. Other than needles, Ran had other issues in his life. I won't say they were either good or bad. I consider them just a part of Ran's personality. I believe that if Ran wanted, he could've been one of the best students in his class, but for him school was mainly a social place to meet friends. When he graduated from high school he entered a private university where his friend met him in between sessions. These meetings were in the garden or cafeteria, but not in the lecture rooms. Finally, at the age of eighteen, he decided that university was not a place for him, so he quit. He found a job as a manager for a casino company in South Africa. Within a very short period he became the most important person in the company, second only to the CEO, who was a very successful and knowledgeable businesswoman. The reason for his success was that every casino Ran was sent to turned into a very lucrative and profitable place within a short period.

In one of my conversations with his boss, she told me, "Ran is a genius in marketing. His ideas are so unconventional that, even though we have doubts, he always succeeds. He has a Midas Touch to turn any failed business into a very lucrative one."

This lady who has been in this business world for many years told me that in all her life, she had never met anyone like him, and he was only eighteen years old when I had this talk with his boss.

Ran was not only good in business, he was much screwed. One day Ravit called from New York and told us that, "You know, today is a very cold day with a severe snow storm, and Ran just appeared at my door dressed in a T-shirt and shorts. Why don't you ask him to get some sense?"

She also told us she was sending us a package from New York. I told her that instead of the package, she should send Ran back to us. Finally, when Ran got on the phone he told us that he had visited a few clinics in Mexico and was impressed by one doctor who treated many patients with HIV. From him Ran received a special tea that gave good results and improved the condition of HIV sufferers. Also during one of his searches, he met a guy in Detroit who manufactured a solution called Cancel, which, according to him, could cure cancer and HIV. He managed to get a few bottles for me. He went to Florida and other states, but couldn't find anything worth mentioning.

At the end, when he was done, I just said only one thing to him, something that I hoped would make him feel how much I loved him. I told him, "Ran, perhaps you are forgetting something. For me the best medication is if you came back home and spent some time with us." Ran did not say anything in response and passed the phone back to Ravit.

Chapter 42

A New Beginning

Back in South Africa things were moving fast. April 27th, 1994, the date of the first free-for-everyone elections in South Africa, was approaching. This day also marked one more thing of importance: it was the day when cellular phones would be launched in South Africa. As far as the elections were concerned, Nelson Mandela was the main presidential candidate for the new South Africa. The white minority was very worried about what would happen during the elections and afterwards. Some of the people were even preparing for a war, buying generators, food, water, and petrol, as if they would be stranded in enemy territory.

The situation was indeed very tense, but there was hope as well. After a long period of negotiations, the new constitution was adopted, and it turned out to be one of the most advanced and liberal in the modern world. There was no discrimination against any background, race, sex, color, or ethnicity. There was freedom of speech and press, and, of course, no more slavery.

In one of our discussions about the elections, Manny noted that the elections and the launching of the cell phones was a big event. Thousands of visitors were expected to come to witness the elections and take part in the swearing-in ceremony of the new president. The idea was that many of them would need cell phones. He said that it would be a great idea to open a cell phone rental company. He suggested that I would hold 30 percent of the company, 30 percent would be his, 30 percent would go to his brother-in-law and 10 percent to one of his sons. I agreed, but insisted that the shares be in Ettie's name because I did not believe I would live for a long time. My other condition was that when Ran came back from the U.S., he would work for the company. Manny agreed and the new company, GSM, was born. Because we had money from the house that we had sold before moving to Houston, I paid for the first few phones for the new company.

While we prepared for the elections, our children were growing up fast. Adele's and Manny's elder son was starting medical school and asked me for advice. The strange thing was that in one of our conversations, he told me that he did not want to study medicine, but was doing it for his father's sake. The reason was that his father had always wanted to be a doctor, but since he didn't become one, he was expecting his elder son to live up to his dream. This is one of the most screwed things parents can do – impose their own dreams on their children. I feel that one should choose the field of work that he or she likes.

*

Late one afternoon, the outside gate bell rang. When we looked out the window, we saw a cab and Ran stepping out of it. Perhaps my message had reached home. It was a real surprise – happiness and joy to all of us. After a short time Ravit too returned from the states, and we were all together again. Ran had brought with him some tea from Mexico, which was supposed to boost the immune system. When I first tried it, I thought it probably would be easier to die from HIV than to drink this tea, but I kept on taking it. He had also brought two solutions from Detroit called Cancel. They had to be combined together to be activated and were believed to cure cancer and HIV. Actually, the solutions were given to him after we promised to run a clinical study in South Africa where so many people suffered from HIV.

To help our cause, I arranged a meeting between Ran and a reporter from the main newspaper in Johannesburg. She published an article with

Ran's photo about the miracle solution that can cure HIV. I had no doubt that we would be flooded with applicants, and there would be no problem in getting patients for our treatment. To my surprise, only five people called in and, including me, there were only six. Nevertheless, we started our study.

I told Ran about GSM and my proposal for him to work for the company. He did not like the idea of working with Manny at all, but agreed to give it a try and was presented with his new business cards as marketing director for the company. Ravit had started to study teaching. She had always wanted to be a high school teacher and work with adults as well. She took courses in Jewish studies and mathematics, and later, she taught them.

*

April 27th, 1994 was the day when all the citizens of South Africa voted for the first time to elect a new president. The air was filled with excitement and many people were celebrated in the streets. Thousands of reporters from all over the world had gathered in the country. The news was being broadcasted nonstop. We were very proud and happy while waiting in a very long line for several hours to vote for Nelson Mandela. The day he won the election was a day that marked a new beginning. There was a new flag, a new anthem, a new constitution, and many new hopes for a better life.

So far everything was going according to plan. There were no disturbances and no bloodshed, or any interruptions in water or electricity. The "screwed" ones who had prepared for war were left sealed in their bunkers.

Nelson Mandela is one of the greatest leaders that this world has ever known. He is a very honorable, intelligent, and educated man who spent most of his adult life in prison believing in the things that he fought for. He and the previous President de Klerk both had brought this historic change to the country and received the Nobel Peace Prize for their efforts.

Dreams of millions became reality, but as always there were still some minority groups that saw it as a national disaster and swore to take back the control of the country into white hands. The inauguration ceremony of Nelson Mandela as the first elected President of South Africa was an event of an international importance – presidents, kings, and heads of states from all over the world came for the inauguration. The historic speech delivered by Nelson Mandela made it very clear to all that peace, prosperity, and freedom to all would be the new ideology in South Africa. We were all proud and happy to be part of this great event.

For us, it had been eighteen years since we had arrived in South Africa. Our youngest son Ori was born there. We had been through apartheid, riots, and negotiations for settlement, and now we were witnessing the establishment of a new country. But was this the end of all the struggles and conflicts? Only time would tell.

Chapter 43

Miracles and Obstacles

Miracles have always been a part of my life. I dedicate this chapter to a few events that I feel were miracles and had a profound effect on my life. One day, Greg, Ran's best friend, came by in his car to pick up Ran. They were about to visit some friends. After greeting us, both Greg and Ran left the house. Only ten minutes later someone came knocking at the door. When we opened the door, we saw Greg and Ran standing outside the door. They seemed scared to death. Both of them were ghostly pale, shivering and unable to talk.

When we got them to talk again, they told us that when they opened the main gate to get out with the car, another car blocked their way and two black guys jumped out of the car with guns. They made them lie in the driveway with guns pointing at their heads and then took off in Greg's car. The screwed thing here was that the main gate of our house was automatic. It closes by itself in thirty seconds. I wondered why this gate didn't close when these robbers were threatening my son and his friend. I believe that had the gate closed by itself, it probably would have caused panic. Who knows? They might have shot the two boys. If this was a miracle, then I was certainly thankful to God for that.

Another miracle occurred involving Ravit. One day she was driving her car on the main highway from Johannesburg to Pretoria. Suddenly the front tire exploded. She barely managed to stabilize the car and park it on the side of the highway. She immediately contacted the Automobile Association (AA) and asked for help. She was told that help would be on its way soon. A white Jeep stopped next to her and out of the Jeep came a man dressed in a white robe. Without saying a word he changed the tire. Before she could say anything he vanished. A few minutes later, AA that told her that the help was on its way and should be there in a few minutes again contacted her. Ravit was surprised and told them that one of their people had helped her a few minutes ago. Their response was that the person who had helped Ravit wasn't one of their people. This was the second miracle that took place and I am very thankful to God for helping my little girl.

The next miracle was a rather strange event. It was when I really started believing in miracles. It happened during one of my trips to Israel. During that trip Ettie was with me. I had not told my family about my HIV, because I did not want them to worry. But parents always know if there is something wrong with their child. My brother noticed something was not the same with me, and he convinced Ettie to tell him what was wrong. After hearing about my sickness, he was so shocked that he started taking tranquilizers. One day, while traveling with my brother in his car, he pulled over by the side of the road and said that he had to tell me something. He said that while he was sitting in his office, out of nowhere in front of him appeared an old man with a long white beard.

The man told him that he was well aware of the reason for his worries. He said that he knew that he was worried about my health. But he wanted him to know that there was no reason to worry, and that his brother would be okay – a certain person would help him. After saying these words, the old man disappeared. No one else saw him. My brother was very sure it was not a dream, and that he wasn't hallucinating. But when he tried to look for this man, he could not find him. Miracles do happen. All it takes is hope, faith, and the desire to accept.

*

Life does not always have miracles in store for people. It also has hidden traps. It seemed liked I still didn't learn my lesson from Avi, who had betrayed me, and later on, his own family. Not only was I being screwed over by people, the whole world of the sick was being fooled by the so-called healers.

While I was in Israel, I met a prominent doctor. He was doing research work in the field of medicine. He was the son of a well-known professor and was considered to be one of the biggest researchers in this field. According to him, after a few years of research of different plants, he and his father had developed an herbal solution than could block the progression of HIV and might cure it, as well. They had already tried it in Germany in a big medical center with very good results on some viruses like flu, herpes, and HIV. It was available for sale in pharmacies. It seemed so promising that I too bought a few bottles for myself to try.

While back in South Africa, about three months had passed since we started the Cancel medical study. The other five people and I took our blood tests, but to our utter disappointment, results were similar to what they were before. There was no improvement at all, but on the other hand, there were no signs of deterioration either. My CD4 count was stable but the P24 was still positive. I met a professor at the University of Johannesburg who was in charge of HIV and infectious diseases and presented to him a case with all the test results; I did not tell him that I was the patient. According to him, the fact that the P24 was positive all the time would bring about a very rapid deterioration in the condition of this patient. When I told him that I was the patient, he was very uncomfortable. After that, our conversation ended quickly.

By the end of July I was on my way to the U.S. where I had planned to visit New York, Detroit, and San Antonio. I had planned to meet the person who had made Cancel in Detroit. When I met him and showed him the test results of the people who were treated, and that there was no improvement, he said, "You'll see, actually! This solution is so sophisticated that it will know in which patients to give good results, and in which not."

With such an answer it was obvious that he was one of those people trying to make money by taking advantage of the desperation of the sick and the terminally ill. There are thousands of such people claiming yet a "New Miracle Treatment." Unfortunately, there are very few who are actually doing something positive. I do not say that I am totally skeptical of these treatments, because I do believe there are many people who really are doing proper research and want to help.

*

While in San Antonio, I met another guy who told me about a solution called Chondriana. It was made out of certain sugars and had to be given intravenously. It was supposed to improve the immune system and extinguish cancer cells and HIV. This drug used to be manufactured in Texas, but after the authorities shut down the plant, the entire operation moved to Mexico and New Mexico.

Another issue was that the price for this solution was very high. Because there were no other "miracles" so far, I decide to give it a try. I gave myself injections, but again without any results.

After meeting many such quacks, I was falling deeper into the trap of "life-saving drugs." Even being a medical doctor, I was following the road of so many other desperate people like myself – trying to avoid the misery and inevitable death sentence.

*

When I returned to South Africa, I saw that GSM, our cell phone company, was growing rapidly. Manny and Ran, with their combined efforts, were building a big company. Ettie was working there as well. In order to boost the company, it required more investment, so Manny wanted to add another partner. It seemed like a smart move, so we all agree that each one of us would give the same portion of his shares the new partner could join.

I met the new partner, Lazer, a religious Jewish guy who wore a yarmulke. He told me that he had graduated as a rabbi from a rabbinical school. His father was a very rich and well known and wanted to invest in the company for his son. According to Manny, Lazer was not bright but harmless. So there was no harm in making him a partner. A few weeks later, a partners meeting was called and the PA of the company joined us. Manny informed us that Lazer was not happy with his shares in the company and demanded 50 percent of the shares, otherwise he would pull out his investments and the company would collapse. He suggested that his brother-in-law and I should drop our shares to 10 percent; he would get 30 percent and Lazer will get 50 percent. I was shocked! I don't know why, but it looked to me like something was not right, and I refused to give an answer on the spot.

For the next few days, Lazer called me several times a day, and even came to see me at my house. Not to meet me, but to get me to sign the contract. He was threatening. He once said, "If you don't sign the documents, then we will dissolve the company and start a new one without you, and you will have nothing left."

I had no other choice but to sign the documents. But I smelled a rat. I soon found out that all the other partners had kept their shares. I was the only one whose shares had decreased. It came as a big shock to me. Frankly speaking, I did not expect my best friend Manny to deceitfully plot with Lazer and go behind my back with this "super religious" partner who later lied under the cover of religion and God. I was really hurt. Manny was my best friend. I had done so much for him and his family. I had treated his mother-in-law, brought her back to life after six years of Alzheimer's, and this is what he and the rabbi did to me.

Does being religious exclude one from judgment for lying or stealing? Can one trust anybody after going through what I had gone through with Avi and now Manny? Is the entire world based on greed and profit, leaving no place for love, trust and faith?

After realizing I had been stabbed in my back, I consulted a lawyer. He informed me that after I had signed the documents I could not back out. From what he saw, it was definitely a fraud. After that day I did not have anything to do with Manny and his family, but Ran and Ettie still worked for the company. I believe a day will come when Manny, Lazer, Avi, and the company will have to account for their actions. One has to pay for one's deeds – this is the law of Karma.

*

After clearing things with Manny and GSM, I decided to move on with my life. We bought a new house and after renovating it, moved in. Though it wasn't as big and luxurious as the previous, it was very comfortable and in a good neighborhood. Things were getting better back home in Israel. In October 1995, I again flew to Tel Aviv to visit my family. Since I was infected with HIV I had minimized my work in South Africa and Israel. It meant that I did not have enough chances to meet my family.

When I reached Israel I saw that the general atmosphere had really improved. A peace treaty had been signed between Israel and Jordan with the mediation of Bill Clinton. At that time, Rabin, a great Israeli-born army leader, was the Prime Minister. He had experienced all the wars. He was the one who had signed this peace treaty and was looking for a way to make peace with the Palestinians.

Due to this effort, he and the Palestinian leader Yasser Arafat won the Nobel Prize for Peace. It was clear that Israel would have to give back the seized territories to the Arabs and it was also supposed to release many terrorists from prison. I believed that if this was the price for peace, then it was worth doing. We were about to celebrate my brother's fiftieth birthday on November the 4th. My mother was not doing well. She had a very clear mind, but her body was barely functioning. She had become so weak that she was confined to a wheelchair, unable to talk. My father was taking care of her in the best possible way.

One Saturday night we were sitting in my parents' house watching TV. Prime Minister Rabin was about to give a speech in the center of Tel Aviv about peace in the Middle East. Everyone was anxiously waiting to hear what would be his next step towards the peace with the Arabs and the new Palestinian State. Only a few minutes into the broadcast, our wait was interrupted by an announcement. "The Prime Minister of Israel was shot by an assassin and was transferred to a hospital where his condition was not known." We all knew that something very bad had happened. A short time later an official announcement was made that Rabin had died from the gunshot. The person who shot him was arrested. He was no Arab terrorist, but a young Israeli who belonged to an extreme religious organization. It surprised me that a Nobel Prize winner and a dedicated supporter of the Israeli movement for liberation who had never been defeated during war was killed by an Israeli. He had paid the ultimate price for trying to bring peace to his war-torn country.

It is shocking, unbelievable, and screwed. The news came like a wave of sadness. My paralyzed mother who was in her wheelchair started crying. Sadly, she could not wipe her eyes with her paralyzed hands, so I did it for her.

After that sad event, I returned home. I was fighting a war myself against HIV/AIDS. Its epidemic was spreading all over the world. Every year thousands were dying and getting infected. It was estimated that two million children in South Africa were AIDS orphans. The older children were taking care of their younger siblings, and in order to survive they had to steal and commit crimes. I wonder if these deprived children were the criminals we should fight, or are all of us party to this crime by not helping them?

*

There was still no treatment or cure. Proper nutrition could help prolong the life of people infected, and so did reducing stress. But the rather screwed thing was, how can you avoid stress when you know that you were about to get even more ill and die? The question was only when.

In 1996 my blood tests showed deterioration. I told Ettie and the children that it was probably the beginning of the end. Hearing this, Ravit started crying. Ettie called her cousin, a doctor in a big research medical center in the U.S., and told him about my condition. He told her that they had found out that a combination of three or more medications, a certain cocktail, could, within a short period of time, stop the progression of HIV and maybe cure the disease forever. A new test was developed to measure the number of copies of the virus in the blood. They found out that by using the combination of medications, the number of particles of HIV in the blood fell rapidly until they become undetectable. I immediately contacted a doctor in Johannesburg, a leading specialist in HIV, and he confirmed the findings of the treatment.

The only problem was that these medications were not available in South Africa. The price was very high, which made it inaccessible to many in need of it. He also told me that one the pharmaceutical companies in Europe was conducting a clinical study with one of the newest anti-retroviral medications. The treatment consisted of three medications. Two of them were well known. The third medication would be given to some participants, and some would get a placebo. If the medication proved to be effective, the company promised to supply it to the participants, which would be the combo of the three drugs. He offered for me to join the study, and, of course, I did. Who wouldn't when death was knocking at the door?

When I joined the study in March of 1996, I had to take about twenty tablets a day, some with food and some on an empty stomach. It seemed very complicated, but it was the only hope I had at that time. The side effects of the medications were quite severe: nausea, diarrhea, pain in the joints, and headaches. A day before my birthday, I had my first blood test since starting the medication. While I was waiting for the tests results, I did not know that there was more bad news in store for me.

Chapter 44

"Sleep in Heavenly Peace"

Late at night my father called to tell me that my mother was in the hospital with severe abdominal pain. Her condition was not good. The next morning, on my birthday, I flew to Israel to see my mother. My brother came to pick me up at the airport. By late evening we were traveling to the hospital. When I got there, my mother was unconscious. It looked like she had an abdominal condition where the blood flow to the intestines was blocked. With her condition, she couldn't have surgery. I asked my colleagues and friends to eliminate her suffering and to give her anti-pain medication.

I stayed by her bedside for two weeks. She was unconscious the entire time, but I had no doubt that she could hear me and knew that I was by her side. I told her about my new medication, about her grandchildren, and many other things she lived for. But the most important thing that I told her was how much I loved her and what a great mother she had been to me all my life.

One evening my wife phoned me and told me that my test results had arrived. The results were extraordinary. My CD4 count was up, and for the first time the P24 was negative. When I told this news to my unconscious mother, I knew that she was happy to hear it.

*

My mother, Nina Shvili, was born in Tiflis [the former name of Tbilisi], Georgia December 25, 1921. Her mother died when she was very young. Georgian was her native language. My grandfather immigrated to Israel when she was three years old. Soon after coming to Israel her father remarried one of his cousins. They had four children all together. After the children were born my mother was neglected most of the time. She never attended school, nor learned how to read and write. In fact, she was forced to go to work and earn money at a very young age. When she married my father at the age of twenty, her life improved. My father loved her very much. Since that day, her husband and children were her first priority. Together with my father my mother did all that was possible to raise us with all the possible luxuries. When I was born, my parents lived in a studio apartment in a very religious section of Jerusalem. In the yard there was one kitchen and bathroom that served five families.

During the war in Israel, and even after it was over, there was a food shortage in Israel. When food was rationed my mother worked at three different jobs so her children would have enough food. Because she had worked hard all her life, we always had everything. When we moved to a bigger apartment my parents used to have on the balcony of the fifth floor a chicken coop so that my brother and I could always have fresh eggs.

The fact that she had not learned to read or write didn't hold her back. Later, she learned to read and write all by herself and then she opened a gift shop in one of the hotels in Beer Sheba. She was the main reason I continued to have the second business in Israel – giving facelifts treatment implied seeing my mother very often.

At 4:30 p.m., May 9th, 1996, I was sitting by my mother's bedside with my hands on her arm. All of a sudden I felt a strong electric current coming from my mother's arm into my hand and it spread throughout my body. All the monitors started beeping, and then it was a flat line. My beloved mother had passed away. For the last time I hugged and kissed her. I was devastated. She was the source of my strength. She reminded me that I was loved. She reminded me that I was strong, and could face any problems in the world. My heart poured out with all the sadness of the world. My only conciliation was that after so many years of suffering, she didn't suffer any more.

The next day, a very hot day with the temperature soaring to 100 degrees, many people attended my mother's funeral at the cemetery. An ambulance stood at the cemetery, and I knew that my mother's body was there. I opened the door and saw her body wrapped on the bottom of the ambulance.

A horrific scream shocked the place. The word "Mommy" echoed in the silent graveyard. If this scream did not open the gates to heaven and did not wake up all the dead in the cemetery, then I am sure nothing else would have. Of course, the person who had screamed so loud was me. During the last rites in honor of my mother, the rabbi read a prayer by my mother's grave. He said, "God is judging you in justice and killing you in justice and will open the gate of heaven for your soul, because the family of the deceased had promised to donate to charity."

Hearing these words, I could not take it anymore, and all my brakes were released. I started screaming, "God is not judging! You are judging and doing it in the name of God! This is not what justice is! A good and loving woman who never harmed anyone suffered so much, and you call it justice! Her soul will go to heaven because she was a good woman, and not because the family will donate to charity!" On screaming in the dead silent cemetery, the rabbi gave me a dirty, angry look and kept praying. My brother and friends barely managed to detach me from my mother's grave and drag me away from the cemetery. I had lost my mother and there was no substitute for her. The only comforting thing was that my mother wasn't suffering any more.

And there were also the encouraging results of my blood tests.

Chapter 45

The Light at the End of the Tunnel

The world was developing AIDS medications. In South Africa, they had started performing the blood tests for the viral load. It is used to show the number of HIV particles in blood. I did not know what mine was before treatment, but from similar cases today, I assume that it was around one million particles of virus per milliliter of blood. This number started to gradually decline and after a few months of treatment, the HIV virus in my blood was undetectable. The clinical study came to an end. Unfortunately, the pharmaceutical company that had promised to supply the participants with medication did not keep their promise. My attending physician added another medication to my cocktail that he got as a medical sample. Finally, I started seeing some light at the end of this dark tunnel.

But the problem was that the situation was a lot more screwed. The drug company had not kept their word, and the price of the medication was ridiculously high. It was about $3,000 a month, and even though our life depended on it, a very few people were able to afford it. 1996 was the year when the treatment of HIV had the biggest turn and, this time, for the better. It was brought by the introduction of the cocktail of medications. This new medication technique changed HIV infection from a lethal disease into a manageable chronic infection, bringing an end to the death of thousands, but only for those who could afford it. Millions of others were unable to get the treatment and would die shortly. Only the rich would get well and survive, while the poor were condemned to misery and death.

I was informed that as an Israeli citizen I might be eligible to get medications from Israel, but it required frequent flights to Israel for blood work and medications. But with the outrageously high price for medication, this to-and-fro flight to Israel was definitely worth it. After a few months of treatment, the test results were still improving, but I felt like my stomach was getting bigger. I looked like I was pregnant. If one looked at my face and limbs, one saw that they were shrinking. They were getting seriously thin, and every vein in my arms and legs could be easily seen. I was becoming a walking circulatory system.

My face looked like that of an old person's. The skin sagged. Most of my buttocks had disappeared, and it was getting very hard to sit – I had to use a pillow. Other blood tests showed a sharp increase in cholesterol and triglycerides. The back of my neck was getting bigger, and it looked like a hump. I was annoyed and confused about what was happening. When I asked my doctor what it was, he said that he didn't see any connection with the HIV infection or treatments.

When I consulted another HIV specialist in South Africa, he told me that it appeared to be the side effects of the medication that was given to HIV patients. There was even a new term in the medical dictionary, "lipodystrophy," that describes this phenomenon. He also told me that some of the patients having this syndrome developed a resistance to insulin and were suffering from type 2 diabetes. To make things worse, he added that some of his patients had heart attacks and brain strokes and some of them even died. He reassured me of one thing – when the new medication came to the market it would have fewer side effects. To help me, he changed my medication hoping it would reduce the effects. The use of the Internet was spreading worldwide, and it was so much easier now to get the medical updates in the different fields of medicine, including HIV. Several blogs were formed where you could get support and knowledge.

After having better results and some good news, I decided to visit my father in Israel. Ravit also joined me. She decided she would attend a month's treatment of exercise and diet in the Wingate Institute, where they treat overweight people.

When I met my father, he looked much better and healthy. He lived in Ganey Omer, an adult community near the city of Beer Sheba, where he had met Neti, a nice lady who was a widow. I knew her already. One of her two sons was a medical doctor with whom I used to work. My father and his new lady-friend seemed to be very happy together, and I was very happy for them. After so many years of caring for my mother so well and after going through all that suffering, he deserved happiness in the later part of his life.

*

While we were there my friend Yossi invited Ravit and me to join him on a visit to Jerusalem. We decided to enter a new tunnel that was discovered underneath a Jewish temple and the Wailing Wall. It was both an educational visit and a good lesson in history. On our way back we stopped for coffee. While we sat by a table in the restaurant, Yossi told me that he had a message for me. Yossi was well known in Israel for his ability to contact the spirit world, and many people consulted with him.

A woman who had joined us on the trip took out a pen and paper and started to right down Yossi's message for me. The messages said: "You are about to go through major changes in your life. You will get an extremely strong power that is unknown to you so far. And with this power, you will be able to help and heal many people with methods unknown until now." At the end, it said: "All this will happen within the next three months." I was surprised to read this message. I did not know what was awaiting me in the future, and neither did it matter to me.

Though I did not see any patients at that time, one of my friends in Israel asked for my help. He said that in the last year his breasts were growing like a woman's (the medical term for it is "gynecomastia"). He told me that he had approached many doctors and the only solution they offered was to have a bilateral mastectomy. In a layman's words, it meant: "remove his breasts." He came to me asking to perform the operation. I was amazed by the doctor's advice. The removal of breasts was not the right treatment in this case.

He had been a good friend of mine for many years, and I knew he consumed large amounts of dairy products on a daily basis. In my opinion, that was the cause for his breast growth. Many people are allergic to some extent to dairy products. In certain cases it has the symptoms of allergy, and in others it can be indigestion or other symptoms. Dairy products make glands, e.g., salivary glands and other glands related mainly to the digestion system, secrete much more, in some cases causing the breasts to grow.

I knew what my friend needed to do. I asked him to avoid any dairy products for the next three months, and if this did not help, then during my next visit I would recommend surgery and would perform it myself. It did not even take three months for his condition to get better. He soon called me and told me that after a short period of not eating dairy products, his breasts returned to normal size and no operation was needed. Before he said it, I knew what his next question would be. "Why did no other doctor tell me this?" The only answer I had was that I was sorry, but I could not do anything about that.

I think that doctors should take the time and effort to pay more attention to patients to find out what really causes their symptoms and what had brought the patient to them. And most importantly, get more information and knowledge about proper nutrition. I have no doubt that most diseases and symptoms are related to improper nutrition. The main problem is that an average doctor studies about ten hours of nutrition in his entire medical studies.

When I returned to South Africa, it came to my attention that Manny and Adel's son, a medical student, accidently pricked himself with a needle while treating an AIDS patient. It was a quite common situation in South African hospitals and clinics – and I am the living, walking and talking proof of it. Fortunately, by that time, by taking anti-retroviral drugs for thirty days, one could eradicate the infection before it even started, and most people would not become infected by the virus.

Chapter 46

On Parenting

Very soon, Ori, a valedictorian, at the top of his class, finishing high school and was getting ready to go to college. His grades gave him the option to choose any field that he liked. He was very interested in medicine. Of course I agreed, but on one condition – anywhere in the world, but not in South Africa. I was afraid that my son, too, would get infected with HIV through a patient. Though I felt justified that it was for the safety of Ori, even today I feel a certain amount of guilt that, indirectly, I stopped him from studying medicine. He decided to study actuary science, one of the most difficult subjects at any university because its foundation is strictly higher mathematics and statistics. I just hope that Ori found his way in life, just as I did.

*

In 1998 GSM was sold and the value of the shares that were stolen from me by my partners was over one million dollars. At least we got some money. The best part about it was that we had no more connections with those crooks. To celebrate the sale of the company, Ettie and I decided to go on vacation to Italy. It had always been one of my favorite countries in Europe. We had a great trip and enjoyed our time together.

A day after we returned to South Africa, the phone rang and Ori answered it. It looked to me that he was a bit pale and scared. When I asked him what was wrong, he did not answer. He just said that he had to go somewhere. About an hour later, Ran called and told us that he was in an emergency room after he injured his ankles while parachuting from an airplane. As a child, you might remember, he used to lie at the bottom of the car, afraid of heights. Now, in order to prove to himself that he was not afraid any more, he started parachuting and doing free falls from airplanes accompanied by his best friend Greg.

He took a bad landing and shattered his ankle. When we arrived at the hospital, it was clear that surgery would be needed to insert a metal plate to stabilize his ankle. I contacted an orthopedic surgeon who was also a friend of mine and asked him to see Ran. After examining Ran and viewing the X-rays, he asked Ran to stay in bed for three days with his ankle elevated so the swelling will go down, and then he would be able to operate. All Ran wanted to do was to run away from the hospital because he was afraid that he would get an injection. He was not just scared of needles, he had a real phobia.

When the swelling finally subsided, my friend operated on Ran and I assisted him. It was impossible to approach Ran with a needle, so the anesthesiologist had to put a mask over his face to put him to sleep before he could be connected to an IV line. To stabilize his ankle, a titanium plate was used with seven screws to attach it to both sides of the fracture. Before Ran was awakened, an injection for pain was administered, but as soon as he woke up all the medication had worn out. All he wanted was to go home where he felt safe and fell asleep quickly.

While he was resting, I went to his room and looked at my son. His fear of heights had turned into free falls from airplanes; he had a shattered ankle, surgery, and a phobia of needles – it made Ran as screwed as his father. We hoped that this experience would put an end to his skydiving, but it didn't. Three months later he was parachuting again, most of the time without us knowing about it. One day he decided to go with Greg on a tour of the U.S. and the Caribbean islands to find suitable places for skydiving. The bulk of his luggage was a personal parachute. We were very happy and took a breath of relief when that adventure ended with no further injuries.

When they returned to South Africa, Ran decided it would be his permanent home. He liked to live and work in that country. He started a new cell phone and communications company with Greg as one of his partners. I had no doubt that he was going to turn it into a very successful company, and it did happen within a very short period. When I heard about the success of my son, I remembered the words of the businesswoman, who once told me that Ran is a genius in marketing – she was right!

*

The transition of government in South Africa went very smoothly, and it brought justice to a very unjust apartheid regime. There was no so-called war, as feared by a small section of the society. The economy flourished, and there was a new upper and middle class emerging among the black population. The merging of many blacks into the areas that used to be only for whites brought a tremendous building boom and a sharp rise in real estate prices. There were many new businesses owned by blacks, Indians, and colored. Hospitals and everything else were open to everyone.

But there were certain areas where there was a sharp decline. For example, crime was on the rise, and it was not just petty crimes like stealing or mugging. People were getting shot for a cell phone or petty cash. Businesses, banks, restaurants, and shopping centers were not safe any more. High brick walls equipped with electric fences were installed to protect property. Extra precautions were taken: windows and doors had bars and every place had an alarm system. Banks and other businesses hired armed guards. Shopping centers and banks look more like an army camp. Driving was dangerous, and when you were stopped at an intersection, there was a constant fear of being robbed or killed. Many residential areas were gated now and armed guards allowed only the residents to get in. The screwed thing was that the media was forbidden to report crimes. It looked like innocent citizens were sitting in a jail of their own homes while the criminals roamed free on the streets. It seemed like the police force was unable to do anything substantial about it. Some police stations even hired security companies to protect themselves.

Due to such conditions, life had become difficult, and many people were leaving the country to protect their families. Besides the standard of living, the level and standard of medical services in public hospitals deteriorated very badly. In order to get decent medical care, one had to go to a private hospital and private doctors. Education standards, too, went down. They were so low that many South African academic degrees were not recognized in other countries. Most of our friends had left the country. Ori was about to graduate from the University of Johannesburg. Ravit wanted to leave for the U.S., as well. It was about time to make a decision. In July 1999 we bought a house in Florida, where we planned to move.

Very soon, Ori graduated with honors and was looking for a place to work in New York. Ravit had attained her dream of being a teacher and she was teaching computer science at a college in Florida. I wanted a change too and decided to retire from medicine and find another occupation in the U.S.

After three weeks of working at a bank in New York City, Ori called and asked me to take a seat. I knew it was going to be a very serious conversation. Ori said that after having worked for three weeks in the bank, he felt that he had not chosen the right profession. Even though he had studied banking for five years, he was about to change direction. I was stunned, but I knew Ori must have thought it over a lot before breaking the news to me. He kept telling me that he realized that five years of the university had cost us a lot of money and wanted to hear my opinion. I told him that if he had to wake up every morning for the rest of his life and hate what he had to do during the day, then it was better to stop right there. I told him that he would have to find something that made him happy and kept him excited enough to get up in the morning to go to work. Once he knew what it was, then we would help him as much as we could. Ori's voice was trembling when he said, "I love you." I replied, "I love you very much, and have a good night."

That day, after seeing Ori in trouble, the guilt feeling of preventing him from studying medicine in South Africa stirred up again, even though we were willing to support him in studying medicine anywhere else in the world. A few days later he told us he wanted to study hypnosis and NLP [Neuro-Linguistic Programming]. I had no doubt that if Ori really put his heart and soul into it, he would be one of the best in this field.

Chapter 47

The Fiasco Factory

Those were days of major changes. Ori had changed his profession and I decided to retire from medicine, I started to look for other things to do. We found a sewing factory in Miami. It was involved in sewing sporting goods for companies in the area. The place was well equipped, was very modern and had about fifty workers. I always liked product industries, and sewing was one of them. Our accountant checked the books of the company that we wanted to buy and said that it looked to her like a very well established business.

Ettie and I started to work at the factory, and in the beginning Ori joined us. After a few months there was no income and we had to invest more and more money to keep the factory going. On a trip to a factory where I used to deliver sporting goods, I met a man with a beard wearing a yarmulke. He looked like an Orthodox Jew. When he heard me talking, he recognized my Israeli accent and started talking to me in Hebrew. He introduced himself as a rabbi. I told him that I was a retired doctor. He looked at me for a moment and said, "A healer can never retire. This is not a profession. Being a healer is a destiny that you have to fulfill. You can take a break, but sooner or later you will have to return to your destiny of being a healer."

*

As far as our misfortunes in business were concerned, the problem was that the U.S. government had lifted import duties from textiles that came from other countries, especially from South America and the Caribbean. The man who had sold us the factory probably knew it. When the taxes were lifted, the factories started sending things that needed to be sewn to Mexico and the Caribbean where they were manufactured for less than half the price of what they would have been charged in America. What an American gets paid for an hour of work is equal to more than a week's salary for the same work in places like Mexico. It was a screwed situation in that the U.S. government forced factories to shut down and fired thousands of workers to support and subsidize foreign countries.

On September 11, 2001, we heard the news about the terrorist attacks in Manhattan and Washington, DC. It was a big shock to everyone living in the U.S. and overseas. Those who pretended to work in God's name killing thousands of innocent people were changing this world forever, affecting the security and economy of the U.S. and the world.

We had no other option but to close down the factory after we lost most of our money. Failed businesses and the severe financial strain brought me back to my depression. This further strained the relationship between Ettie and me. As arguments and conflicts at home were intensified, I found an easy way out by escaping to South Africa instead of staying and trying to resolve them.

Chapter 48

The Circle of Cancer

A feeling sparked in your mind will translate as a peptide being released somewhere. Peptides regulate every aspect of your body, from whether you're going to digest your food to whether you're going to destroy a tumor cell.

- Candace Pert

The rabbi who had told me that a healer couldn't retire but can only take a break or a vacation was right! Within a few months my supposed vacation was over and I was practicing medicine again. My interest in HIV, the immune system, and cancer led me to search for ways to improve the general health of patients or to eradicate these diseases.

As a result, I started to work and study the field of Electro-Medicine. I found out that by giving certain electrical pulses of different strengths and frequencies, one could treat certain diseases, and these impulses could also be used occasionally to kill organisms and cells. As I looked deeper into this issue, I found that one of the biggest researchers in this field lived in California in the 20's and 30's. He had developed a microscope with which you could see that cancer cells contained a form of microorganism that caused the cancer to grow. Then he developed a machine that used radiation to destroy cancer cells.

His name was Dr. Rife. Unfortunately, something very strange happened after his work was made public. Due to bizarre and mysterious circumstances, his lab was burned down, all the equipment was destroyed, and all the protocols of his research and work disappeared. In that incident, one of his assistants was burned, too. Rumors said it was a conspiracy by the medical establishment and the FDA. All his work was gone in a few moments and Dr. Rife suffered immensely. He died in San Diego years later as an alcoholic, penniless. Though all of his work was destroyed, some documents miraculously survived. They showed that he had managed to cure many types of cancer in patients he had treated.

Dr. Rife had discovered with his microscope that in every cancer cell there are microorganisms, though it was not clear if those were viruses, bacteria or other forms of microorganisms. Today it is very well known that some forms of cancer can start as viral infections in certain areas, e.g., cervical cancer. Today, many machines have come to market claiming to use Rife's methods for treatment of cancer. Some work with sound and some with radiation. Most of them provide no results.

My major drive to work in this field of medicine came up after I met David, an American in his thirties. David was usually deep in his research work. He was what I would call a bit eccentric. I met him in South Africa where he claimed to have been infected with HIV for ten years and was doing fine with no medication. He explained to me that he lived and maintained his health by using a device that he had been treating himself and other patients with.

According to David the machine sends electrical currents through the body, killing the virus. He showed me the test results. The viral load went down from millions to about 500. I was getting medical treatment myself and my viral load was undetectable. It was not possible to see what this machine would have done for me.

Then I met a young woman who had contracted HIV from her boyfriend who himself had died from AIDS. She could not afford any medication and her health was deteriorating very fast due to AIDS. Her

CD4 count was around 10. She had been hospitalized many times with opportunistic infections, which are typical for AIDS patients.

After we demonstrated the machine on South African TV, some people approached us for the treatment. The young woman was one of them. She stayed on the treatment for two months. Sadly, we did not see significant reduction in her viral load. It was very obvious now that David was rather screwed, and in a bad way – the machine did not work. Unfortunately, the young woman died from AIDS a short time later.

Though the project ended there, my research did not. I read many articles about two doctors in the state of New York that had developed a device that filtered blood while passing electricity through the blood. The principle was that by doing this, the HIV virus was being destroyed, but I couldn't get in touch with them. No one seemed to know where to find them.

A few weeks later, one of my friends arranged a meeting for me with Martin, an electrical engineer. Both of his parents had died from cancer while he was a child, and he was sent to an orphanage. Together we tried to develop a machine that would destroy cancer cells by using different frequencies and forms of electrical waves. These signals would then be converted to sound frequency, which would destroy certain enzymes that were very specific to cancer cells. This way we could disintegrate the cancer cells without harming normal cells in the body.

The human body is a good conductor of sound. The bones, the muscles, and the body fluid move the sound waves everywhere in the body, and we hoped to exploit this to destroy cancer cells wherever they were. We were confined to a balance between the number of cells that could be destroyed and the ability of the body to secrete those cells without harming the liver and kidneys.

In all my years working as a doctor, I had treated thousands of cancer patients with surgery. It was very clear that if one could find the cancer in the early stages, the best method to stop it from spreading is to remove it. But in more advanced stages, only a few types of cancer respond to chemotherapy and radiation. Some types of cancer can be cured or can go into remission for a very long period by using those methods. Often, radiation and/or chemotherapy have little therapeutic effect while having adverse side effects.

In every human body there are cells that can potentially turn into cancer cells. A well-functioning immune system recognizes them and gets rid of them. When the immune system fails or does not function properly, these cells grow and create a cancerous growth in a specific place. From there, the cancer spreads to other areas. In all the cancer patients that I have investigated, I found that eight months to three years prior to the diagnosis of cancer, they had a major emotional event that affected them emotionally and physically, e.g., death of a family member or friend, depression, divorce, financial strain or any other terrible event. For the improvement of the cancer patient the problem that caused the mental trauma had to be addressed.

The other issue is nutrition. It's a well-known fact today that nutrition is a major factor in our health. Improper nutrition is one of the most prominent causes of diseases, including cancer. I have not seen any sick patient whose body was not acidic, and that means a low pH. The normal pH in our body is around 7.4, and in almost all diseases this pH goes lower, presenting a major risk factor. The deficiency of some vitamins like D, A, C, and E can cause certain diseases, including cancer. Some of these vitamins are known to be very good antioxidants, and can improve cell function and prevent cancer.

In every human body there are free radicals as a result of physiological functions like digestion and others. These free radicals can disturb normal functioning of different systems in the body. With all this in mind, I formulated a treatment program that consisted of four major parts listed below to treat cancer patients.

1. Proper nutrition, along with the elimination of sugar, dairy products and oils (with the exception of olive oil). Then, I planned on using food ingredients that would increase the pH in the body, something like quinoa, a species of grain-like crop grown primarily for its edible seeds. They contain a balanced set of essential amino acids, making it an unusually complete protein source among plant foods.

2. The daily intake of vitamins, minerals, and other food supplements to reduce free radicals. They would be used to boost the immune system and to improve the functions of all the systems in the body.
3. A unique feature: the treatment of the emotional problem that triggered the disease.
4. A therapeutic treatment utilizing the Dolphin Machine. I found out that about thirty minutes a day, five times a week, gave the best results, and gave the body the chance to get rid of the toxic byproducts.

Some types of cancer can be identified in the blood by checking for cancer markers. Different types of cancer have different markers. Usually, high levels of these markers mean that the cancer is spreading. One of the well-known markers is the PSA, which may indicate prostate cancer when it is above a certain level.

During the treatments I discovered that the cancer marker in the blood may go up to very high levels, probably because of disintegration of cancer cells. In certain stages the level will stabilize and start to drop, indicating that the tumor is getting smaller and would hopefully disappear.

The treatment with the machine was painless and did not cause any discomfort. The procedure that we followed was: A small transducer was put on the skin, and it transmitted sound frequency into the body. One heard something like a high-pitched noise coming out of the transducer. Most severe cancer patients were relieved from pain within seven to ten days after the start of the treatment. They would then be able to discontinue the use of pain medications.

When we started the treatment, we did it mainly in advanced stages of cancer where the main goal was to stop the pain. The machine that we developed transmitted certain frequencies and shapes of electrical pulses, which were then converted to sound waves by the transducer. Before working with humans, we experimented on cell cultures and found the right frequency to destroy cancer cells. We had to make sure that normal cells were not harmed. Our device was based on the same principle as the sound machines used for physical therapy. After having satisfactory results with cell cultures, we moved to terminal cancer patients. Because there was no more hope, these people came to us and asked for some form of relief. They had the attitude that they had nothing to lose, and if we were able to relieve them from the pain they were suffering from, then it was more than they could have asked for.

I chose to name the machine The Dolphin because dolphins are believed to have healing powers by transmitting sound frequencies.

One of our first patients was a woman from one of the African countries. She suffered from a very advanced lung cancer. Her husband, who was a professor, had brought her for the treatment. Before she came, she had numerous courses of chemotherapy and radiation, with no improvement. In fact, the radiation had damaged her lungs and heart. When she came to us she was in pain, including her bones. She needed high dosage of morphine to control her pain. Her nutritional state was very poor. She looked malnourished and extraordinarily underweight. It was scary – she was as light as a child.

After the first week of treatment, we saw a lot of improvement, i.e., the pain was not as severe as it used to be. A few days later it disappeared completely. Her appetite improved, and she started to eat more. By the end of the first month, she gained weight and started feeling well. She had become so fit that she could take care of herself. The woman, who could not spend an hour without high doses of morphine, was now driving and participating in taking care of her children.

Her condition kept improving. X-rays and scans showed that the cancer was shrinking. After three months she returned to her country and her husband informed me that she was doing very well. She was functioning again as a woman, a mother, and a wife. Unfortunately, her damaged heart could not take her new lifestyle as a healthy woman and she had severe heart attack months later. She died due to the heart attack, but the autopsy showed no cancer in her body. We had been able to cure her from the cancer, but, sadly, the weak heart ended her life.

Another case came when my insurance agent contacted me. He was sitting with one of his clients who had come to settle his affairs because he was going to die soon. When asked about the cause of his death, the man explained that he was suffering from pancreatic cancer. He had been bedridden and was in severe pain. He was unable to eat, and was waiting for death to end his misery. My insurance agent advised him to go and see me. Perhaps I might help him.

His wife wheeled John, who was in his fifties, in a wheelchair. John had come to South Africa years ago and used to work in the auto industry. He looked gravely ill. He had lost a lot of weight, his skin was hanging, his complexion was pale yellow, and he had difficulty talking. His wife told me that about six months earlier, he became jaundiced, and was diagnosed with advanced pancreatic cancer. At that stage, surgery was not an option and the oncologist recommended chemotherapy, hoping it would extend his life for a few months.

The first course of chemo was very hard on him, and with it came all the usual side effects: nausea, vomiting, severe weakness, hair loss, and ulcers of the mouth. All this made it more difficult to eat. He was unable to eat even the little bit of food he had been able to eat earlier. By the end of the treatment there was no improvement in his condition. Further tests showed the cancer had spread to the liver.

Another course of chemotherapy was recommended, this time with much stronger agents. After a few treatments he suffered acute renal failure. He had difficulty breathing and lost consciousness. He had to be hospitalized. His family was told he was going to die in a few days, but he got better and was discharged so he could die in his home. He took large doses of morphine to ease his pain. He was bedridden and disoriented.

I asked John only one question. "Do you give up or are you ready to fight?" He responded with no hesitation. "I am ready to fight and get better." When I saw the determination in that man, my promise to him was that I would fight with him. After I explained the treatment to him and his wife, they readily agreed.

As per my planned treatment, the first step was to improve his nutrition by giving him vitamins and supplements to rebuild his body and his immune system, which had been demolished by chemotherapy. Then we introduced thirty-minutes-per-day, five-days-a-week therapy using the Dolphin Machine. When his condition improved we would deal with the emotional problem. The other condition was that while on treatment he could take morphine only when needed, and not routinely like he used to. His wife immediately started to give him the proper food and supplements, and we proceeded with the treatment.

Within a few days his condition started to improve. He was able to get in and out of bed by himself and was able to walk on his own. His appetite improved and he was getting the right nutrition. Within the next two weeks, he started driving again and came by himself to see me. The best part was he did not need morphine any more. He was pain free.

When his condition permitted and he was able to concentrate, we had hypnosis sessions that revealed the deep emotional problems he had. Those problems mainly involved his children. Fortunately, he managed to resolve his emotions issues.

As expected, the cancer markers, which were very high, went down. A CT scan showed that the cancer growth was diminishing, and some of the metastasis that was very obvious in previous scans had disappeared. I asked John to get his medical file with the prognosis that his oncologist had given him. The screwed event that followed next was that when John went to see the oncologist, the doctor was surprised to find him alive and doing so well. He refused to give John his medical file. When I contacted the oncologist (he was a very reputable doctor, and I had known him for years) asking him for the medical files and all the previous tests and X-rays, he refused me as well!

I was amazed by the screwed thoughts that might have been in the oncologist's head. I explained to him that according to the law, he had to give all the reports to the attending doctor, and if he denied me, then I would approach the proper authorities to lodge a complaint. The same day we received the files. The least I had expected from that guy was to ask why John got so much better and did not die as he had expected him to. Sadly, no such query came from him.

Unfortunately, this was a common reaction from other doctors over the next few months. About three months after starting John's rehabilitation treatment, he was fit enough to return to work. He and his wife decided to return to Germany a few months later, and he started working again in the auto industry. Tests later performed in Germany showed no evidence of cancer. Four years after his treatment he told me that he was doing great.

After hearing of my success, a physician from another country asked me to take six of his cancer patients. The main object was to relieve them of severe pain. In all of them the pain disappeared within ten days of treatment.

Two of the patients died within a short period. One of them was a young woman in a very advance stage of breast cancer. The other was an older woman with kidney cancer. The good thing was that a ninety-year-old lady with breast cancer that had spread into the armpit recovered completely. There was no more evidence of cancer, and she died four years later at the age of ninety-four of factors unrelated to cancer. The other two patients I treated had major improvement, and the cancer growth shrunk; but because of family problems, they could not carry on with the treatments.

The only dark spot was that the medical community, in general, was notoriously skeptical of the new, and the so-called "unproven" methods and remedies. To be fair, the stakes are high, and it is often the best policy to err on the conservative side. I understood the risk, but even I wasn't prepared for the response that I got with my new take on the big C – cancer. I was told, "Don't mess with it."

Not many doctors were interested in my treatment methods. I had even received a very strong negative message from the entire industry. One day, a doctor from New York contacted me, asking for more information about the cancer treatments I was practicing. I was elated. It was the very first time another doctor had shown interest in my so-called "screwed" methods. I was happy that, though the industry may not welcome me, at least it was finally of interest to the medical community.

I bundled up a package of information about my patients and their treatment, including X-rays, test results, and outcomes. A short while later the doctor took the time to call and let me know that he was very impressed by what I had sent him. In fact, he called to congratulate me on what he considered to be a breakthrough. Well, at last I got a little validation. Hearing his words, I went on thinking that this could be a real turning point, and maybe the medical scenario would change.

Then the doctor took a deep breath and said, "You know, of course, that the cancer industry in the U.S. is a two-billion-dollar-per-day industry."

He went on. "This includes doctor visits, x-rays and other diagnostic procedures like surgery, radiation, and chemotherapy." He paused for a moment. I had no clue where he was going with this line of thought.

He continued. "No one in this industry, especially the drug companies, would like to see revenues from diagnosis and treatment go down. Of course, everyone is interested in prolonging the life of patients, but no one wants to see the complete eradication of cancer." Those words hit me like a bomb. I couldn't believe my ears. And yet, I knew he was talking about the biggest obstacle faced by anyone using alternative medicines and treatments.

I said to him, "I get what you're saying." I was trying my best to keep my temper in check. I continued, "But you can't be serious that *no one* wants to see cancer eradicated. What about the physicians and researchers who have devoted their lives to finding a cure?"

"Their lives are well funded by that work," was his serious response.

"And what about the patients and their families whose lives have been ended or forever altered by the disease?" I asked.

"Well, of course, they wouldn't choose cancer if they had a choice – that's not the issue," he retorted. "The issue is that your treatments will not be welcomed by the cancer industry, and you have no chance of getting your methods approved."

His final bit of friendly advice was to stop treating cancer patients. I was so angry I had a hard time controlling myself. Wasn't this screwed again? How can people not want to cure cancer? I wonder if any of these so-called industry people were suffering from cancer, what their answer would be then? I did not listen to him and continued my work helping others live a healthy and painless life.

*

I had many encouraging results. One day, out of the blue, a man who introduced himself as a member of the royal family of a Middle Eastern country contacted me. He told me that he had heard about my cancer treatments and asked if I would be willing to travel immediately to London to see his sister, the princess. He said that she was suffering from an advanced lung cancer that had spread to her liver and bones. I was a little nervous, but mostly curious. The next day I took off for London.

My heart was filled with the anticipation of what was about to come. When I landed at Heathrow Airport, I took a taxi into the city where I was supposed to meet the Prince at a very luxurious upscale hotel. When I met him he was cordial, but very abrupt, quickly ushering me to a car that took us to his sister. She was staying at a private home located in an exclusive neighborhood only a few minutes away from London.

On our way, he filled me in on some of the details as the car navigated through the dense city traffic. From what he told me, the princess was in her fifties and had been diagnosed about a year earlier with lung cancer. By the time it was diagnosed, the cancer was too advanced for surgery. However, the princess had traveled to the U.S. for a round of chemotherapy and radiation. Unfortunately, it had not helped, and the cancer was still spreading. Two of her vertebrae were in danger of collapsing because of the cancer, which would most likely lead to paralysis.

Her condition was very serious. Most of the doctors she had consulted did not expect her to live for more than a few weeks. By the time her brother called me the princess was living on large doses of morphine to control her pain. The screwed part of this story is that she had been told that the only thing the medical community could do was to try to keep her comfortable until she died.

When we entered her room, Her Royal Highness was in her bed surrounded by her children and grandchildren. To my amazement, she was puffing on a cigarette. "If you are going to tell me to stop smoking, you might as well turn around and leave the room," she snapped at me in a very gravelly voice that suggested she'd been smoking since the day she was born. I had quit smoking only a year ago myself, and, trust me, kicking myself in the butt had not been easy, even though I witnessed the ruthlessness of tobacco on a daily basis. But there were still times when a cigarette sounded too good to refuse. I had to take my chances and gain her trust, so I used it as a tactical gambit.

"I wouldn't presume to tell you something like that," I said. "In fact, if I may borrow a cigarette from you, I'd like us to enjoy one together." She looked surprised, then cheerfully handed me the pack. Someone stepped forward quickly to light it, and we each took a long drag. While she was inhaling deeply and enjoying the smoke, I was feeling like I was about to get sick. Anyone who has smoked after a long non-smoking spell can understand what I mean. The first few puffs made me dizzy, then the old addiction kicked in, and I was again enjoying it. We sat together smoking while I explained the terms and conditions of her treatment. She agreed to almost everything. but expressed concern about the strict diet I had asked her to follow.

The princess asked me to speak to one of the three chefs in the kitchen so that they would have detailed instructions regarding what she could eat and how her meals were to be prepared. By the time I left, I felt good about our rapport and her level of trust in me and her belief in the success of the treatment. After all the details had been sorted out, I made an arrangement to fly to Johannesburg the next day to get my equipment so I could get things in motion immediately – the princess had no time to lose.

When I returned to my room in the evening I found a large, gift-wrapped package on my bed. It turned out to be a beautiful, state-of-the-art laptop computer. It was a gift from the prince. While talking to him he had noticed that I had not brought a laptop with me. When he inquired about it, I explained to him that I was not a big computer fan and did not use a computer except for looking up medical information. I left my computer at home so my wife and kids could use it. He didn't accept that story. He thought that as a doctor I needed to have my own personal computer, so he got one for me. This is one of the perks of being royalty, you can pretty much get whatever you want. I will admit that it was rather nice to be on the periphery of that world – at least the royal gifts were rubbing off on me. From that day onwards there was a special connection between my laptop and me. Now I can't even imagine going through a day without it.

Three days later I returned to London with my equipment and my definitely non-royal-sized entourage, which included Martin, the electrical engineer who had developed the Dolphin Machine, accompanied by his wife. To my surprise, when we arrived at the royal residence, we were denied permission to begin that day or any time in the near future. I couldn't believe it. What might have happened to change things so drastically in the space of three days?

*

A few hours later I found out that nothing had changed. The real problem was that I had again run into good old traditional medical stonewalling, as usual. After knowing that I had come to treat the princess, in their best conciliatory fashion, the treating physicians graciously invited me to take part in a meeting that had been arranged in one of the hospitals in London. Attending that meeting were the three oncologists who had been treating the princess, including one from the U.S. who had prescribed her chemo and radiation. The purpose of the meeting was to find the proper course of treatment for the princess.

"Proper course?" Was this some kind of a joke? As I remembered, it had been decided three days earlier when the princess herself had sent me back to Johannesburg to start things in motion. Well, I guess I was wrong again. During the meeting the American doctor said that even though there had not been any improvement with previous rounds of chemo and radiation, he believed it would be best to administer another course of chemotherapy. He acknowledged that it wouldn't do any good at this point and would certainly generate a lot of severe side effects, but it would give the patient the feeling that something was being done for her.

I couldn't believe what he was saying, and what I was hearing. There sat a prominent American oncologist, and he was recommending treatments knowing that not only wouldn't they work, but also that they would add to the patient's suffering. It sounded more like a painful placebo, and a really painful one. The next screwed thing to happen was that the other doctors concurred with his opinion, though, at least, they did so with regret and expressed willingness to consider or explore any other possible options.

When I saw their hesitation, I recognized a potential opening, and immediately jumped in. I presented my treatment methods to the other doctors, explaining the different components of the process. I told them about some things that could, actually, make some difference from the way they had done things in the past, for instance, improving nutrition, adding supplements, providing emotional treatment, and using the Dolphin Machine. I barreled through the rationale without letting anyone else get a word in edgewise. The main reason for my aggression and continuous data-firing was that I was afraid that if I stopped, they'd never start listening again.

By the end of my presentation, I said, "Even if it only relieves the pain without clouding her thinking, wouldn't it be worthwhile?" After having asked such a question, I knew none of them would answer it. So I said, "Of course it would. None of us wants her to be in more pain, and we all want to make the quality of her remaining time the best it can be."

I knew they had no valid argument. This lifted my sprits even higher so I kept talking. "I can't promise specific results because each patient and each cancer is different. The thing that I can promise, however, is to give a chance to improve the Princess's condition without negative side effects." After having spoken for such a long time without letting anyone utter a word, I paused and looked around the table. I could hardly breathe. I knew this was one of the most important moments in the future of cancer research and treatment.

Finally, one of the British doctors cleared his throat, and said, "I don't believe...um... What I'm about to say..." Looking at his colleagues, and then facing me directly, he continued, "I think your treatment makes more sense in this case than starting another course of chemotherapy."

Well, at least I had been able to score a point. The discussion that followed was long and intense. It steered from polite and scientific to personal and sometimes inflammatory. When the dust finally settled, the four other physicians had talked themselves right back into treating the Princess with another course of chemotherapy. Sadly enough, no one had the courage to dissent, despite knowing the fact that they were about to add to the suffering of a patient. They looked like four undertakers waiting to bury her. They were too afraid to change their own professional status quo, and refused to think out of the box.

After the meeting, I told the prince that I was leaving London the next day. To my surprise, he asked me to stay a few more days, because he did not agree with the plan to administer another course of chemotherapy. He wanted a little more time to discuss it with his sister, but he made sure that I understood one thing – that the final decision about the treatment would be entirely the princess's.

The next morning the American doctor met with the princess and convinced her to have another course of chemo. As I had expected, he did not tell her he did not expect any improvement. Naturally, the princess already knew what the side effects would be. Fortunately – or unfortunately – the pre-chemo blood tests indicated that her white blood cell count and platelets were seriously low as the result of previous chemotherapy. That made another course of chemo far too dangerous. When I learned this, I again saw the door opening for me – if only a crack. Due to the failing health of the princess, I wedged my foot in as boldly as any door-to-door salesman would have done if he believed in the value of his merchandise.

I suggested to the prince that this might be the best time to bring in a physician whom I knew well and trust implicitly. He specialized in holistic treatments for cancer. He lived in Miami, Florida, but I knew he'd welcome the opportunity to see the princess and combine his methods with my treatment. The prince agreed, invited the doctor, and then denied both of us access to the princess. This seemed to have become sort of a pattern. I knew the only thing we could do was explore and visit the different places in London and, finally, make plans to return to the U.S.

Just before we were to leave we had a brief meeting with the princess. We didn't know what to expect, but the meeting was cordial, with no other doctors around. I believe that was the key because both the princess and her brother were almost afraid to go against traditional medical advice. We were able to get her to agree to give our methodology a try.

We seemed at last to be back on the right track. We still had to overcome opposition from the other camp of doctors. It was two more weeks before I was permitted to start the treatments. The main problem that I was facing was the princess's obstinate obsession with her unhealthy diet. I knew that my chances of winning her over on this issue were as likely as getting her to quit smoking. I had to compromise. The princess also objected to the number of vitamins and supplements that I prescribed, so I had to modify them as well. Despite all these roadblocks, as soon as we started the treatment her condition began to improve. Within two weeks her pain had gone almost completely. However, at this late stage of her illness, after months and months of pain, she had already become addicted to morphine. I did what I could to, reduced the doses of morphine, and she was quite responsive. At one point she was able to get out of bed and play for a while with her grandchildren. As her birthday approached, she was looking forward to a welcome visit from some of her family.

During the treatment, I got to know the princess better. She loved her family. She loved food. And she loved to gamble. All this had led her to plan a big birthday dinner party at one of the largest casinos in London. As her doctor, it was wonderful to see her looking forward to something exciting and uplifting for a change. The members of the royal family arrived and they proved to be friendly, generous, and supportive.

I was privileged to have spent a lot of time with Her Royal Highness in between the treatments, and it gave me a chance to catch a glimpse of the lifestyle of the rich and famous. Our time together demonstrated that regardless of our life status, we are all driven mostly by the need for good health and the happiness of those we love. The princess had been a daughter, sister, mother, and grandmother. The people who rallied around her as her illness took its toll were the people who had truly loved her throughout her life.

But all good things come to an end, and so did the princess's victory lap of fighting the disease. One evening the doctor who was in charge of the pain management for Her Royal Highness came to visit her. He talked with her and told her that if she was going to die soon anyway she should take as much morphine as she wished. Even though her pain had decreased during the past two weeks of treatment, his logic was that she shouldn't take any chances in case it came back. As someone who had suffered so much pain in the past, she was sufficiently scared of that possibility and allowed several large doses to be administered. The next day she was unconscious, and the following day she passed away.

All this seemed unfair to me. The Princess and her family had been denied their last few days of what could have been a peaceful and memorable time together – all of it because of a doctor's ego that wouldn't let him admit that, perhaps, there was a better way to treat her than the one he'd always advocated. This was a big defeat for me. I had envisioned a healthy princess, laughing and playing with her family, but she was no longer with us. Frustrated and depressed, I returned home, feeling as though I had lost yet another battle.

I know that I do not have the answer to totally eradicate cancer. I also know that there is an equally *dangerous threat* to our health and wellbeing: *the lack of openness to alternative treatments on behalf of mainstream medicine.* I had gone to London with proven ways to improve the princess's final days and maybe more, yet I was met with resistance, fear, even hostility. Even though I was armed with many examples of how my treatment had improved and even cured some patients, it seemed to me that the doctor who called from New York was absolutely right. My treatments, which had a real potential to cure people of pain and misery, were not welcomed by the so-called cancer industry.

What this industry doesn't know, however, is that I'm accustomed of going to where I'm not always welcomed. I'm used to talking even when it seems as though no one is listening. If I look at this as a war with the entire medical establishment, I have no chances for victory. I'll have to look for other opportunities, make inroads in different places, explore other dimensions and make certain that I keep on moving forward, even though the so-called medical industry will be throwing stones at me. I know that I believe in myself. I know that I can do it, and I'm committed to see where this persistence takes me.

*

In April 2004, our whole family went to Johannesburg to celebrate Ran's 30th birthday. His partners threw a lavish party for him. The venue of the party was a beautiful restaurant. We all had a great time. The food was good and there was live entertainment. It was one the most beautiful birthday parties I had ever seen. Among the guests I met a married German couple: Ann, a lady in her thirties and Pitt, her husband, in his forties.

Both of them were tall, blond, and had startling blue eyes. The fact that drew my attention was that Pitt's neck was so huge, and it looked like he was unable to put his arms down – they were elevated all the time.

I asked Ran, "What is wrong with Pitt? Why can't he put his arms down and why is his neck so enlarged?" It turned out that Pitt had leukemia, a type of blood cancer. He had been suffering from it for the last two years and refused to go through chemotherapy. The big lymph glands in his armpits prevented him from putting his arms down, and as far as his neck was concerned, it was so gigantic because of the enlarged lymph glands. I thought I could be of some help to him, so I was introduced to Pitt and Ann. Pitt told me that he had refused chemotherapy and was searching for other ways to treat his cancer. We decided to meet the next day and discuss it further.

The next day Pitt arrived and brought all the blood test reports that he'd had done and the reports of other tests and scans. His condition was not good. The cancer was in a very advanced stage and had involved most of the lymph glands in his body. But his general condition was reasonably stable. He was still working full time. I described the treatment, and he asked me to start straight away. As per my treatment plan, we started with his diet to cleanse and improve the functions of every system of his body and to increase his body's pH. We changed his diet and added vitamins and supplements. Along with that, he was getting a therapy treatment with the Dolphin thirty minutes a day, five times a week.

Within two weeks his condition improved. His lymph glands shrank, and he was able to put his arms down. His neck was still swollen, but not as much as it was the day I had first seen him. He was able to sleep well at night, something he was unable to do earlier because of the pressure on his glands while lying down. When his condition improved, we decided to find the emotional cause for his cancer. Under hypnosis, I regressed Pitt to where the problem had started. He started crying and shivering as if he was very cold. When I asked where he was, he described a cemetery in Europe. It was the month of December and it was snowing. He was at his father's funeral. His father had passed away a few days earlier from a heart attack. Pitt blamed himself for his father's heart attack because Pitt and his family left Europe and moved to South Africa.

When we clarified the problem, it was very clear that his father had suffered from heart problems for many years before Pitt left Europe, and the deterioration in his father's health was not that unexpected. I assured him that he had nothing to do with it. In another session of hypnosis, I asked Pitt to go forward and see himself free of cancer. This time, he described a place in Johannesburg where he, along with his wife and son, were celebrating. This time he was very healthy, free of cancer, and had a big smile on his face. I told him to give me the date when he will be free of cancer. Pitt said, "By the end of December 2004, I will be free of cancer." We carried on with the treatment for three months. He strictly followed the diet, took all the supplements, and his condition improved. By the end of July, I returned to America. Pitt's last blood test results before I left showed a remarkable improvement. His lymph glands had returned to normal size.

On the 31st of December 2004, around midnight, Ran called us from Johannesburg and wished us a Happy New Year. In the background we heard the sounds of celebration. They were having a New Year's party, and the loud music and noise told me that they were having a good time. Before we hung up, Ran told me that someone wanted to talk to me. He put Pitt on the phone who gave me the good news: the blood test results from the previous day showed that he was cancer free. Pitt and Ann became our very good friends.

Because I visited South Africa at least once a year, I used to see them during my visits. Pit was working full-time, and his health was good. In 2007, during one of the dinners with us, I was amazed to see him. He had gained a lot of weight and had stopped the diet I prescribed to him. It was clear to me that if he kept on doing what he was doing, he would get sick in no time at all. Since I was concerned about him, I told him and his wife so. His reaction was that, though he really wanted to stay healthy, it was very difficult for him to stick with his diet and healthy lifestyle. He then reassured me that there was nothing to worry about because his blood tests were normal.

He thought that the cancer was gone. I, however, was of a different opinion. A year later, we met again. Pitt had severe back pain and walked with crutches. He spent most of his day in bed and had stopped working.

The doctor was treating him for a slipped disk in his spine, and there was no improvement in his health at all.

After I gave him anti-pain treatment with no improvement, it was clear to me that the pain was not due to a slipped disk, but most probably due to swollen lymph glands from cancer pressing his nerves on the spine. On hearing my diagnosis, he refused to accept it because the blood tests were normal. On his birthday, in May 2008, Pitt passed away. It was more proof that the will to live and the discipline required to maintain a healthy lifestyle are the best treatments, but once you ignore this reality and give up, the disease will return. Most patients say they really want to get better and stay healthy. Unfortunately, if we look deeply inside and are honest with ourselves, we see that is not always the case.

*

Recently I was invited by a doctor-friend in Israel to visit two middle-aged female patients. They were being treated for advanced pancreatic cancer. They were at about the same stage of the disease and were receiving similar treatments. When I saw them, they both looked like people who had progressed to the advance stages of cancer. It was heartbreaking to see that one of the two women looked very depressed and lifeless – there was not a single sparkle of hope in her eyes. When I spoke to her and asked her how she wanted to proceed with the treatment, I was never given a straight answer. She informed me that she had to consult with her family, which consisted of her husband, brother, and daughter.

When I insisted on knowing what she was actually feeling inside her heart – and that excluded what her family was thinking – her response was, "I don't know." She used to be a businesswoman, ran two very successful businesses, and it seemed like she had found her place in the world, something that a lot of people had never been able to find. Suddenly, her life began falling apart when she got sick six months earlier and was told that she had a cancer of the pancreas and only a short time to live.

She transferred her career to her husband because she was unable to continue working in such a fragile state. I recommended a specific diet as well as supplements to help her deal with the inevitable physical deterioration. She told me bluntly that she could not stick to such a diet or swallow so many pills. When I asked her where she saw herself six months down the road, I knew her answer just by looking in her weary eyes, but I still needed to hear it out loud. She said that all the doctors had told her she would not live more than three months. I was certain at that point that she had already given up her fight against this disease and had given up her life. The fact was that she did not want to improve her condition and was wallowing in self-pity. She was hoping for an elusive magical pill, and I felt that it was best not to treat her because, despite of all my efforts, I could not make her think she could get better.

The other patient was also a very successful woman. She ran three interior design businesses. She too was diagnosed six months earlier with cancer of the pancreas when she had severe jaundice. A stent was introduced into her body, in order to allow the flow of bile, and the jaundice went down for a short period of time. Another stent was introduced and the jaundice ended up going away. That woman had a very long medical history. About five years earlier both of her breasts were removed due to breast cancer. During that exhausting time in her life she still managed a full-time job.

Under hypnosis, we went back to the place where the cancer started but she could not see very much in this vision. The only thing she kept saying was that her mother was bothersome. When I asked her age, she said that she was a young girl. Eventually I asked a painful question, one that not everyone wants to disclose right away. I asked her if she was abused. She responded by saying that she was not physically abused, but her mother talked too much and had a tendency to run her life to the point where she was unable to take it anymore.

Her voice was shaky. I sensed she was not ready at this stage to take the conversation any further. We stopped talking about the past and started discussing the future. The future sometimes can be as terrifying a place to envision as the past. I asked her where she felt that she would be in six months. She described an apartment on the beach where she and her husband were standing on the balcony overlooking a beautiful view of the ocean. Her husband was very happy to see that she had recovered from cancer. She was in good spirits, and the best thing was that she was cancer free.

When I asked her if she lived by the beach now, she replied, No, but had plans to move there in the future. When I told her about the treatment, it invoked a very enthusiastic response (unlike the other woman who was waiting for a magician to come and cure her without any medication). She agreed to everything and wanted to start right away. Her condition improved and she planned to stick to a healthy lifestyle, including proper nutrition, even though it would be a challenge because she was working fulltime, and felt stressed out and very tired.

When her oncologist predicted that she had three months to live, her first major decision – instead of buying a traditional coffin – was to purchase a condo on the beach. I was not surprised when she actually found the one that she had told me about during our hypnosis session. The last time I saw her, her scans showed that the tumor was shrinking. She was strictly adhering to my diet plan and was doing well. The only thing she was still not ready to cope with was her emotional problems.

The other woman, according to her doctor, deteriorated quickly and passed away a few weeks later. The most significant difference between these two seemingly the same medical cases were the patients' general attitudes towards life and the will and determination to get well. My treatment might have helped, but the most essentially critical point was the patient's attitude. It was about a person's entire willingness to heal him/herself, and do whatever it took to improve his or her condition, taking into account three different levels of a healing process: physical, mental, and emotional. Medical treatments such as surgery, radiation and chemotherapy, can improve one's condition, but they may never bring full recovery, and could even be reversed unless the mental and emotional aspects are completely addressed and resolved.

While I was treating the lady in my friend's office, I noticed a man who was also receiving treatment. He had an IV line attached to his arm. The right side of his body was in tremors and convulsions. I asked my friend, the doctor, what was wrong with this patient, and he told me that since

1997 the patient had suffered from Parkinson's disease and, unfortunately, even with all the treatments, he was not doing well. I told my friend that I did not believe the patient had Parkinson's. We were introduced, and shortly afterwards the patient told me that he would like to have a hypnosis session in order to find out what the real problem was.

Under hypnosis, he regressed to the time where it had all started, back to May 1997. He started crying and told me that he had lost his house, business and been divorced. It turned out that was when he got sick. It also appeared to me that he had a lot of secondary gains from being sick. First of all, he was getting disability checks every month, and since his remarriage he did not have any responsibility for his two young children. He didn't drive, and even the smallest daily personal care routines such as combing his hair were completed by someone else. It was very clear that the problem here was not Parkinson's disease. Parkinson's does not get to this stage in one day. It is usually a gradual progressive disease and rarely effects on one side of the body.

Under hypnosis, I told him that two minutes after he wakes up, the tremors would disappear and he would have a new chance to be without it. It would be his decision to go back to being sick or start living a normal life again. If he chose to get better it would require more treatments. Two minutes after waking up, the tremors and convulsions disappeared. Within two days he stopped the medication and started playing with his children and driving again. The only thing he did not do was return to work. When I met with him again at my friend's office, he said good morning and goodbye, but it looked like he had some kind of resentment towards me. He did not ask for any more treatments and told the secretary that he didn't want any more, either. For about ten days he did not have tremors, but it was very clear that soon they would come back. Unfortunately, his condition went back to where it had started and he fell ill again. The reason for this was that this man was accustomed to living with sickness, and like every person, he had a free choice to either be free of sickness or remain sick. He chose the latter.

Chapter 49

Different Kind of Healing

I will always remember the December of year 1996, when my friend Yossi told me that I possessed unconventional healing powers, and within three months I would have the great ability to heal and help many sick and suffering people. Since that strange day, you would be surprised to know that I have heard similar things from different people who had been living in various parts of the world. During the years when I worked with Martin on developing the Dolphin Machine, he told me that it was not the machine that healed the patients, but was something that I possessed. Even one of the most rational people in my life, Ettie, confessed to me often that whenever I touched an area of the body that was hurting, the pain would disappear almost immediately.

My life is full of such examples. Here are some of them. One beautiful evening in Florida, Ravit, Ettie and I went out to have dinner in a restaurant with a good friend of Ravit's. While we were waiting to be seated, a young man stormed into the place. He looked rather over-excited. His eyes bulged out, he was breathing heavily and had a red face. Ravit's friend was shocked and told us that it was her son, and he was often having similar attacks.

No one really knew what caused his attacks or what to do about them. The guy sat down, and it seemed as if he was about to faint. Ravit's friend asked me to do something, so I instinctively put my hand on his forehead.

Then something unexpected happened. His breathing slowed and he began to relax. His eyes closed, and the color of his face returned to normal. It seemed to me as if he had reverted back to the usual calm state. After about a minute he woke up and looked deeply into my eyes. His eyes were like a child's, full of wonder, and he asked me what I had done to him. I told him that I did not do anything except put my hand on his forehead. Hearing this, he said that he had never felt so much at peace in his entire life, until the moment I put my hand on his forehead.

Another similar incident happened when my friend Mark invited me to dinner. This is where I met Steve. The next morning Mark was leaving for the north, and Steve was supposed to take him to the airport. Steve asked me to come along, and, after leaving Mark at airport, we would drive around and visit a flea market. The next day we took Mark to the airport. Suddenly I had an intense urge to tell him something. I had a message for him from a blue-eyed young blonde woman who had short cut hair. She had sunken cheekbones and a blue ribbon in her hair. In her message, she wanted to comfort Steve by telling him that she was happy, and there was nothing more that he could have done to help her. She wanted to let him know that he would always be in her heart, and every ounce of her body, mind, and soul belonged to him for all of eternity and thereafter.

On hearing this message, Steve was shocked. For a moment it looked as if he was about to lose control of the car. His face turned white and he started crying uncontrollably. He told me that lately he had been thinking about her, but she was not alive anymore. Steve even mentioned her name, and I gently told him that I knew she had a violent departure from this world. However, she wanted Steve to know that she was doing well and so was their son. There was total silence in the car, but anyone would have been able to tell that Steve was having difficulty driving. I was upset that I had just met him, and all of a sudden I needed to transfer an important message to him from his deceased girlfriend. It was not that I had any control over it – I just had to let it out.

After a few minutes he was more relaxed and told me the story of how he met the love of his life years ago. After graduating from high school, he met this girl. They fell in love and she got pregnant. He was sent to the

Vietnam War, and during his time in service there was no contact between them. He did not know what had happened to her or their unborn child. When he returned from Vietnam he found out that her parents had forced her to have an abortion. After a short time she married another man. Her new husband was very abusive and violent, so violent that in one of his impulsive acts of rage he murdered her. He was arrested and found guilty of murder. Since then, Steve lived with severe guilt. He always thought that he didn't do enough to help her and the expected baby. Lately, he had been thinking about her a lot blaming himself for her death.

I can't explain what happened in the car, but I know there is a deep connection between the soul world and us. We all get messages. We should listen and be ready to accept and embrace them.

The next day Steve came for a visit and was limping. When I asked what was wrong, he told me that for the last ten years, he had experienced pain in his right knee. After numerous treatments by different doctors with no improvement, he was told that the best option was to go for a knee replacement surgery. Without any medical insurance, it would have taken a lot of money and he did not have that much money. I offered to examine his knee. As soon as I placed my hand on his knee, he said the pain was gone for the first time in ten years. He was free from pain and this was after one minute of my touching his problem knee. In utter shock, he asked me what I did. For the next few days he was completely free of pain. One day he told me that he tripped off a stepladder and hurt his knee again, but in a few minutes, it stopped hurting and he felt well again.

From these emotional experiences that connected us in ways that many others cannot quite understand, Steve and I have became close friends.

There were other instances that still seem unexplainable to me. But it was evident that these things did happen for a reason. I don't know how or why, but when I tried to use these powers deliberately, they do not work. My medical background and Western education are always whispering in my ear. They keep telling me that this kind of healing cannot be done, and I am probably blocking myself. I've also been told that as long as I try to rationalize and see it scientifically, I won't be able to help anyone. It's only if and when I let everything unfold as it is meant to that I'll be able to help those who are suffering, and truly embrace my true nature as a healer. All I can say is that I'll be waiting patiently to see what's in store for me.

*

On one of my trips to Israel, my father seemed to be very happy with Neti, his lady-friend he had met after my mother passed. They had been together for ten years and were very happy. It was really nice to see my father so happy again, after all the misery and suffering he had gone through while my mother was sick. Neti was a very nice woman, and they both came to visit us in South Africa where I did a treatment on Neti's face. When she met us, she was much wrinkled. After the treatment she looked much younger. Her son, also a doctor, sometimes came to visit us, and we used to work together before I had known Neti.

On the second day of my visit my father came home and minutes later the phone started ringing. It was Neti. She said that she wasn't feeling well. My father left immediately to see her, and an hour later he came back pale and told me that Neti had a heart attack. The ambulance had come and before he was able to reach her, she had a cardiac arrest. The medical team resuscitated her, and when her heart started working again, she was transferred to a hospital. My father and I went to the hospital straight away where we met her son.

Neti was still in the room where they had put a stent in one of her coronary arteries to restore the blood flow to her heart. The attending cardiologist told us that her condition was stable and she would be transferred to intensive care, but it was too early to know the extent of damages to her heart. The next day Neti looked much better, but, just as a precaution, she was kept in the ICU. For the next few days it looked as if she was recovering well. But her pulse was irregular and the cardiologist decided to administer electric shock to stabilize her heartbeat – a well-known procedure that usually takes seconds, but it has to be done under general anesthesia to avoid any pain.

Her heartbeat returned to normal, but the next day she seemed very lethargic to me. When I inquired about it, the doctor and her son told me that this was a result of the anesthesia. Since I was just a visitor, I did not say a thing. The next day there was no improvement. I contacted her son, an M.D., and told him that, in my opinion, there was a blockage in the blood flow to her brain, which can happen after a heart attack. He said that he would talk to the doctor, and let me know what was going on. When we left the hospital, I asked my father what he expected was going to happen with Neti. He was very optimistic and had no doubt that she would recover soon and return to normal life.

Since I did not want to break his heart, I explained to him as gently as possible that it might get worse and he had to be prepared. His reaction, as expected, was the usual, "You are screwed and have a wild imagination." He was certain it was going to be okay. I wanted everything to be that way. I prayed and hoped that he was right, but still, deep in my heart I knew I was not wrong. An ultrasound was performed to study the blood flow to her brain and her son informed me they did not find any severe blockage. It remained the same as about two years ago. For the next few days her pulse was stable, but she seemed to be even more lethargic. The day before I left, I went to say goodbye to Neti. It was the day she was transferred from the ICU to the geriatric unit.

Before I left, Neti apologized for not taking me out to dinner. She said that the last ten years with my father were the best years of her life. On our way home my father said that this was the proof that I was wrong. (He meant screwed.) Neti was out of ICU, and everything was going to be all right. The next day, early in the morning, my father answered the phone. It was Neti's son. Last night Neti had a brain stroke and passed away. Before I left Israel I attended Neti's funeral. I did not understand. Was I the only one who saw things the other doctors failed to see? Was it because they did not know what to look for? Similar things happened to me in the past and are still happening.

Chapter 50

Back to Atlantis

In one of my regular visits to Johannesburg in the spring of 2003 I met a young architect, Joe. He was mainly involved in the construction of clinics and hospitals using ecologically sound materials and techniques. He also incorporated the use of traditional Chinese Feng-Shui at his work. We got along really well. He told me about a place on the outskirts of Johannesburg where a spiritual community of about thirty people was living on twenty acres of land.

They wanted to move their site to a smaller location and were looking for a buyer for the land and the existing buildings on it. The catch was that, until then, the spiritual leaders of that place had refused to sell it to any random, greedy developer, who would most likely raze the site to build townhouses or condos. This land was their child, and just like an adoption agency that scrutinizes the background of potential parents, these people insisted that the potential buyer should cherish the spiritual nature of the place and protect the sanctuary of the surrounding natural environment.

When I heard about such conditions, I thought that they might be interested in selling the land to this "screwed" doctor who had a firm belief in healing people. Joe and I visited the location, and indeed, the place was just as gorgeous as he had described. The natural surroundings were pristinely preserved. When I took a look around, I was filled with wonder for the beauty of the place. The jacaranda trees were in full bloom. When we walked on the narrow paths it felt as if we were walking on a purple carpet of flowers. It was purple above in the sky where the trees were in full bloom and purple on the ground where the flowers fell. Not only was it a delight for the eyes, but you could smell the sweet fragrance of the jacaranda flowers in the air, and hear a beautiful choir of exotic birds singing in the diffused sunlight that seeped through the trees – just as if you were in paradise.

At a distance there were a few small red brick houses that surrounded the main building, which was the place where all the meetings, group meditations, and other social and spiritual events took place. The place looked a bit run down. When I met the leaders they confirmed the architect's story that the land would only be sold to someone who would preserve it. I was immediately inspired by the potential of this place and decided to meet with local experts and investors in Johannesburg specializing in the fields of conventional and holistic medicine, spirituality, and alternative energy such as sun, wind, and water. The best thing was that all of us shared the vision of creating a community where we could live a healthy, productive life in harmony with the environment.

Within a few days and after a few intriguing and productive meetings, we came up with a groundbreaking plan to build a unique medical center for integrated medicine around the lake on the premises of the current center. We planned that it would be a place where traditional and alternative therapies were freely intermixed for the optimal result of each patient. One of the names suggested for the center was Atlantis.

We planned that this center would have clinics to treat a host of ailments. We would have experts in healing and rehabilitation; we would use many specialties of Western medicine, along with traditional Chinese medicine, traditional African medicine, Chiropractic, Nutrition, Mental Health, Homeopathy, and other modalities of healing. These various practitioners would work together, fully cooperating with each other, providing the healing, and, most importantly, teach others and learn themselves. The idea was to ensure that the treatments would not be given simply to erase the effects of various symptoms, but would be performed in an integrated fashion that targeted the harmony of the body, mind, and soul.

Along with the various experts, the volunteers and I worked on this idea together. The more we planned, the more this center grew bolder in concept and scope. We planned other finer details for short-term outpatients and for longer-term inpatients. These patients were to be accommodated in a satellite hotel that was to be built adjacent to the center. The complex would also have a shopping plaza with entertainment and fitness centers. These facilities were to focus their natural products and services on healthy lifestyles and spirituality with special emphasis on whole food, proper nutrition, and exercise.

As required by the current landowners, and per my wishes, in an effort to conserve nature and the environment we decided to obtain as much power as possible by alternative means like solar, wind, and geothermal sources. There would be classrooms and auditoriums where the aforementioned practitioners would share their knowledge through various workshops and seminars.

We even planned to build primary and secondary schools where the latest and most advanced methods of teaching would be used for the children of this community. The remainder of the property would be used for homes in which all of these healers, experts, and vendors, along with their families and some other families and individuals looking for this kind of lifestyle would live. We even considered methods for halting the potential decrepitude of aging with a multitude of opportunities for seniors in the community to work and volunteer in order to maintain their mental and physical skills.

I had a vision that this dream of mine would be wildly successful and would be copied all over the world to provide healing for thousands or even millions of people. I saw this as a sister-project to "Patch Adams' The Gesundheit! Institute" shown in the 1998 movie *Patch Adams* starring Robin Williams, but, of course, without the supposed "clowning around" that was the part of the movie. With an actual hospital and with a very fair pricing model for our treatments, I saw a huge potential in the idea. When the actual bidding began, we offered a fair rate for the land but were countered with some obscenely high prices, so our talks with the spiritual leaders of this community fell apart. We could not compete with large investors taking advantage of the booming property market in the new South Africa. The owners decided to sell the land to conventional developers who, of course, decided to build condos on the site. As I saw it, greed had overpowered the spirituality of those people.

As far as my plans and dreams were concerned, they were lost. My hopes to see integration between different modalities of healing crashed and burned like the actual Atlantis falling into the ocean. After the talks fell apart, I left Johannesburg. The question that I continuously asked myself was, if we could indeed create communities like the one I had envisioned, would it be akin to raising Atlantis out of the abyss? Was this a goal that we really wanted to accomplish? I wondered if it was true that Atlantis disappeared because its capacity for technology exceeded its level of spirituality? Given the fate of that city, it was clear that this was not what we were looking for. But then again, what if deep underneath this dream we were really looking for such a world where we all could live in happiness, harmony, health, prosperity, and cooperation in a verdant, abundant, and unspoiled nature? Was this the world John Lennon was talking about when he sang, "Imagine all the people sharing all the world?" I believe that our environment, our world, and all humanity are desperate to see this happen. I pray and hope that some of you, look forward to the same world and aspire that one day we would be able to make this dream a reality.

Chapter 51

I Found God

"For you can't hate love no matter how much you try. But you can't love hate no matter how much you cry!"

-Patrick Stafford

This is perhaps that part of my life that has made all the difference. The place where one might see illusions lifted and lives changed. I do not say it made a seer out of me, but yes, it did help me be a better person. Though I was not a religious person, many times I tried to read the book *Conversations with God* written by Neale Donald Walsch. As expected, I was unable to do so. All I did was read a few pages and stop. Then one day I felt like giving it one more try, and that's when something magical happened. For the next few days and nights I could not put the books down. After having been through so much in my life, I felt like the book was written for me. Trust me, it does not happen on a regular basis that I connect so deeply with something. When I finished reading the books, I decided to listen to the audio version in the state of deep relaxation, and it was one of the most incredible experiences I have ever had.

There were moments when I felt like God was talking to me.

Today, without any doubt, I can say that it is the best book I have ever read. That book changed the way I saw God, the way I saw myself, and the way I saw the world. The book changed everything, and, most importantly, it changed my perspective towards life.

What was the God that I discovered, the God that was talking to me, the God that I believed in? My answer to this question would be that, my God will not judge, will not punish, but will unconditionally love. This God is nothing else but pure, unconditional, and unlimited love. I believe and I am not afraid to say it out loud. Whoever we are, and no matter what faith we believe in, the only thing for the sake of God that we could do is LOVE.

Our love is embodied. Our sexuality is the physical, intellectual, emotional, and spiritual capacity to give and to receive love. The reality is that having affectionate feelings for another is not enough. We cannot love truly without our whole selves, without our bodies. The Love that I talk about must be physical as well as emotional, intellectual as well as spiritual.

One thing I believe is that the capacity to love is not just a gift from God. Actually, it is God's presence alive and active in our very being. We embody God when we love. To be a lover is what is meant when we say we are created in God's image. To be a lover is to know God. There is no such thing as unholy love. Pure love knows no boundaries, no barriers, and no limits. It is the nature of love to push us out of selfishness, fear, and ignorance to overcome boundaries and barriers in order to love the other person.

This love is free without restraints. Loving someone is a human right that cannot be regulated by law, religion, or culture. There is no government, no religion, no cultural custom that has the authority, the power to tell us who we must love; and, there is no government, no religion and no cultural custom that has the authority, the power to tell us we cannot love someone because of her or his race, ethnicity, religion, class, family, or gender.

I believe that to love someone is to be connected to that person on a deep and spiritual level that defies and ignores all social categories and classifications of people.

I appeal to you with all my heart and soul. Please let no one tell you that your love is unnatural, immoral, unhealthy or sinful because your love does not conform to his or her prejudices and fears. Love between persons is more than normal, more than wholesome – it is divine.

Trust your love. Believe in it. It is love that makes a marriage and a family, not government and not religion. Honor your love as precious and innately holy. Do not wait for others to honor it. Your love does not depend upon someone else's approval or acceptance. The more you honor your love, the more others will understand your love and honor your love.

Trust your love. Believe in it, and we will change the world!

You must believe that we all are parts of God. We are love, and we were given a free choice to do whatever we like to do in our life. According to our choices, our life will be, and so are all the consequences that come out of our actions.

One of the most important things is to love oneself. Unless we love ourselves we can never love anybody or anything else and can't be loved. When we love ourselves, we can love a partner, child, friend, family, society, and the world we live in. Love is the origin of good, light, happiness, and joy. Everything good comes out of love. Fear is the opposite of love, the origin of dark, hate, jealousy, suppression, greed, and war. All negativity originates in fear. In the place where there is love and light, there cannot be fear and darkness.

I have seen it happen. Many times with hypnosis I have regressed people to their past life and progressed them to a future life. In different lifetimes we have lived in different places. We have been of different religions and a different sex and occupation. Our soul will choose to experience different things in different lifetimes in order to evolve and get to a higher level. Whatever we do in our lives, the final destination is love. Our soul is eternal. We were never born and would never die.

Moses, Jesus, Muhammad, Buddha and others, who have been the greatest teachers to have ever walked this earth, have always preached love. How could a different religion turn love to fear? In order to control the masses, some religious people introduce fear, fear of a judging God, fear of hell. If you don't pray, don't follow certain religious rules, and don't contribute money to a specific religion, God will punish you, and you will burn in the fire of hell. Only the followers of this religion will go to heaven.

Are we not all sons and daughters of God? Will a father throw his children into fire because they belong to a different religious group?

Throughout history, more people died in religious wars than any other wars. The Spanish inquisition tortured and killed innocent people in the name of God. Suicide bombers kill themselves with innocent people in the name of God, and that, too, because of a hollow promise from their religious leaders that by doing so they will secure their place in heaven. Sadly, some of these people that serve God have also been abusing and molesting young children.

I respect and honor all religious people that truly believe in their religion as long as it is their free choice, and as long as they do not force it on others. We all have a free choice, and we can chose to be religious or not, and choose which religion is the right one for us. The point is that we are all different. If we were all the same like clones of each other, the world would be a very boring place, and we would not be able to function. The beauty of life is that each one of us is unique. We have to honor and respect each other and all the different choices we make, and most importantly, we should not harm each other physically, mentally, or emotionally just because of a different choice someone made in their life. Most religious people, like priests, rabbis and others who serve God and the communities, do believe in the mission of bringing love, help, and prosperity to their followers.

Finally, I would like to say that I believe that there is only one God for all of us. And this God is pure, unconditional, and unlimited love. Love is the only reality to live by.

I love you.

Chapter 52

On My Own

After I came back from the failure of the Atlantis project, I heard about a treatment for people infected with HIV. Actually, it was not the treatment of HIV as such, but for those who had lipodystrophy syndrome, which involved treatment of the sunken face. As I have mentioned earlier, the side effects of some of the medications given to people infected with HIV can cause a change in fat distribution of the body. What happens is that the fat under the skin almost disappears from the face, upper and lower limbs, and the glutei region and accumulates in places like the abdomen and lower part of the back of the neck and chin.

There are other changes that can't be seen, such as high cholesterol and triglycerides, insulin resistance, high blood pressure and much more screwed stuff. As a matter of fact, no other disease or infection in history (well, except leprosy in old times) was associated with a stigma like that with HIV. In many countries, especially in Africa, people infected with HIV are beaten up and even killed. Their only crime is they were infected with the virus. They were isolated based on their physical appearance called lipodystrophy, which was like an HIV+ stamp: sunken cheeks, eyes and temples, hanging skin. Generally, an HIV patient looks very similar to a person suffering from malnutrition.

*

I had heard of a possible treatment. It was given in Tijuana Mexico, just across the border from San Diego. A synthetic polymer was injected as filler to the sunken area of face, and within minutes the HIV stamp was removed from the face. The treatment was approved in Europe, but not in the U.S. I went to see what it was all about and was very impressed. All they did was give small injections into the face, and behold, the face looked normal again. The major problem was that the treatment was very expensive, about $5,000 just to do the face. Some people had infections and other complications. Some were covered by insurance to treat lipodystrophy. Fortunately, new medications to treat HIV have fewer side effects, and in many cases, there was even a reversal of some symptoms of lipodystrophy.

One more things happened in San Diego. I met Glenn. Glenn was fifty years old and was infected with HIV by his partner who died from AIDS thirteen years ago. Glenn was fortunate because he did not need any treatment – his CD4 count and viral load were still good. Not many people are so lucky as to have such a good immune system to control the virus, making the progression of the infection slow. Some people are even resistant to the infection even after being exposed to the virus many times. Cases of immunity to HIV were first discovered in Kenya where some prostitutes were exposed to the virus many times and were still not infected. Later on, similar cases were seen again in Europe, especially in Northern Europe. After having seen so many cases of immunity, scientists managed to isolate a specific gene that prevented infection by the virus. I just hope that one day with gene therapy a vaccine and cure will be developed.

Glenn and I became very close friends. About a year later, when I went back to San Diego to visit him, we spent a week together and decided that I should move in to live with him. My relationship with Ettie had deteriorated to such an extent that we had no communication … well, except for occasional fights. Things were so bad that it was clear to me that we couldn't carry on like this, not without destroying everything good that we had and without affecting our children, whom we loved so much.

So one day I decided to leave. When I told my family about it, the children accepted my decision and told me that I was doing the right thing. Ettie did not object, but was very angry. In May 2005 I loaded my car and drove to San Diego. I met Glenn in Alabama and together we drove to California. While on our way we visited Sedona, a magical place in the red mountains of Arizona. I found it to be a very spiritual center for the new age movement. What I did not know at that time was that in the next few months I would be visiting those places again because Ori was moving to live there.

During the trip I discovered a different Glenn. He was not the same Glenn I'd met earlier, or perhaps I was the one who had changed. Glenn lived about thirty minutes north of San Diego. During part of the week he was out of town for his work. When he was at home, he refused to meet other people, except his family,

I, on the other end, liked being with people. I had never felt so lonely. It was like total isolation from society. Being alone, far from the city, with no friends, and with nothing to do in my profession … all had a terrible effect on me. It pushed me back into severe depression.

After nine months of trying to cope with this new environment, I could not take it anymore and decided to return to Florida on the way to South Africa. In Johannesburg I lived with Ran. He had become a successful businessman. The big part that he played in building GSM, the cellular phone company that we were partners in, exposed him to the business community. After GSM he opened a new company with some partners, and within a short period of time, he turned it into a large and successful organization. At the age of twenty-six he was already a brilliant businessman, dealing with the South African government and the community. He had again proven to be a genius at marketing. The strange thing, though not so strange for me, was that his motive was never financial gain, but rather the challenge, the love to improve and build. His partners, friends, and employees knew that every assignment he took on himself would be done in the best possible way, and he would always help and support them with good advice, financial assistance, or any other help. His employees loved him. He knew everyone, including their family, but at the same time they were afraid of him, as they knew that he would demand from them what he demanded from himself. And that would be: do things the best way and with no compromise.

If one were to ask me what was the only right thing Ettie and I had done? I would say, and I feel Ettie would agree, raising three incredible children, Ravit, Ran, and Ori, that we love and are proud of. There is no bigger satisfaction to us as parents and as humans.

*

One day Ran told me that he met a businessman. He was the most incredible man he had ever met. Hearing this from Ran made me very curious. I wanted to meet him, too. At the beginning Ran refused to give me his name or any contact information, because he kept all his business contacts confidential. After a long discussion, he agreed to give me the person's phone number. I tried many times to contact him and left a message for him to call me. Then one day John did call me. I introduced myself as Ran's father and told him that Ran said very nice things about him, and I would like to meet someone who, according to my son, was the most incredible person he had ever met. John sounded very friendly and nice. He invited me to have lunch with him the next day and asked if there was any food that I did not like or was allergic to. After my conversation with John, I felt a strong urge to convey a message to him from a deceased woman. I did not understand the message, so I wrote some things down on a small piece of paper to show to him the next time I'd see him.

The next day I had lunch with John. He lived in a beautiful house. Everything in his house was tasteful and classy. He was a man in his sixties, pleasant and friendly, a very successful businessman and very good chef. He had prepared lunch that deserved to be served in a ten-star restaurant. I consider myself to be a good cook, but when I ate the food that John had prepared, it was more delicate and tasteful than anything I had eaten before. How about hot corn soup topped with saffron ice cream served in a small dish supposed to be eaten with a very small spoon? Sounds strange, but it was awesome.

During lunch, we had a nice conversation. Afterwards, I apologized, telling him that I was not completely crazy, though some people thought that I was screwed beyond repair and I have a message for him. He was anxious to hear the message. I first described the lady who gave me the message, and, to my surprise, John's immediate reaction was, "This is my late mother."

I finally gave him the paper with the message, and told him that I did not understand it. John did. He knew what it was all about. He became very emotional. When he calmed down a bit, he told me his life's story so I could understand what the message was about. When I left John, I agreed with Ran. He was indeed an incredible man. And this meeting with John was like a ray of light in the darkness of the depression that I was falling into.

Chapter 53

Depression

After coming back to the U.S, things went downhill for me. We lost most of our money in the textile business we had opened in Miami. As a result, we had to sell our house. There seemed no hope in the immediate future and we faced financial insecurity. In my personal life, things were even worse: after thirty-five years of marriage, Ettie and I got divorced. After a rather disappointing attempt to move to San Diego and the outcome of the Arab princess's cancer treatment in London, I was getting weak. All these misfortunes pushed me over the cliff, and I found myself in a state of deep depression. I was falling, falling deep into this deep black hole, hopeless, with no place to escape. The depression had veiled my vision of the future, and all I saw was the sad dark present to live in. It is known that the higher your IQ is, the higher are your chances of suffering from depression. Was it the IQ? Was it my mother's genes or just a way to escape from reality? I wish I knew the reason.

At that time, all I knew was the feeling of hopelessness. I was praying every night not to wake up in the morning: waking up would mean facing yet another day of darkness. The problem with depression is that there is a sense that nothing good is coming, not today, nor tomorrow, and, probably never. I remember when my mother was depressed, I tried as much as I could to help her, but I could not. I had the feeling that if she wanted to improve and help herself, she could come out of it. Here was I, her son, facing the same situation, unable to get out of it.

My children expected me to do something about it. I remember expecting the same from my mother. I was paralyzed by the depression. As a physician, as a person, and mostly as a patient, I can assure you that depression is the worst disease to fight. It affects every cell and system in us, and no matter whoever you are, the results can be disastrous. When you are physically ill and in pain, you know what is wrong. You can take medication to ease the pain. While in depression, you don't know the reason for it, and most medications will help very little or won't help at all.

It is a well-known fact that about 40 percent of Western society suffers from depression to a varying degree. We do not know what the cause of depression is. The theories of chemical imbalance in the brain have never been proved. The levels of serotonin and norepinephrine as neuron transmitters believed to be one of the reasons of depression were never proved. Most treatments are based on trial and error. Latest research shows that there is no big difference in treating depression with antidepressants or by placebo. It is true that depression hurts. The emotional pain is so strong that it becomes physical, but no medication can control this pain. The pain, the dark hopelessness, and the inability to function and control your life make you sick. You can be surrounded by family and friends that love you and try to help, yet still feel so lonely.

Every Thursday night there was a meditation at Terry's house. There used to be an open meditation followed by discussions, usually about the book *A Course in Miracles*. At the end of the evening there was another meditation. I forced myself to get out of the house and attend that meeting. By the end of the evening, Terry announced that on the weekend he would be giving a seminar. The topic of the seminar was: "It is all in the mind." Terry told us that he would be teaching how to resolve any physical or emotional problem by using our mind in the proper way.

I had nothing to lose, so I decided to attend the seminar, and it turned out to be a very enjoyable, interesting, and informative event. We had a lot of meditation sessions and relaxations, and Terry showed us how in the state of deep relaxation we can reprogram our mind and change negative patterns of behavior, addictions, and any physical condition to create the state of well-being and happiness. There was nothing new to me in the seminar. This is what I had been telling my patients for many years. The saying "You teach what you have to learn" was true.

Then came the Sunday evening. I was lying on the sofa when Ran came home. He asked me how the seminar went. I told him that it went very well.

"So, what did you get out of it?" he asked.

" I got out of the depression," I answered.

"When?" he asked with a surprise.

"This minute."

I fell asleep feeling such a relief. The nightmare was over. I was healthy again. In the morning I woke up to a beautiful African morning. The sun was shining and so was I. I was happy, full of energy, knowing that all was going to be all right.

So by now, all of you know that I am screwed, and was it, perhaps, the reason how in minutes, I turned depression into happiness? It was like turning a switch or pressing a certain button inside, with no medication at all.

So, where did the theory of all the chemical imbalances in the brain that trigger depression go? If they are imbalanced and out of control, how can one balance it in a minute? Does that imply that depression is only a state of mind, a deep dark place for anyone to avoid? A place where there is no love or happiness? I can't answer all these questions. What happened to me seemed like a lesson to teach me that, like any other healing, it would have to come from inside. It was a very painful and cruel lesson and I certainly do not want to repeat it ever again. What I still do not understand is how somebody with so much experience and medical knowledge can sink so deep, lose control and not find a way to get out of it.

Since coming out of depression, many things happened. I would not say everything got better, but yes, something indeed happened. In 2006, Ettie and I legally divorced. After the separation, Ettie moved to Ohio. Since the separation, we have become really good friends. There were no more fights or arguments, as the children rightly observed. It took our divorce to become good friends. During that year our children, Ettie, and I met in Sedona, Arizona for a family vacation. We had a wonderful week visiting Arizona, the Grand Canyon and Las Vegas.

The thing that I still do not understand is when people get married, they are joined – supposedly – "till death do they part." But why don't they stay married only as long as both are happy, and separate when one or both of them are not happy in the relationship any more? Such separation could eliminate the suffering, fights, and arguments that may destroy all the good and love they have been sharing. The children will be happier realizing their parents are good friends rather than witnessing daily fights and arguments between an unhappy couple.

*

By the end of that wonderful week, Ettie returned to Ohio and Ran to Johannesburg. Ori stayed in Sedona, while Ravit and I returned to Florida. It was time to start a new chapter in my life. During our marriage we always had large, spacious homes. This time, the children and my friends convinced me to move to a condo. I decided rented a condo in a nice neighborhood.

For the first time in my life I had my own place. As a child I lived with my parents; when I was a student I shared an apartment with other students; when I got married, we lived as a family in different houses in different countries. Now I was on my own. I could furnish the place and decorate it according to my own taste.

It was very strange to come home to an empty house, to wake up in the morning when no one was around. I was sure that it would take time to adjust, and I was sure that one day I would find the right partner to share my life with. It was so easy to make new friends when the children were young. Even when we moved to another country, we made friends easily with other children's parents, neighbors, and people we met at work. All had changed now. The children were gone. I was not working as I used to. The Internet had become the main source to date and meet people.

I visited many social groups and met many lonely people. Most of them complained about being lonely, but they were not ready to take any action.

Instead of going out, they usually stayed home feeling sorry for themselves. The fact that I am infected with HIV made it even more difficult. The stigma and fear of HIV would cease the potential of future relationships. As a result, I decided not to tell anybody about my HIV status unless it was necessary. I am sure that many of my friends and associates will find out about it for the first time in this book.

One of my friends told me that as a resident of Florida, with no income or insurance, I could get medication for HIV from the county where I lived. I applied for assistance from the Ryan White program, and was approved and referred to a clinic specializing in the treatment of HIV. After the initial blood test, I met for the first time the physician that would be my personal doctor. He was a young and very knowledgeable guy. He specialized in the treatments of HIV. I was impressed by his medical knowledge, his devotion, his open-mindedness, his friendliness and willingness to help. The entire staff of the clinic was very friendly, professional, and helpful to me and the rest of the patients. They provided free and highly qualified medical aid.

I would like to thank you, Care Resources of Fort Lauderdale, Dr. Robert Heglar, and my case manager Jean Alexandre. You have made a big difference in your patients' lives. I pray and wish that similar facilities and help are available to the millions of people who are infected with HIV and cannot get treatments and/or medication.

Chapter 54

A Message from a Dove

D olphins have always fascinated me. According to many studies, dolphins have strong healing powers, especially for children with neurological defects, brain damage, and mobility problems. It was the reason why I named the machine that we had developed for treating cancer patients the Dolphin, utilizing the principle in our treatments that is very similar to the sound waves transmitted by dolphins. I've been so fascinated by dolphins that I've always wanted to swim and play with them.

One weekend I was pleasantly surprised when my friend Steve told me that we would be going to the Florida Keys to swim with the dolphins. I was really excited. On our way, we stopped at one of the Florida Keys to see an old boat that was in the movie *The African Queen*. I carried a digital camera due to my love for photography. There we were, standing by the boat, and I was taking pictures.

I love the ocean. I love feeling the salty breeze on my face. As I was taking pictures, a white dove appeared in front of me on the boat. The bird was pure white and beautiful with black sparkling eyes. I was able to get very close to her, and she seemed to be posing for me. A young couple standing next to us, said, "Look, she is posing for you." Steve told me that the dove was giving me a message. "Did you get the message?" he asked. When I looked in the black beautiful eyes of the dove, I saw a tiny spot of light in the middle. For some reason, the first thing that came into my mind was that there is a light at the end of the tunnel. So, was this the message the dove had delivered to me? Deep down inside my heart, I knew that it was.

After the message from the dove, we continued our journey through the Florida Keys to swim with the dolphins. When we got to Dolphin Cove in sunny Key Largo, it was a beautiful Florida winter day – the best season in Florida. The temperature was perfect. The sun was shining. The sky was so blue. Tropical trees, flowers, and shrubs surrounded us. The ocean was very calm, and the natural lagoon open to the Florida Bay provided the natural habitat to the bottlenose dolphins and other marine animals. The trainer gave us instructions of what to do and not to do while swimming with the dolphins. The water was chilly, but the adrenaline rush compensated for the cold. There were only six of us in the group. We swam and played with the dolphins. I hugged, kissed and got kissed by these incredible creatures.

There were two female dolphins with us in the pool. It was really an unforgettable experience. The beauty, the incredible strength and energy radiating from those mammals, could not be described. After getting out of the pool, the dolphin that I hugged and kissed came to the side of the pool, so I could touch her again. It felt that we had made a connection. The trainer almost had to drag me out of the water because I couldn't say goodbye to my new friend. On the way back, Steve told me that he had never seen my eyes so shiny and full of joy than during my swim with the dolphins. The video and pictures that were taken on that day prove it.

While searching the Internet for dolphins, we found a group that was called The Dolphin Meditation. They met every Wednesday evening. I called Jimmy, the moderator of the group, and he sounded like a very nice man. He invited us to come and join the group. There, we met about six other people, members of the group. Jimmy introduced me to the others as Ammi – my nickname, which I had never revealed to him before. He talked about me as if he had known me for most of his life. All I had told him the night before was my first name. He said that I was "given a gift of incredible healing power" and included details about my past that were very accurate. He mentioned that I didn't need to touch a person to be healed. "All the healing could be done by the mind," he explained. "As soon as I start acting from my heart and not from my brain, this healing power would manifest even more so." He told me that by trying to find a logical and scientific explanation for my power, I was blocking it.

Here we go again. I wonder what gets into people who say such stuff about me, I thought. This guy barely knows me, and he is telling me what I've been told so many times before. I was absolutely stunned. Steve was convinced that during my telephone conversation with Jimmy I told him everything about myself because he was so accurate. Yet, the only thing I said the night before while talking to him on the phone was my full name, Amnon Goldstein. Prophesying about my powers, Jimmy told us that I was the chief healer in Atlantis. According to him, I was the one who told the leaders of Atlantis that unless spirituality would be advanced, the place would be extinguished.

James said that my healing powers were so strong that I could actually do things like grow limbs on people with no limbs, and then he said that the only thing blocking me was my analytical and scientific background. When James finished talking, it looked like Steve and I were the only two people in the room that were shocked and amazed. The rest of the group was not. Then Diego reached in his pocket and pulled out a crystal. He gave it to me and said that the crystal was with him for a long time. "I knew I had to give it to somebody. The minute I saw you," he smiled, "I knew it was you who should have it. As soon as you start acting from your heart you'll be able to change the world."

Wow! I mean, really, I, "the screwed one," had the world on my shoulders? This was all I needed to get screwed-up even more. As the evening progressed, we found out that Jimmy was channeling a dolphin called Sea Spray. When channeling, he went into a trance. His voice changed and he delivered messages to the people present in the room, as well as general messages. According to Jimmy, the dolphins were guides to all of us. At the end of the evening I was still undecided if these people were even more screwed than I was. The fact that Jimmy could tell so much about me without even having met me was astounding. For the next few months Steve and I attended the group meetings. We enjoyed them and learned much. For personal reasons, Jimmy stopped the meetings.

I remembered the day I was sitting with Dr. Ron having coffee when a strange man had approached us and told us that he knew us from Atlantis, where we were fixing heads. Was it déjà vu, or was there a hidden message?

Chapter 55

The Power of Crystals

In the spring of 2008, our good friends Bob and Helen had Ravit, Ori, and I over for dinner. Bob's mother had passed way recently, and he was renovating the house. After a delicious dinner Bob showed us the renovation work that had done on the house. He showed us crystal chandeliers that hung in their house for fifty-five years. While we were admiring their beauty, Bob said that is was about time to get rid of them. I was shocked. How could anybody get rid of such a beautiful chandelier? Immediately, I offered to buy it. Bob, however, did not want to sell, but said he would send it to me with Ori. As for me, I have always liked crystals.

Jimmy told me that my attraction to crystals originated in Atlantis, where the main power supply came from crystals. Without having the slightest idea what he meant, this sounded even more screwed than my being from Atlantis.

A few days later, Ori delivered the crystal chandelier to my place. As he took it out of his car, some of the crystals fell out of it. I asked Ori to put the chandelier in the veranda, because it was very dusty. I had planned to clean it first and then put it up in my house. Ori left the main piece in the veranda. The pieces of crystals that had broken off found their way to my coffee table. The next day, while talking to Ori and Ravit, I told them that I was not feeling well. As I was talking to them, I started feeling very tired and nauseous. I was unsure what was wrong. It was nothing major, just a general malaise. Ravit and Ori wished me well and good luck because the next day I had to go to immigration in order to get my American citizenship.

The next day, early morning, I went to Miami for my appointment with the immigration officials, testing my knowledge of American History and government. I wanted to avoid busy traffic, so I arrived about an hour early. I was sitting in my car in the parking lot listening to music and smoking with the windows of the car down. All of a sudden a torrential rain started. I closed my window and left my cell phone lying on the other seat because no cell phones are allowed inside a government building.

I entered the building all soaked and wet. The lady who interviewed me was not friendly at all. She tried the best she could to make me fail, but I passed the test anyway and was scheduled for a final appointment. As I got back to my car, I found that the car was flooded. I had not closed all the windows. My cell phone was soaking wet, and I couldn't even call my children to tell them about the interview as I had promised to do.

First, I put the cell phone on the dashboard to dry it out and left all the windows open to dry the inside of the car. As I entered the highway, the cell phone suddenly slipped out of the car window and was smashed by the car behind. With so much ominous stuff happening around me, all I wanted was to get home to lie down. When I made it home, I tried to open the door to my apartment, but could not. The reason being that I was trying to open the door to the wrong apartment in the wrong building. Finally, I was home and after calling the children, I crashed into my bed and was soon sound asleep.

In the morning, I still did not feel well, and I still had no idea what was going on. Since I had nothing better to do, I decided to do some cleaning, so I put the crystals that were on the coffee table out on the veranda with the chandelier. I did some housecleaning, had something to eat, and when my kids called to ask how I was feeling, I realized that I actually felt very well.

In the evening, Steve and I were sitting outside in the veranda having coffee and a cigarette. I was feeling fine. All the nausea and the general malaise were gone. When I looked outside, I realized that one of the trees in front of the veranda had turned yellow. I jokingly told Steve, "I think that the tree is a bit confused. Instead of being green in springtime, he looks like a tree in the fall." Steve agreed.

A few days later, I decided to disassemble the chandelier and soak the crystals in salty water to clean them. They say crystals should be soaked in salt water for a few days in order to clean them from negative energy. Two days later, when Steve and I were again sitting in the veranda, we noticed that the tree that turned yellow had become green again. I also remembered that earlier when it had gone all "goofy and confused," the chandelier was pointing towards the tree. Once I removed the crystals, the tree fully recovered. To be quite honest with you, if I had not seen it all happening with my own eyes I would not have believed it. It is strange how much energy the crystals can store. The crystal chandelier had been hanging at Bob's place for over fifty-five years. It had witnessed both of his parents' illnesses and death, Bob's divorce, his head injury, and so on. It had not been a happy home for years. I hope that with the crystals gone Bob and Helen would be much happier in their home.

Chapter 56

AG18

My friend Steve called me all excited one day about a new product, an instant facelift cream, that, according to the advertising, brings immediate results. I decided to give it a try and ordered this miracle online. Steve's face was very wrinkled and his skin was thick and sun damaged. He really was an ideal model for it and I was quite anxious to see what results we would get. When the cream arrived, I covered half of his face with it and within three minutes ... nothing happened. There were absolutely no changes. The right and left parts of his face looked identical. Not only did it not do what it was supposed to do, but when I looked at the ingredients, I was convinced that it could damage the skin if it was used often. It was a good experience because it gave me an idea to invent my own product that would have a facelift effect without causing damage to the skin. I started the research and made a few different formulas to find out if it was really possible to create something of the sort.

After two years of work, I came up with the formula that I called AG18. Steve and I decided to have some fun with it and went to a big shopping mall. We approached a salesman that was working in one of the kiosks. He was selling beauty products. When we asked him if he had any products that gave an instant facelift, he said yes. The next thing we asked him was if we could try it on Steve's face. He agreed. We immediately applied the cream on half of Steve's face, and as expected, we did not see much of a change. After having tested his product, I put my cream on the other half of Steve's face, and guess what happened? Within less than two minutes the wrinkles and lines on Steve's face disappeared. He really looked about twenty years younger – on one half of his face. It was more of a miracle for the salesman. He got so excited that he called people around to come and see the miracle. Before we knew it, we were surrounded by a crowd of people. Everyone wanted to purchase it. When I explained to them that it was not for sale yet, they became very upset. Everyone wants to be part of the success story.

The following Wednesday we decided to take the cream with us to the Dolphin Meditation Group to get the opinion of the two of the ladies there who worked as makeup artists at Neiman Marcus. Their reaction was the same as the standing ovation we received at the mall. They told me that it was the best face-lifting cream on the market. When I compared it to other products on the market, I did not find any that gave the same effect and improved skin texture as well. The best part was that the more you use this cream, the smoother and nicer your skin will become.

After an extensive search, I found a reliable and professional cosmetic manufacturer in Florida that is producing AG18 cream for me, which is now being successfully marketed. My customers, both men and women, find that it not only gives them more confidence to face the world. but also improves the quality of their skin.

Chapter 57

❦

The Overweight Epidemic

I magine a situation where an epidemic strikes the world and 30 percent of the Western world goes from healthy to being sick. From what I see, after that epidemic strikes, every country would go into a state of national alert, and I am talking like World War-type of an alert. The first thing I am sure of would be that all medical services would operate in top emergency mode. Scientists and researchers would work day and night to find a solution to treat and cure the disease. To avoid the spread of the disease, schools and universities would close down and so would other work places. The media would report about the situation every few minutes. All in all, it would be a state of panic and despair. To add to the efforts, billions of dollars would be reallocated from less important trivia like wars, space research, and, probably, even from security and education.

All the money would be used to fight the epidemic. If the epidemic were airborne, most of the countries would close their borders, airports and other means of transportation. People would not even talk on the phone anymore for the fear of getting infected. Public places would be closed down, just like during SARS, Bird Flu, and Swine flu. The economic and social effects would be felt for many years to come. The main effort would be to find treatments, a cure, and to educate the public, especially children, on how to behave, what to do and what not to do.

Thanks God, nothing of the sort has occurred, and hopefully it will never happen. There are no viruses or bacteria spreading around the world. Our food is not contaminated with lethal microorganisms – only with pesticides, hormones, and other toxic materials – and most of the time our food tastes pretty good. We all enjoy eating it and a lot of it. We like to eat food that is high in calories, fat, and sugar.

The epidemic that I am talking about has in reality already infected about 40 to 50 percent of the Western world. The best news is that it is not an infectious disease. The worst part is that not much is being done about it. The world is still the same, although the media is paying some – but not nearly enough – attention to it. There is yet to be declared a national or global emergency.

The epidemic I am talking about is the overweight and obesity epidemic. It is affecting children, adults, babies, and seniors. As I said, about 50 percent of our population is affected. The thing is, people are not dying on the streets, and many of them will develop "symptoms" only later in their lives. There will be symptoms such as high blood pressure, diabetes type II, cardiovascular diseases, arthritis, liver and kidney diseases, respiratory problems, and many more. As the years go by, the epidemic is spreading and affecting a larger part of the population.

Food has become a major part of entertainment. Almost every happy occasion, as well as even the unhappy ones, involves consuming food. When children behave, they are given candy. We are being brainwashed daily by all kinds of food scams. In fact, the major cause of diseases and death in the Western society is improper nutrition, and in the underdeveloped world, undernourishment and starvation.

Progress in technology and transportation has reduced the amount of physical activity we all do. Factors such as getting away from the nature, pollution, and chemicals affect the food we eat and its nutritional value. Every physician will tell you that a proper diet is a balanced diet, but I wonder how many will tell you what a balanced diet is.

I would like to say that I am not judging or criticizing, only bringing the facts the way I see them. We all know something very drastic has to be done to control this epidemic, and it has to be done very soon. In the last few years, steps have been taken in the right direction. Manufacturers of food have to list ingredients and calories; restaurants have to present the number of calories of different dishes on the menu. It's true that some positive steps have been taken – certain drinks and foods are not allowed to be sold in schools, and people have become more aware of the dangers of being overweight. To my regret, the epidemic has affected many families, including my own daughter.

When Ravit was born, she weighted about four pounds. At that time, she was considered an underweight baby and was put in an incubator for a few days. When she was about a year old, she started attending kindergarten for children of working parents. In the kindergarten, the young children received professional care, including the meals. But as soon as Ravit returned home, her mother, and especially her grandmothers, would feed her again, just in case she did not get enough food in the kindergarten. At the age of two, Ravit was a very happy, beautiful, and overweight baby. Each year her weight would escalate. In 2003, when Ravit was thirty-two years old; her weight was 370 pounds. She had a condition called *morbid obesity*, along with many of the symptoms that went with it. She suffered from type II diabetes, joint pain and hypothyroidism. She had a problem breathing, especially during sleep; and on top of it she suffered from severe depression, a serious disease in itself. She also faced many other problems, like discrimination in the workplace because of her weight, social isolation, and worst of all, the inability to find a mate and partner.

Ravit belongs to the 50 percent of the population that is overweight to one degree or another. The main reason is an addiction to overeating. As one of my professors in med school said, "There is no being overweight without overeating." This is the real problem. About half of the population of the Western civilization is addicted to food. "Which restaurant did you go to last night? How was the food? The food was to die for" and so on and so forth. The standard for having a good time very often is synonymous with having good food. Popcorn, cotton candy and sodas have become major attributes of the American pastime that is spreading around the world.

Can you imagine going to the movies or circus, attending county fairs or kids' birthday parties in the parks without anyone of those "irreplaceable items?" Even countries that guard and protect their customs and language, like France, for example, are adopting American terminology and enlarging their vocabulary by adopting terms like "le popcorn" versus standard French "le maïs," "le Big Mac," "le McDo's," "le cheeseburger", etc. In less than a decade, 40 percent of all French are obese or overweight. The problem that exists in France, in the U.S., or elsewhere, is that help is very limited compared to other addictions like alcohol or drugs.

Back to Ravit. During her school years, she was on almost every diet imaginable. It was obvious that the only diet that she liked was the "see food" diet: You see food, and you eat. Or, if you don't see it, you look for it and then eat it. We all knew that something had to be done about it, and very soon, or else things would get out of hand.

Ravit met a mother and daughter who had a gastric bypass. They both lost a substantial amount of weight and became Ravit's good friends. Seeing the changes that had happened to them, she decided to have the surgery done by the same surgeon who operated on her friends. Being a surgeon myself, I joined Ravit for a consultation with the surgeon in Miami. I was rather impressed by him. He was very young, but reliable and already experienced in this field of Bariatric Surgery.

Bariatric surgery is a relatively new field in surgery and it is growing as quickly as the epidemic of obesity is. Many of the people that we met during our meeting with him were young, including teenagers. The two main surgical procedures in bariatric surgery are the gastric bypass and the adjustable gastric band. The new kid on the block is the gastric sleeve. They are one of the most frequently performed procedures for morbid obesity in the U.S. The gastric bypass uses both a restrictive and a malabsorptive surgery techniques; in other words, it restricts food intake and the amount of calories and nutrients that the body absorbs. In addition to creating a smaller stomach pouch, the surgery changes the body's normal digestive process. As a result, food bypasses a large part of the stomach and a part of the small intestine.

The lap band procedure does not require stomach cutting or stapling, or re-routing of the gastrointestinal tract to bypass normal digestion. The procedure involves implanting a silicone ring containing an inflatable cuff, known as a gastric band, around the upper portion of the stomach during a minimally invasive surgical procedure. Once the band is in place it can be adjusted to restrict the amount of food a patient can eat.

The adjustable gastric band is used to create a smaller stomach pouch that can hold only a small amount of food, reducing the stomach's food storage area. The band also controls the amount of food that can pass from the newly created, smaller upper stomach pouch to the lower part of the stomach. The smaller the stomach, the quicker people feel full, and the slower food moves between the upper and lower portions of the stomach during digestion. As a result of this, people feel less hungry, eat less, and lose weight.

The biggest advantage is that it does not change the anatomy of the digestive system permanently. According to the needs of the patient, the tightness of the band can be adjusted easily by taking out or adding fluids to the band. Both of the procedures could be done today using laparoscopy techniques and with only small incisions into the abdomen. The best part is a speedy recovery and fewer complications. The bad part is the price for each procedure – $20,000.

As a surgeon and a father, I did not like the gastric bypass, which, in fact, was a very long and mutilating procedure that cannot be reversed. Also, the chances of complications are much higher. In many cases, the anastomosis between this new stomach and the intestine will get bigger. It will dilate, leaving no more restriction for the passage of large amounts of food.

I was restless after learning about the procedures. To know more, I contacted a surgeon in Israel. In my opinion, he was (and still is) one of the best and most experienced bariatric surgeons in the world. According to him, about 60 percent of the people who have had gastric bypass stop losing weight within a year. Since the procedure did not help the patients much, he stopped performing that operation. The only operation that he recommended was the adjustable gastric band. He told me it takes him about fifteen minutes to perform the surgery, and it was fairly uncomplicated.

Like her stubborn father, Ravit wouldn't listen. She said that unless she can have the same operation that her friends did, she would do nothing (as if having an operation was fashionable). We did not have any choice but to agree to the gastric bypass, chiefly because the alternative of doing nothing was much worse.

Ravit's friends had the surgery paid for by the health insurance company. Ravit, too, applied to her insurance company to pay for the operation and submitted all the necessary medical documents. And guess what? She was refused and was told that the insurance company had changed their policy and operations like this would not be covered. This led to a rather screwed-up situation. Those insurance companies were ready to pay for years of complication and health problems resulting from morbid obesity, which would be many times more expensive than paying for the operation.

Ravit filed an appeal, and after getting medical documents from a cardiologist, psychiatrist, her personal physician, and her endocrinologist, we appeared before the committee. They denied her the operation. The bureaucrats working for the insurance company had made their decision, and without any medical quantification they still had a legal right to decide what was good or bad for the patient.

In desperation, Ravit approached the local Channel 6 News and asked for help. They sent a crew to interview her, and took many pictures of her wearing a bathing suit and other people in similar condition. Before the program was aired, they asked the insurance company to provide their comments, but they refused. Finally, it was on the air, but did not help either.

Many desperate patients who needed surgery were traveling to other countries where the cost was only about a quarter of the cost in the U.S. While we were exploring other possibilities, Ravit received a call from the surgeon's office. She was invited for a meeting with the surgeon. To her surprise, when she arrived there, her brother Ori was waiting for her and presented her with a card attached to balloons. The card was from her brother Ran wishing her a Happy Birthday and had a gift voucher for a gastric bypass surgery. Ravit was happy beyond any limits. The historical day of her surgery was scheduled for October 28, 2003, which also happened to be Ravit's birthday. Little did she know that it was not the end of the battle.

All these years as a surgeon, I had never seen anybody going for major surgery in such a happy mood as Ravit. She did not have the usual fear that people going under the knife had. She was really, really happy. We, on the other hand, felt rather nervous and tense. Ettie, Ori, and I were in the waiting room next to the operating room in the Miami hospital while Ravit was undergoing the gastric bypass. We were sitting there all tense, when we received a call – it was Ran. He had arrived from Johannesburg to be at his sister's side when she woke up after surgery.

Ran's arrival indeed eased a bit of the tension, but, being a parent, there was really nothing that could have helped me with my worries until I saw Ravit happy and comfortable after the surgery. I knew the operation should take about two hours, but even after two hours had passed, we did not hear anything from the surgeon. Then came back the "screwed" thoughts of a doctor. I started thinking about all the things that could go wrong with the surgery and the anesthesia, especially when the patient was so overweight.

When I performed an operation, if the surgery stretched longer than planned, I made sure that a nurse informed the family about the progress of the operation and the condition of their relative. I was expecting the same from the surgeon operating on my daughter, especially since we were in a private hospital and had a private surgeon. He did not do so.

It was about four hours later when the surgeon came to inform us that all had gone well, and Ravit was doing fine in the recovery room. It was indeed a great relief! A day later Ravit was discharged from the hospital after the surgeon came to see her briefly. Frankly, I was very disappointed by his post-operative care. It is not all about preparing the patient for the surgery and actually doing it – a healer keeps caring even after the surgery.

One day after the surgery Ravit and I went for a short walk near our house. I was really amazed by her speedy recovery after such a serious procedure. I was a surgeon for more than twenty years – this laparoscopic technique was like science fiction. During my years as a surgeon patients used to stay in the hospital for seven to ten days, connected for a few days to tubes and IV lines.

Modern surgery has become so advanced and has made life so much easier for patients. Look at Ravit! After the operation she was not only able to walk well, but also eat, although only in very small portions, mainly consisting of concentrated proteins and some supplements. Finally, the surgery started showing its effects and within the first three months she lost thirty pounds. With her weight going down, the diabetes that she suffered from disappeared and so did the joint pain and the breathing problems. Her depression gave way to hope. My daughter started seeing the light at the end of the tunnel, a long stretch covering some thirty human years, from the age of two to the age of thirty-two.

Over the next three months Ravit shed another thirty pounds and then suddenly the weight loss stopped. During all that time she was going for follow-up visits to the surgeon who had operated on her. To my surprise, except for the day after the operation when he had only spent five minutes with her, the surgeon who had performed the operation never saw Ravit. During all of her visits to the surgeon's office she was seen by the physician's assistant or a nurse. I did not expect anything like this from any surgeon, especially not from someone who had charged us $20,000. I called the surgeon's office to let him know what I thought of it. It was only after I presented myself as a physician, that the surgeon agreed to talk to me.

I told him that in my opinion, the anastomosis between the new stomach and the intestine had been dilated. After hearing from me, he promised that he would see Ravit himself during her next visit. He also said that if this was the case, and if the anastomosis was too big, then there was nothing much that could be done about it. He did not see Ravit during her next visit or any other time.

To my sorrow, what I was afraid of had happened. Ravit did not lose any more weight – the happiness and hopes that had followed the operation were replaced by depression. This desperation and depression made her lose all hope. She accepted the fact that she would be overweight for the rest of her life, and there was nothing that she could do about it. The only good thing that had happened after this operation was that Ravit did not gain any more weight, and all the symptoms that she had due to her obesity disappeared.

In 2006 I decided to move in with Ravit for a while. During all this time, I did not give up on finding a solution for her weight problem. I hoped that by living with her I would be able to convince her to have another operation, the one with the adjustable gastric band.

Since her operation, Ravit was seeing a psychologist. The doctor's name was Sandy, and she was a very nice lady. She had helped Ravit a lot. Sandy managed to convince Ravit to have the operation. This time I took no chances. I knew exactly who would be the surgeon operating on Ravit. I knew him personally. He was from Beer Sheba, Israel. I talked with him on the phone several times, and then we decided to do the operation at the end of April 2007. The price of the operation in Israel was $5,000, which was a steal compared to $20,000 in the United States. The price was not the main reason for choosing to do the operation in Israel. I knew that this surgeon was one of the best and most experienced bariatric surgeons in the world.

In April 2007 the whole family went to Israel. It was a nice family reunion. Before the operation, Ravit met the surgeon himself and not one of his assistants. He took the time to explain the operation, the risks and benefits, the postoperative care, as well as proper nutrition. The best thing was that he answered all the questions that Ravit had. On the morning of the operation the surgeon came to see Ravit and informed her that she would be the third person on the list for that day, and made sure that she was ready for the surgery.

Unlike in the U.S., the operation lasted less than thirty minutes. As soon as he left the operating room the surgeon came outside and informed us that all had gone well and Ravit would be back in the ward as soon as she woke up. The next morning, after the surgeon visited Ravit (again!), she was discharged home to be seen again in three days to remove the stitches.

The recovery from the procedure was very fast. Three days after the operation the stitches were removed by the surgeon himself, and Ravit had a chance to meet other people who had the same surgery in the past so she could see and compare results.

The first filling of the band was supposed to take place a month later, so the surgeon invited me to the clinic to see and learn how to fill the band and change the amount of fluid in the band if needed. Good things followed the operation. Immediately after the operation, without even filling the band, Ravit started losing weight again. As a result, everybody was happy and we had a chance to spend two wonderful weeks with the family in Israel before we returned to Florida.

It was really a wonderful experience. The surgeon and his team had done everything possible to give the best service, support, and guidance. After a great time in Israel we happily returned to Ravit's new condo in Florida. A few days after our return I told her that my mission was accomplished. After all, I had managed to make things better for my dear daughter....

After this operation, Ravit lost more than a hundred pounds but a new problem arose. After having lost more than 50 percent of her body weight, Ravit was left with hanging skin folds in the abdomen, back, breast, arms, thighs, and buttocks. Some things just don't get better that easily. To remove the excess skin, it required long and costly plastic surgery. Again the price was $20,000. Ran, the savior, again came to her rescue and gave his sister a special birthday present – the amount needed for the plastic surgery.

On October 28th, 2008, on Ravit's 37th birthday, another surgery took place. Once again she moved to the operating room like she was going to a party, all happy and smiling. This girl never took surgery very seriously, I suppose. This time it was a seven hour long operation. And guess what? As we were sitting in the waiting room, Ran arrived from South Africa, yet again, to be at his sister's side. Every time a member of my family showed this kind of love for one another, it made me proud of Ettie and myself for raising such wonderful children.

At the end of the operation the surgeon came out and told us that Ravit was doing fine. The surgery went as planned, and he removed about twenty-one pounds of excess skin and fat from Ravit's body.

This time things were not as easy as the last time. The recovery from this surgery was very long and painful. The infection that she developed during the operation on one of her breasts had to be treated for a few months, and that included many treatments in a hyperbaric chamber.

Some scars as a result of the infection would require more surgery in the future. But no matter what had happened, Ravit looked stunning. She had gone from a big fat lady weighing 370 pounds to a 180-pound beautiful, attractive, happy, and optimistic young lady. She was always smiling and cheerful, and if one looked closely, one could see a new spark in her eyes.

Even now, she carries a picture of her the way she looked when she weighed about 370 pounds. It serves as a reminder for her (and to show off as well).

Finally, the long nightmare had come to an end. She was ready to start a new chapter in her life. In April 2010, Ravit had another plastic surgery, mainly to fix the scars on the breast. This time she developed an infection again. A few weeks after the surgery we flew to Israel to celebrate my niece's wedding. It was a wonderful and happy family reunion. Unfortunately, two days before the wedding, Ravit was not feeling well. She had a high temperature and developed a red rash all over the abdomen and chest.

To me, who had seen so many infections of this sort, it was obvious that she had developed a severe postsurgical infection. I took her to see a friend who was head of one of the surgical departments. He suggested waiting and seeing what would develop, as he had not seen anything of that sort before. I objected and decided to start right away with broad-spectrum antibiotics. I contacted a friend from medical school. He was now a Professor of Dermatology. I described to him what was happening and he gave a diagnosis immediately over the phone. It was erysipelas, a superficial bacterial skin infection that characteristically extends into the skin lymphatic system, and streptococci are the primary cause of erysipelas. He agreed to go along with my treatment and suggested adding another antibiotic. Within two days the fever came down, and Ravit was able to attend the wedding happily and cheerfully.

Unfortunately, due to the economy in the United States, the college where Ravit had been teaching computer science closed down and she could not find another job in the U.S. She started to look for work in Johannesburg. Before she left for South Africa, she asked me to help her pack. She always carried a lot of stuff (but then, I suppose, all women do so). When I opened one of the bags, it was full of junk food and sweets.

She explained to me that it was for as emergency, in case there was a plane crash. I almost crashed myself hearing her reply.

When she was back in South Africa, Ravit was happy to meet her old friends. She told me that nobody could believe their eyes when they saw the new Ravit.

Though she had lost weight, Ravit's food addiction was not over. She still buys all kinds of junk food and stores it in her drawers. I wonder if she's saving it up for the apocalypse. If it weren't for the gastric band that prevented her from eating too much, she would have gained all the weight that she had lost.

Food addiction is one of the worst addictions there is. No one can avoid food – it will always be there. The thing about drugs and alcohol addictions are that one can avoid them totally. But no one can avoid food. The temptation is right in front of you all the time. It is my deepest hope that in the near future we will be able to find a solution and treatment for this epidemic, and then there would be no overweight people and no more suffering due to something as essential as food.

Chapter 58

My New Home

I t was 2009 – the so-called "Great Recession" had hit the United States and most parts of the world. It was the biggest recession since the Great Depression of the late 20's and early 30's. Was this a part of the bad things that we had to go through in order to get to the good? Only time could give an answer to this question.

The lease on the condo that I was renting was about to expire. Since I had always lived in big spacious houses (except when I was a child), I did not particularly like my condo, where people told me what to do with my property and charged money for it. One night Ravit was staying overnight at my place, and the next morning a sticker was glued to the windshield of her car saying that she needed a special permit to park her car overnight. Why do I need a permit from anyone, and why should anyone be telling me if my daughter or anybody else could spend the night at my place?

Due to the recession, and since real estate prices were dropping very quickly, I decided to look for a house to buy – and I did find a house. It was a nice property right on a golf course, a foreclosure. It was very run down and had severe water damage. Its floors looked like it was a minefield, but it was very spacious. Seeing such a challenge, my creative juices started to flow, and once again my wild imagination went into a high gear. This was going to be *my* house for the first time. I was free to do whatever I wanted to do with it. I could shape it in any possible way I wanted. The funny part was that the way I saw things was not the way others saw it. When Ravit and Ori came to see the place, Ravit started crying, and said that even her "screwed" father couldn't live in a place like this. Ori just kept quiet.

I didn't understand their disappointment. I had renovated quite a few houses in the past and they turned out very nice. I do have to admit that none of the other houses were in such bad condition as this one was. When my friend Steve saw the place, he said, "Well! At least the garage door works!" Yeah, right! As if that amount of sarcasm could have stopped me. My friends were absolutely sure that this time I was really losing it.

After long negotiations with the bank, I got the house for a good price. I knew renovating this house would keep me busy and out of trouble for a while. Ran helped me financially and I bought the house in December 2009. Renovating this house was a lot of hard work, but certainly a lot of fun. The house required full renovation. Everything had to be renewed from floors and ceilings to the bathrooms and the kitchen.

The best thing about this venture was that I did most of the work myself. It saved me a lot of money. I even designed my own furniture. The end results were stunning. The house looked beautiful. I had never received so many compliments in my life, not even when I saved people from death.

This is definitely the most beautiful house I have ever lived in. One of Mark's friends, who also happened to be a well-known interior designer, came to see my house when I had bought it. When he saw the house after I was done with it, he couldn't believe his eyes. He said, "If you are as good a physician as a house renovator and designer, then you are an excellent doctor." To hear this from him was a real compliment. I am very happy in my new home, hoping to share it and my life with a loved one.

Chapter 59

Healing Versus Treating

Each patient carries his own doctor inside him.

-Albert Schweitzer

In my forty years as a physician, and in different fields of medicine, I have treated thousands of patients. When I was a young doctor I believed that Western modern medicine could heal, cure, and help, or at least improve, the condition of most of my patients. What I knew at that time was just the tip of the iceberg. Today, after having practiced medicine and gained much experience, it has become clear to me that there is much more to the human body that we don't know than what we do know. When I say "human body," I do not mean only the physical body, but I refer to an integration of body, mind, and soul. I refer to an entity that functions in harmony and balance as one.

One of my friends used to say that medicine is the second most accurate science in the world – the first is the Bible. Modern Western medicine does not see a person as one complete unit, but as a combination of organs and systems. One physician would treat the heart, another treats lungs, digestive system, hands, feet, and so on.

A physician who has been trained and specialized in the hands, would not treat the knees or feet, either because he does not know how to treat other parts, or because his insurance carriers won't cover him if he treats things out of his specialty. Gone are the days of the family physician, someone who really knew the patient and his family. Today, a health physician treats mainly minor illnesses. He follows up with the patient, fills out the prescription and refers him to another specialist, when necessary. How many physicians today will have the time to sit with the patient, to take a full case history, to find out about the patient's lifestyle, his nutrition and his emotional and mental state?

Most physicians cannot do that today because they won't be able to earn enough income, or, perhaps, they won't be able to see as many patients as expected by their employer or healthcare provider. A great teacher of mine said that 90 percent of diagnosis could be done by just talking to and examining the patient. He also said that a good physician is the one who knows when not to give treatment, but lets the body heal itself.

Today this would be an unacceptable treatment! Patients expect physicians to prescribe medication for their medical problem. As a young surgeon I was told that unless I could see it in the operating field, it does not exist. My problem was that I never saw the human soul in the operating field. I never felt the feelings, the conscious, and many other factors of my patients. But does that mean they do not exist? What I did see in the operation field was a local injury or effect due to many other causes that required further investigation and treatments.

I learned that there are other forms of medicine, like Chinese medicine, which is called alternative medicine, primitive medicine, unacceptable forms of medicine, holistic medicine, integrative medicine, natural medicine and many more. So many different names and forms of medicine indicate one thing: that we are still looking for the proper form of medicine.

What I feel is that most other forms of medicine do see the human body, mind, and soul as one unit functioning in harmony with the surrounding nature and environment. Does that make them primitive, or are we practicing an incomplete form of medicine? Why do we even have to choose between one form of medicine or another, rather then take the best from each form and combine it to form a good medicine? Don't we all like to find the best way to help the sick and the needy? As healers, that's what we should be concerned about.

Western medicine has changed a lot in the past few years. Many things that used to be undoable have become reality. With the arrival of computers and new diagnostic methods, minimally invasive surgery and implantation of organs, the new forms of medications and treatments, the way we treat our patients has improved tremendously. We are achieving many improvements in the condition of patients resulting in better quality of life and extended lifespan. With the mapping of the genome, genetic engineering, stem cell research and many other discoveries, many new methods of treating and eliminating certain diseases have opened up for mankind. The future looks good and promising.

Many times, I asked physicians and scientists, how many diseases we can actually cure? I do not mean just a temporary symptomatic relief, but a total cure. The answer has always been the same: very few. Though it does not sound very encouraging, I don't see it as a failure of medicine but a step towards better medicine in the future.

We still know little about the human mind and its power to make us sick and to heal.

In my first year as a surgical resident, I entered a patient's room to prepare her for vascular surgery in order to restore circulation of blood to her leg. The patient was in her forties. She was in a good health and the operation was low-risk with good chances of a speedy recovery. The patient told me that she would die during this surgery. I saw it as natural fear of surgery and the unknown, and told her that everything was going to be okay. I really believed in what I was telling her. During the operation, there were unexpected complications and the patient died on the operating table.

I am sure that similar things have happened to many other surgeons as well.

Today, about forty years later, I still remember that case very clearly. Since then, whenever it was possible, I did not operate on patients who believed that he or she would die during the operation unless they changed their thinking and started believing that they would survive the surgery. This can be done with help from us, the physicians. We have to get to the stage where we treat a patient as a person and stop giving just symptomatic treatment. We should be healing, and not just treating symptoms.

I have been asked many times, "What is good treatment?" I believe that good treatment is treatment that helps the patient get better. It can be medical or spiritual help, such as praying, or anything else that offers help and hope. This help can be given by anyone: a physician, a friend, a rabbi or a priest, a child, or anybody else, as long as it improves the condition. *Not every physician is a healer and not every healer is a physician.*

One of the greatest teachers that humanity has ever known was Jesus Christ. Though I was born Jewish, and did not know much about the New Testament, I was well aware of the story of a lady lying sick on the floor believing that if she would touch Jesus she would be healed. When she touched Jesus and was healed, Jesus' followers saw it as a miracle, but Jesus told them that her belief had healed her, not him.

The main power to heal is the patient's will, the belief and readiness to be healed. We, the healers, can assist and advise, but every healing is self-healing. We are all energy, and so is the entire universe. We have to find a way to restore the uninterrupted flow of energy in our body, and by doing so we will heal.

For many years we have heard more and more about anti-aging medicine. New clinics have been opening all over, and many products are sold as anti-aging for billions of dollars. To my "screwed" mind, I see this term as very deceptive. Aging is a natural, normal part of life. The only way to avoid getting old is to die young. Everyone who is born will grow old and eventually die. We all would like to get old in dignity and health. We'd like to eliminate degenerative diseases, hormonal imbalance, aesthetic appearance, and other negative symptoms that have become part of aging. But we cannot stop the aging process, just like we cannot stop time.

CONCLUSION

Hope is itself a species of happiness, and perhaps the chief happiness, which this world affords.

-Samuel Johnson

Almost all books have a conclusion, but at the same time, a conclusion is also a new beginning. It is like a new quest both for you, who have followed *The Path of a Healer* until the very end, and for me, as well.

As I look back over the last two decades, it becomes very clear that our world and society are going through major changes. These changes are not limited to just one aspect of our life. They are everywhere. Most of the events that have happened lately seem to be of a negative and destructive nature. It looks as if everything around us is collapsing, as if everything is moving toward an end.

*

The great thing in the world is not so much where we stand, as in what direction we are moving.

--Oliver Wendell Holmes

*

The sad thing is that more and more people think it is not right to bring children into this world with such an abundance disasters, unhappiness, suffering, and uncertainties. Some are talking about Armageddon, the supposed end of the world. Some have even predicted that it will be at 11:00 a.m. on December 21st, 2012, the day the Mayan calendar will end.

In one of the chapters of this book, I have asked the question, "Do bad things happen for a good reason?" Well, from my experience, I'd say, "They do." When bad things happen, usually, we are unable to see what good can come of them. We want to have a reason for all our problems. But, sooner or later in our lives we come to understand the reason, the purpose, and the lesson to be learned.

As I'm writing this, two cards from the tarot deck come to my mind: "the death card" and "the tower card." Although I'm not a great believer in tarot cards predicting the future, I do believe that these two cards signify what we all are going through and what the outcome will be.

The Tower: Difficult Times

This card can indicate an event or period of time that could be challenging and difficult, but as it has happened often, one disaster leads to a new victory. When everything seems to be crumbling around us, it can be very difficult to believe that things can and will get better. Despite the destruction or collapse of certain aspects of our lives, these very events we curse now can often lead to brand new possibilities. The life lessons we learn from this turbulence help us to rethink and approach our lives with newfound wisdom. We learn not to make the same mistakes again. *The tower* represents something in our life that will challenge or has challenged us. It will be up to us to choose how to get over it and learn from the experience. Beware, the tower also serves as a warning that a certain choice or decision could lead to disaster.

*

It is not the strongest of the species that survive, nor the most intelligent, but the one most responsive to change.

--Charles Darwin

Death: New Beginnings

The death card does not represent a physical death. It is a card of experience, a transformation. It represents an event or series of events or circumstances that may cause great disruption and possibly upset us, but will ultimately lead to a transformation that changes our outlook and approach toward life and the world as it is. These events make us change our course and tactics, and eventually achieve great success.

There is a myth where a sacred firebird, after having lived for five hundred years, builds itself a nest in the branches of an oak that then ignites. From the ashes a new, young phoenix or phoenix egg arises, reborn to live again. To my mind, this myth gives the best, allegorical interpretation of the meaning of *the death* card: rebirth, immortality, and renewal. When something in our life comes to an end, the transformation may be painfully challenging, but from the ashes comes a new growth.

Let's take a brief look at the last decade of the twentieth century. The USSR collapsed and the Berlin Wall fell, symbolizing the end to the Cold War. Instead of building more nuclear weapons that could destroy the world with the push of a button, we witnessed the beginning of a dialogue to control the threat of nuclear proliferation. Many countries became independent. East and West Germany became reunited to become Germany, one of the leading economic powers in Europe. The European Union established in 1993 by the Treaty of Maastricht united twenty-seven European democratic nations to work together on economic, judicial, and security issues with a single market and a single European currency, the Euro.

When I see these positive changes, I feel that maybe it is the beginning of the unification of the entire world.

We see China turning almost overnight from a third-world country into the second largest economy in the world. It is only a matter of time before freedom prevails in China.

We witnessed catastrophic natural disasters and unusually high levels of seismic activity: earthquakes and tsunamis in southeast Asia, the devastating earthquake in Haiti, and volcano eruptions in Iceland that paralyzed air travel in most of the Europe. There is a lot of evidence of global climate change due to a number of factors, mainly greenhouse gas concentrations.

The climate change can account for abnormal temperatures, record-high temperatures in summer and record- low temperatures in winter.

We've had the worst oil spill in U.S. history in April 2010, as a result of the explosion at a BP offshore drilling rig where over 205 million gallons of oil were spilled into the Gulf of Mexico. It was the biggest ecological disaster this country has ever experienced. It's very clear to all of us that we can no longer carry on destroying our planet, our home. It's time to clean up the mess we have created. There's no time to be lost. It's up to us to make these changes and take steps to force politicians and lawmakers to accept the recent scientific discoveries that are utilizing alternative and environmentally friendly sources of energy, such as solar and light energy, wind and water power, and wave and geothermal energy. It's interesting that China today is leading the world in exploration for clean, efficient, and non-toxic sources of energy.

We are facing the biggest recession since the Great Depression. The global economy is no longer the problem of a single country, but the result of the interactions between the countries of the world. Consequently, a bill regulating financial institutions in the United States became a law.

I feel that the worst is probably not over yet. We are still undergoing major changes. It is probably true that only after we have hit the bottom, can we start climbing back up again.

In the field of medicine, we have witnessed major progress. Earlier, better, and more precise diagnoses of many diseases are the result of today's new diagnostic methods and very sophisticated equipment. New medications and treatment methods have improved people's lifespan and general quality of life. It seems that these days there's a lot more acceptance of different forms of healing and medicine. Alternative medicine is being integrated much more into mainstream medicine. However, the overuse of antibiotics has resulted in development of bacteria that are resistant to antibiotics, and the side effects of medications have made us look for new ways of treatments, in other words, less toxic and more natural.

The HIV/AIDS pandemic has claimed the lives of millions and is still doing so. Many forms of cancer are on the rise. On the brighter side, the immune system has become a major subject for research and understanding. It has laid the foundation for research of most diseases and their healing.

It has become quite obvious that we cannot separate the mind from the body. For the first time we actually see the reverse of the saying "Healthy body, healthy mind." A healthy mind is equally as important as a healthy body. Sickness and health start in the mind. It's up to us to make the right choice. I feel that today it is very important to realize, "Heal your mind, and it will heal your body."

In surgery, which is a field that is very close to me, things that sounded like science fiction have become reality. Minimally invasive, almost bloodless surgeries like laparoscopic surgery have become the standard in many operations. Many surgeries can be performed today with minimal opening of the abdomen, chest, joints, and other parts of the body. The results are better health, fewer complications and a speedy recovery.

The mapping of the human genome, genetic engineering, and stem cell research are some of the fields of the future of medicine. These things will change our understanding, diagnosis, and treatment of all diseases.

Unfortunately, the big pharmaceutical companies and insurance companies still control the health system. By doing so, they are controlling our health, but that too is changing – slowly but surely. With the new healthcare law that is still very far from being good, I believe we have taken a step in the right direction.

We are all becoming more aware of nutrition and its effects on our health and wellbeing. More and more people are starting to realize that proper nutrition can prevent and even cure many diseases, and it is the key to controlling the obesity epidemic.

It has become very obvious to every nation that its future depends on education, and major changes are occurring in this field as well. The spread of the Internet and telecommunications throughout the world has made it easier to get information in every field of life. All this has made knowledge more accessible to most people.

A major change that has occurred in last few years is that spirituality is no longer linked only to religion. More and more people have turned from being religious to being more spiritual.

By now you know that I've been labeled as *screwed, crazy, hopelessly optimistic, hopelessly romantic,* etc. I can accept most of them except for *hopeless.* I really do hope, and I know that a better future is coming. I agree with the prediction that the world is coming to an end – to an end of screwed–up wars, greed, political corruption, bribery, hunger, disease, poverty, child mortality, destruction of the planet, etc. Out of these ashes will arise a new world, a world where there's "nothing to kill or die for"; a world of peace and global partnership where there's universal primary education for all; a world of health and happiness, spirituality, freedom, and equal opportunities for everyone; a world where humankind lives in peace and harmony with their environment and protects his fellow living beings that have the same right to live as they do.

Finally, if there's one thing you can gain from my book, I hope it is this: through all of life's screwed events, it is love that sustains us and gets us through the troubling times; love of self, family, community, and others.